GEORGE WASHINGTON

BENEDICT ARNOLD

Courtesy of Bill Stanley, president of the Norwich Historical Society
Previously unpublished portrait of Benedict Arnold, in oil by Doug Henry

George Washington

AND

Benedict Arnold

George Washington

AND

Benedict Arnold

A TALE OF TWO PATRIOTS

DAVE R. PALMER

Former Superintendent of West Point

Since 1947
REGNERY
PUBLISHING, INC.
An Eagle Publishing Company • Washington, DC

Library of Congress Cataloging-in-Publication Data

Palmer, Dave Richard, 1934–
  George Washington and Benedict Arnold : a tale of two patriots / Dave
R. Palmer.
    p. cm.
  Includes bibliographical references and index.
  ISBN 1-59698-020-6
  1. Washington, George, 1732–1799. 2. Arnold, Benedict, 1741–1801.
3. Revolutionaries—United States—Biography. 4. Generals—United
States—Biography. 5. American loyalists—Biography. 6. United States.
Continental Army—Biography. 7. United States—History—Revolution,
1775–1783—Biography. 8. United States—History—Revolution,
1775–1783—Campaigns. I. Title.

E312.25.P3 2006
973.3'30922—dc22
[B]
                                                                    2006014666

Published in the United States by
Regnery Publishing, Inc.
One Massachusetts Avenue, NW
Washington, DC 20001
www.regnery.com

Distributed to the trade by
National Book Network
Lanham, MD 20706

Printed on acid-free paper

Manufactured in the United States of America
10 9 8 7 6 5 4 3 2 1

Books are available in quantity for promotional or premium use.
Write to Director of Special Sales, Regnery Publishing, Inc.,
One Massachusetts Avenue NW, Washington, DC 20001, for information
on discounts and terms or call (202) 216-0600.

Dedicated to the memory of

THOMAS E. GRIESS,

*whose vision and energy restored the study of history
to a prominent place in the American Army's blueprint
for developing leaders of character.*

CONTENTS

CHAPTER ONE

PHILADELPHIA

———◆•◆•◆———

SUSPENSE STIRRED PHILADELPHIA'S STEAMY LATE SUMMER air. Something called a Continental Congress was coming to town. For weeks, conversations in America's largest and most cosmopolitan city had turned on little else. Ordinarily stoic citizens contemplated the event with open curiosity. Tavern patrons speculated endlessly over possible outcomes. Innkeepers probed travelers for news from elsewhere. No one quite knew what to expect from the assembly of delegates streaming in from colonies north and south of Pennsylvania, but the folks of Philadelphia sensed nevertheless that it would surely be a momentous happening. They understood that the meeting was not exactly legal, and suspected that it might even be treasonous, which added to the feeling of nervous anticipation. It was August 1774.

The gathering was the bitter fruit of an acrimonious decade marked by oppressive acts passed in faraway London. Americans deemed these acts absolutely "intolerable," and they often reacted with violence. The latest such affront had been a kick to the colonial stomach from a hobnailed boot—the occupation of Boston by the British army and the replacement of home rule in Massachusetts with what amounted to martial law.

Representatives from British colonies up and down the Atlantic seaboard crowded dusty roads, converging on Philadelphia. Canada, the northernmost colony, and Georgia, the southernmost, declined to participate, as did Nova Scotia and the British islands of the Caribbean. But twelve colonies forming a solid line stretching from Massachusetts to South Carolina had delegations on the way. Reacting sharply to the military takeover in Massachusetts, these twelve had agreed to develop a united response to what they saw as Britain's sustained attacks on their way of life.

Among those heading for Philadelphia were two men who had not yet met, but whose destinies would be intertwined in the most remarkable ways over the next six years. One, Benedict Arnold, was from Connecticut, and the other, George Washington, was from Virginia. The two had much in common, including admirable attributes that would soon propel them into leading roles as warriors in the coming Revolution. But the very essences of their natures and characters were also quite different. Their relationship was fated to soar on eagle's wings of trust and fame—and to crash on jagged rocks of treason and infamy.

A novelist might have portrayed them as star-crossed. But even the most creative of storytellers would have been hard-pressed to pen the true tale of these two patriots, a tale all too real—and perhaps rather too bizarre—for human invention. For as we shall see, in spinning this story, truth needed no help from fiction.

A committee of Connecticut's legislature had selected several of its members to serve as delegates to the Continental Congress, but only three chose to go—Silas Deane, Eliphalet Dyer, and Roger

Sherman. Two others filled out the group: Samuel Webb, Deane's stepson and personal secretary, and Benedict Arnold. Not being a member of the legislature, Arnold was not an official delegate. At the age of thirty-three, though, he already ranked among Connecticut's more prominent citizens. A very successful merchant in the port city of New Haven, Arnold had married into one of its distinguished families. He was an acknowledged leader in the local resistance to Parliament's actions, and was deeply involved in New Haven's chapter of the Sons of Liberty—a blustering and sometimes riotous anti-British organization. Silas Deane, a man of intrigue then as well as later in the Revolution, and Arnold's close friend and fellow agitator in the Sons of Liberty, had invited the younger man along to add radical heft to the delegation's representation, and perhaps to dampen the impact of Sherman, who was thought to favor a more conciliatory stance toward London. In late August, the five gathered in New Haven to start their journey.

There was high excitement in the Connecticut city. Just days before, the congressional delegation from Massachusetts had passed through. That group, including John Adams and his firebrand cousin, Samuel Adams, had attracted boisterous crowds. "Every bell was clanging," wrote John Adams, while citizens clustered in doors and windows "as if to see a coronation."

When Arnold and his Philadelphia-bound colleagues climbed aboard Silas Deane's carriage, they were sent off with rousing cheers from well-wishers thronging the New Haven Green. The coachman pointed his horses down the road from Connecticut through New York and New Jersey to Pennsylvania, more than 150 rutted miles and many ferry crossings away.

The five road-weary, rumpled travelers rolled into Philadelphia on the final day of August. Representatives to the Continental

Congress filled rooms all across the city, some in inns, a few in private homes, others in boarding houses. Except for Roger Sherman, the Connecticut group lodged together.

The youthful Connecticut businessman who sprang so lightly from Deane's carriage surely caught the eyes of curious onlookers. Arnold was not tall, being for that time about average or somewhat less in height, perhaps some four or five inches above five feet, but he had an acrobat's powerful build and carried himself with the agile grace of a natural athlete. With piercing gray eyes, thick dark hair, deeply bronzed skin, and a prominent nose and chin, he was handsome in a rugged way. He had what men called a commanding presence. People noticed him. To go along with his compelling physical appearance, he possessed unusual powers of mind and personality. Quick-witted and articulate, full of energy almost to restlessness, bursting with confidence bordering on arrogance, Benedict Arnold was a force to be reckoned with.

Soon after settling into their new quarters, the men from Connecticut assembled with other emissaries to establish some preliminary rules for the conduct of the Congress. Nearly half the delegates, however, were still on the road, so they had no choice but to wait until the following Monday, September 5, to formally open the proceedings. They planned to hold their sessions in Carpenters' Hall, the guildhall of the city's Carpenters' Company, rather than in a government-owned building because of the extralegal status of the gathering. Arnold and his colleagues spent some of Friday and Saturday seeing the sights of the bustling city. Philadelphia had a large store of places to captivate the curiosity of visitors. Based on their written comments, New Englanders were particularly enthralled by the city's insane asylum, tucked away inside the basement of a major hospital; lawyer John Adams was astounded to discover among the inmates one of his former clients.

On Sunday they went to church—three times. Throughout those waiting days, however, as late-arriving members joined and anticipation mounted, delegates continued to huddle. At dinners and other gatherings, strangers from across the colonies became acquainted and probed one another on the issues, forming alliances and identifying strategies for the forthcoming Congress.

George Washington was among those who checked in just before the Congress's opening day, and so missed the preliminary rounds of caucusing. He and two fellow representatives from Virginia—Patrick Henry and Edmund Pendleton—had rendezvoused at Mount Vernon before taking Washington's carriage to Philadelphia, arriving on Sunday, September 4, after a swift four days on the road.

Virginia's envoys to the Continental Congress were members of the House of Burgesses, their colony's legislature. On August 5, 1774, that body—calling itself a convention after the governor dissolved it for alleged impertinence to the British government—cast ballots to determine which members to send. The seven with the highest number of votes were chosen, and all seven Virginians accepted their duty and went to Philadelphia. It was primarily Washington's military reputation that secured him a place, for he had not been a notable leader in the Burgesses, having throughout his many years of service there taken a backbench role in debates and having compiled a less than laudable record of attendance. Even so, with talk of fighting in the air, he placed third in the polling, behind Peyton Randolph and Richard Henry Lee.

Washington was one of his colony's wealthiest citizens. He had gained a fortune in land acquisition and agrarian pursuits and had also made an exceptionally advantageous marriage. Perhaps more important, he was very well known, thanks to his military exploits in the French and Indian War. In fact, Colonel George Washington was probably the most famous man in colonial America after Benjamin Franklin, and by 1774 the forty-two-year-old planter was an avowed radical who had completed a personal transition from being an Englishman who lived in America to being, quite simply, an American.

Colonel Washington appeared younger than the delegates had anticipated, but he looked every inch the soldier. The first thing one noticed about Washington was his stature. In an era when a man six feet tall was rare, Washington stood a towering six feet, three inches. Well-muscled and long-limbed, obviously possessing great strength, he was erect and trim, exuding energy. His hands were huge, so big that observers often commented on their size. Moving with athletic ease, a litheness unusual in so large a person, he was Olympian. In an age when nearly everyone rode, he was conceded to be the most graceful of horsemen. With blue-gray eyes set in deep sockets, strong features framed by a broad face, fair skin that never quite tanned, and reddish-brown hair held back in a tight queue, he had manly good looks. To say that he was impressive would be an understatement. When the soldier from Virginia entered a room, everyone was at once aware of his presence.

The Congress remained in session nearly two months, not adjourning until late October. In those busy weeks, delegates accomplished more than they had expected. They condemned Britain's "intolerable acts" as unconstitutional and pledged economic sanctions against Britain until the acts were repealed. They denounced Britain's stationing of troops in American cities, prepared petitions to the king, and talked warily of armed resistance. One decision had far more impact on the future than all the others combined: the members agreed to convene a second assembly the following spring. What became the First Continental Congress set May 1775 as the date for the meeting of the Second Continental Congress. That body would eventually decide to declare independence and wage war.

American leaders got to know one another during the sessions of the First Continental Congress and in the social life of Philadelphia. Well-to-do Philadelphians launched a seemingly endless round of ostentatious banquets, dinners, receptions, and coffees (teas were no longer politically correct because of the British tax on tea). In mid-September the city's State House was the scene of a glittering banquet in honor of the Congress, during which a staggering thirty-one toasts were offered and drunk. But the constant daily dinners were also extravagant affairs. Leading citizens appeared to compete with one another in the flaunting of wealth and status. "A most sinful feast again," moaned John Adams, already given to plumpness and fearing for his rapidly expanding waistline. He described for his wife a typical day in the Congress: work hard from nine to three, and then "go to dinner with some of the nobles of Pennsylvania at four o'clock and feast on ten thousand delicacies, and sit drinking Madeira, claret and burgundy 'til six or seven."

In their diaries and letters, the delegates gave prominent mention to Judge Edward Shippen as a host. Not only was his fare sumptuous, but his elegant home was graced by three lovely daughters, accomplished and poised young ladies who could more than hold their own with their father's distinguished visitors. The youngest, Margaret, called Peggy, a lively and flirtatious girl of fourteen, was especially popular. That September precocious Peggy Shippen thoroughly charmed both Benedict Arnold and George Washington. They were fated to cross paths again and again—in both love and war.

By fate or coincidence, John André, a young officer in the British army, disembarked at Philadelphia's waterfront that same

September. He was on his way to join his regiment in Canada, and would become the fourth person to play a leading role in the dark drama of Arnold and Washington. There is no indication that he made the acquaintance then of Peggy or Arnold or Washington, but André's route took him up the Hudson River past the site that would be central to his future service—and his death.

Neither Arnold nor Washington had much impact on the conduct or course of the First Continental Congress. As he was not a delegate, Arnold's influence was obviously limited to discussions outside the formal sessions, where his primary role was to support the virulently anti-British positions of Silas Deane. Nevertheless, his feisty, volatile nature had ample opportunities to exhibit itself.

Washington, for his part, listened attentively but seldom spoke, projecting a thoughtful seriousness. That restrained demeanor actually made him stand out in a gathering of political leaders for whom talking bordered on obsession. Those who gauged the tall, quiet man included Arnold and his compatriots from Connecticut, as indicated in a letter written by Silas Deane. The Virginian, Deane reported, was not the best of orators, although he spoke "very modestly in a cool but determined style and accent." As the only person in the Congress with any appreciable military experience, Washington did attract attention. John Adams, himself a key player in that First Congress, did not list Washington as an important delegate, but he repeated a story that had the wealthy Virginian declaring he was ready to raise a thousand men at his own expense to march to the aid of Boston. That the story was false did not keep it from adding to the burgeoning radical reputation of the man from Mount Vernon.

No one recorded when Washington and Arnold first met or what they talked about. Washington was sparse in describing his activities in Philadelphia, while Arnold, besides being a lax note-taker, was present only in an unofficial status. But meet they surely did that September, if for no other reason than that the attendees themselves worked hard to become acquainted with their colleagues from other colonies.

The First Continental Congress adjourned on October 26. Washington and Arnold, hearing the distant thunder of darkening war clouds, turned their attention to military preparedness in their respective colonies. John André, rather oblivious to the signs of gathering conflict, was enjoying his adventurous travels in the remote interior of North America. Peggy Shippen, missing the fun of having so many captivating guests at dinner, was anticipating with girlish delight the round of holiday balls soon to start.

The fifth major actor in the unfolding tale of triumph and tragedy was not a person at all. Rather, it was Philadelphia itself. The City of Brotherly Love would provide the sinister stage where patriotism would transition into treason.

Chapter Two

Family

THE FIRST WASHINGTONS AND THE FIRST ARNOLDS SAILED from England in the mid-1600s. Settlements in the New World were new, few, and sited near navigable water that permitted easy access for ocean-going ships, the sole and tenuous link to the mother country. Beyond the beaches stretched a wooded wilderness reaching farther than any Englishman had explored, and hiding what secrets no one knew. Native tribes inhabited those vast forests, sometimes befriending the European newcomers, sometimes turning terribly hostile. Quite obviously, one had to be both brave and adventurous to settle in so forbidding a land. Such boldness ran in the blood of the Arnolds and the Washingtons.

John Washington, the great-grandfather of the future president, became a Virginian more or less by accident. Sailing as second officer aboard a trading ship bound for America to pick up a cargo of tobacco, he entered the Chesapeake Bay around the start of 1657. His voyage was jinxed. The ship ran aground in the Potomac River on the last day of February, and a gale sank it soon afterward, temporarily stranding the seamen on the wrong side of the Atlantic. While waiting for the vessel to be raised and repaired, its crew had time to explore the new, primitive land. Twenty-four-year-old John Washington liked what he saw and decided to stay, ending his career as a merchant mariner but establishing the Washington line in Virginia.

Seventeenth-century Virginia bubbled with opportunity. Land was plentiful and virtually free for the occupying. Careers beckoned in every field, promising grand rewards for daring souls who did not shy away from labor, danger, or the lack of common comforts.

John Washington fit the pioneer profile ideally: rugged, a natural risk-taker, hardworking, and possessed of an abundant spirit of adventure. It helped that he was also motivated by stark necessity. Although he had been born into relative gentility, with family circumstances all but guaranteeing him a life of privilege, his father, a parish priest named Lawrence, had chosen the losing side in the English Civil War. In the turbulent aftermath of that conflict, the Washingtons had lost everything, forcing John to seek his fortune on his own. Still worse, both of his parents had died by the time he started the voyage to Virginia. Having nothing to fall back on in the Old World made the possibilities of the New all the more attractive to the ambitious young man.

One more inducement for John to remain in America was Anne Pope, the daughter of one of the colony's leading citizens. When they married, Anne's father staked his new son-in-law enough land and money to start farming. John turned his boundless energy to improving his lot, and succeeded handsomely, gaining wealth and expanding his landholdings at every turn. He focused on the area called the Northern Neck, a body of land lying between the Potomac and Rappahannock rivers and stretching vaguely into uncharted regions toward their headwaters. Among John's many acquisitions was a tract of some 2,500 near-wilderness acres far up the Potomac, alongside a stream called Little Hunting Creek. There Mount Vernon would one day stand. John also served in leadership roles in his church, in his county, in the Burgesses, and as an officer in the militia. He was competent, shrewd, driven, not overly scrupulous, and perhaps just a bit of a rake. His innate toughness matched the rough-hewn country itself. By the time of his death, two decades after starting from scratch, the first American Washington had rebuilt his family's status to about what it had been in the Old Country—landed gentry, not among the very upper class, but solid and respected in the larger community.

Lawrence, John's eldest child and George Washington's grandfather, inherited the better part of his father's considerable estate. As his namesake in England had been, he was more a man of intellect than of action. Schooled back in England (one of the benefits of having well-to-do parents), he became a lawyer and prospered in that pursuit. Like his father before him, he served in the House of Burgesses and in other community and colonial leadership capacities. He also continued what was to become a family tradition of marrying well, taking as his bride the daughter of Augustine Warner, a politically influential leader in the colony. A capable if not an aggressive manager, Lawrence increased the family holdings modestly before he died young, in 1698. He was not yet forty, and left a widow, Mildred, and three young children. The second son, Augustine, who would become George Washington's father, was only three at the time of his own father's early death.

Women did not normally remain widows very long in colonial times. Mildred soon remarried, choosing as her next husband George Gale, an Englishman engaged in the tobacco export business. Before long, Gale moved his family back to the mother country, where Augustine and his older brother began their schooling. At that moment the odds were high for that branch of the Washington family to revert permanently to life in England, which would have removed George Washington from the list of our nation's founding fathers. But once more fate intervened. Mildred died before her children could become firmly rooted in the Old World. Lawrence's will had directed that a Virginia cousin would raise his offspring if Mildred died before they reached adulthood. So, under court order, the three siblings crossed the ocean again. Augustine was ten.

Blond, attractive, and outgoing, Augustine grew into a widely admired young man, apparently known to his friends as "Gus." Unusually tall and strong, he was a gentle giant whose most remembered personal trait was kindness. But he possessed in full measure the Washington bent of aggressive ambition to better himself. As the second son, his part of the family properties had not been large, so he had much to achieve. In 1715 he married Jane Butler, who brought a small inheritance to the union. Together they started with fewer than two thousand acres, a small holding at that time in colonial Virginia. But like his grandfather John, Gus worked diligently to expand, and had considerable success. Blessed with a winning personality, he also began to make a name for himself as a leader, serving as a county judge at the age of twenty-two and thereafter being a church vestryman, a militia officer, and a sheriff. He and Jane had four children: Butler (who died young), Lawrence, Augustine, and Jane. Having prospered, the couple could afford to send their boys to The Appleby School in England, which Gus had attended before being returned to America.

Life was going well for the Washingtons, although, like so many land-rich and cash-poor Virginians, they struggled constantly to generate income. In addition to farming, Augustine's enterprises included pursuits as diverse as running a grist mill and involvement in iron-mining. As it turned out, however, he was not an especially gifted businessman, so his finances were always shaky. Then adversity struck. His wife died, leaving him in need both of money for his ventures and a mother for his children.

The new widower did not have to look long or far. The name of Mary Ball came quickly to his mind. At twenty-three, she was quite available, being well past the normal marrying age. Moreover, she had come into a tidy inheritance as a result of a series of deaths in her family. That she was attractive was a bonus. Augustine began courting her straightaway.

Mary had a rather unusual background. Her father, Joseph Ball, had emigrated from England in his youth, had done well, and had raised a family. Then, as a widower nearing sixty, in an act thought scandalous by some, he had married Mary Johnson, a young, illiterate widow. That marriage produced Mary Ball. Joseph died when the girl was still a toddler, and her mother, after a third marriage and being widowed yet again, died when her daughter was twelve. Mary went to live with a guardian named George Eskridge, the closest thing to a father she would ever know.

Orphaned early and raised as an only child, with scant education and precious little parental discipline, Mary grew up to be strong-willed and tart-tongued. That might explain her being single—her headstrong personality very likely chilled the ardor of would-be suitors. But Augustine was not deterred. At thirty-six, and personally easygoing, he apparently concluded that he could cope with Mary's independent streak. The two were married in March 1731. Accompanied by Augustine's three children, they moved into a small, unpretentious home he had built near the spot where Popes Creek runs into the Potomac. Eleven months later, just past mid-morning on February 22, 1732, their first child was born.

With the most often-used names for Washington males—Lawrence and Augustine—already given to her husband's first two sons, the new mother felt free to name her child after her surrogate father, George Eskridge.

————

Seventeenth-century England was marked by war, rebellion, lawlessness, religious persecution, economic chaos, the Black Plague, and the burning of London. More than six decades of convulsive internal strife precipitated a massive migration out of the island kingdom. Not only did it lead the Washington bloodline to America, but it also provoked the departure of the Arnolds.

Seeking religious freedom, William Arnold and his family gave up their economically favorable circumstances in England and sailed with other Puritans to Massachusetts in 1635. William's first son, almost twenty years old when the family reached America, was the initial Benedict in an unbroken string of Benedicts, right down to Benedict V, the Revolutionary War hero—and traitor. Discovering that the religious atmosphere of Massachusetts was itself oppressive, the Arnolds soon moved on, following Roger Williams, who was establishing a tolerant new colony he named Providence. There, in what became Rhode Island, the Arnolds found the spiritual freedom they had been looking for—and a robust environment for acquiring considerable wealth. William promptly laid claim to extensive tracts of land, and within a few years his family stood among the top tier of settlers in the colony. The Arnolds' status in America quickly surpassed what it had been in England.

Although William lived nearly four decades after settling in Rhode Island, his son soon eclipsed him in both prestige and power. The first Benedict's stewardship of the Arnold lands greatly enhanced their worth, while his marriage to Damaris Westcott forged ties with another of the colony's important early families. Moreover, Benedict was charismatic. By the time he was in his thirties, he had become an acknowledged regional leader, widely looked upon as the obvious successor to founder Roger Williams. Repeatedly elected to the governorship, Benedict Arnold served longer in that position than anyone else before or since. So great was his renown that upwards of a thousand people reportedly flocked to his funeral in 1678.[1] If that estimate was even close to accurate, the assemblage was an enormous turnout in an age when population was so sparse.

The wave of respect for Benedict I carried his son and namesake into positions of opportunity and influence. Benedict II held high seats in both judicial and legislative bodies of the colony, and appeared well positioned to follow in his father's path. But he was a spendthrift who squandered his chances. Having neither the entrepreneurial skills nor the political acumen of Governor Arnold, he let the family lands and influence slip through his fingers and had little to bequeath to his descendants other than the Arnold name. Compounding these financial shortcomings, the next Arnold—Benedict III—died early, pre-deceasing his father by eight years. Benedict III left his widow, Patience Cogswell

---

[1]   John Washington, his contemporary—though they never met—had died in 1677.

Arnold, and their several children in severely straitened circumstances. Benedict IV was still a boy when his father died. With no patrimony to support him, he became an apprentice barrel-maker, a trade essential in the shipping business, which promised steady work in maritime New England. When he reached adulthood, Benedict IV moved west to Connecticut, a less crowded colony where he could start anew. He opened shop in Norwich Town in 1730.

He had chosen well. The town was bustling. An inland seaport, its wharves were located along a cove carved by the Yantic River not far from where it joined another stream to form the short but stately Thames River, which empties into the Atlantic on the eastern side of Long Island Sound. Sitting astride the main road from Boston to New York City, Norwich Town was also a hub connecting the river port with settlements deep in the northern interior. The town was thus a quite strategically placed center of commerce. It held ample opportunity for an ambitious young man who burned to recapture the former glory and wealth associated with the Arnold name.

One of the very first persons to hire Benedict was Absalom King, a ship captain and trader. Captain King quickly took a liking to the eager, bright, hardworking newcomer. Before long, the barrel-maker was sailing as a trading assistant with Absalom. A quick learner, trustworthy, and with a good head for business, he soon graduated to the command of voyages on his own. A typical trip for King's vessels would be to depart New England loaded with lumber and salt meat, trade that for rum and molasses in the Caribbean, and then exchange that cargo in England for manufactured goods bound for America. Benedict prospered as a seagoing trader, establishing his own reputation and improving King's business at the same time.

Then death scrambled affairs, as it so often did in colonial days. Returning from a trip to Ireland in 1732, Captain King died at sea. As a friend of the family, and a business intimate of the captain's, Arnold had the sad duty of consoling King's widow. Childless, she was sole heir to Absalom's ships, warehouses, wharves, house, and other properties. Hannah Waterman King walked among the area's social elite, being related through her father to one of Norwich Town's founding families, the Watermans, and through her mother to one of the town's most prosperous families, the Lathrops. She had standing in local religious circles as well; she was noted for her piety even in a Puritan setting, where piousness was more or less obligatory. What's more, she was pretty. Benedict wasted no time before paying court, and successfully. They married in 1733. With that single stroke, Benedict Arnold IV became not only a prominent citizen in the community, but one of the richest men in town. Only three years earlier he had left Rhode Island owning little more than a winning personality, a large measure of cleverness, and a burning desire to make something of himself.

In the next few years he expanded King's shipping business significantly—and garnered the nautical title of Captain Arnold. He soon established his home in a mansion fully befitting his new-found status. Sitting on five elm-covered acres along the way from the Norwich Town wharves to the village green, the three-storied structure, with twelve generous rooms and eight fireplaces, was so large that it required a barn-like, gambrel roof to cover it. Affable as well as affluent, Captain Arnold held many community service positions, from surveyor to selectman. By the time he had lived a decade in Connecticut, he was one of the colony's more respected and successful businessmen.

The one cloud in the sky of Arnold's new life was the absence of heirs. At a time when homes were considered to be woefully incomplete without children—indeed, when family futures often depended upon large numbers of offspring—the halls in the spacious Arnold house echoed emptily. The couple seemed unable to have children. Hannah had given birth twice while married to Captain King, although both infants had died. But she remained barren through her first five years of marriage to Arnold. Finally, she became pregnant and bore a son, Benedict V. But their happiness was short-lived, for the baby died. Hannah, distraught, turned to the church for solace. Already deeply devout, she grew ever more so over time. Perhaps it was her prayers, or perhaps it was the deep freeze of the coldest winter in memory, but on January 14, 1741, Hannah gave birth to a hardy boy, who survived. As was often the practice—in order to retain family names—the new baby received the name of his dead older brother, Benedict V.

At birth, Benedict Arnold and George Washington had much in common. They entered life just a few years apart as American subjects of King George II. Born into families with long-established records of local and regional public service, they carried names highly regarded in their respective colonies of Connecticut and Virginia. The parents of the newborn boys were solidly situated, enjoyed financial success, and gave every appearance of being able to provide the two infants a substantial start in life, including a sound education when the time came. Hannah Arnold and Mary Washington must surely have thought their sons' futures, in their part of the expanding British Empire, looked promising indeed.

CHAPTER THREE

CHILDHOOD

———◆•◆•◆———

WHEN GEORGE WASHINGTON ENTERED LIFE, IN THE farmhouse on Popes Creek, he was the family's fourth surviving child, having two half-brothers, Lawrence and Augustine, and a half-sister, Jane. Lawrence, the eldest, was away at school in England. The infant grew into a toddler in a jostling household crowded with people—the family itself, slaves working in and around the house, passing strangers, visiting relatives, business colleagues of his father's, even occasional Indians. Almost at once the number and mix of children began to change. Augustine sailed to join his brother Lawrence in England before George could walk or talk. A new baby, Betty, arrived in 1733. Another, Samuel, came along the following year. Then, on a chill January day in 1735, Jane died. For the first time, George, just a month short of three, personally encountered the grim finality of the grave, and he found himself the oldest child at home. Later that same year George's father decided to move the family a few dozen miles north along the Potomac to a plantation he had purchased from his sister, land that had been in the Washington family for the better part of a century.

There, on a high, level bluff overlooking a sweeping curve of the Potomac River, Gus had built a story-and-a-half home. Typical of frontier structures at the time, the simple, rectangular house had four rooms on the ground floor, separated into two pairs by a central passageway. Two large, external chimneys, one at either end of the building, gave draft to angled corner fireplaces inside all four rooms. Smaller garret rooms in the attic above the first floor provided additional sleeping space. That modest, remote home—later named Mount Vernon and still later much enlarged—would provide George Washington his earliest boyhood memories. It would also be the site of his death sixty-four years later.

For the next three years that remote plantation encompassed George's world. The mile-wide river in his backyard and virgin forests beyond the cleared fields in every other direction were the boundaries of civilization as the lad personally knew it. His father traveled, to be sure, including trips to England, bringing back exciting tales of strange and distant places, but such adventures were beyond the ken of a child who had never seen anything other than his own isolated and limited surroundings. Life on a wilderness plantation in 1735 turned inward. Still, there were people aplenty. Slaves, many of whom George had known all of his life, were around in good numbers, while a continual flow of visitors added variety and interest. And the family kept increasing. John Augustine, called Jack, was born in 1736, and Charles in 1737. George, barely five, was then the oldest of five siblings in what surely must have been a noisy, hectic household.

The following year brought two events that would have a deep and lasting impact on the impressionable six-year-old. First was

Lawrence's return from England after he had completed his education there. That formerly mysterious figure, whom George had heard so much about but had never met, turned out to be a tall, dark, sophisticated young man. Immediately capturing the affection of the awestruck boy fourteen years his junior, Lawrence remained until the end of his own short life an object of George's admiration and emulation. Their relationship would shape the future president perhaps more than that of any other single person.

The second event sprang from a need to uproot the family yet again. To remain profitable, Augustine's iron-mining operation required more of his direct attention than he could give it from the Potomac plantation. Accordingly, he acquired a large tract of land some thirty miles distant, across the Northern Neck near the new town of Fredericksburg. There, in December 1738, the family moved into a house very much like the one they had just vacated, with four rooms on the first floor and two more up a steep staircase. Sitting just back from the banks of the Rappahannock and overlooking a ferry crossing site, the new home was called Ferry Farm.

The new Washington home, closer to roads and businesses than the previous one, saw even more visitors. One can glimpse the bustling nature of the family's day-to-day life by considering just one item in an inventory made of their furnishings: beds. The six-room house contained a surprising number of them, thirteen altogether, with three standing in the parlor alone. It might be assumed that not every guest always got clean linen, for the family had only sixteen sets of sheets for the thirteen beds. Overnight visitors were commonplace, and the Washington children met plenty of strangers.

Fredericksburg, founded only eleven years earlier, was the first town young George had ever seen. Small and raw, even in comparison with other towns in colonial America, it nevertheless held a magical attraction for a youngster whose entire life up until then had been spent on remote farms. Established as an inland port primarily to serve planters in the burgeoning Northern Neck, the town boasted a wharf, warehouses for tobacco, a courthouse, a jail, a half-built church, a scattering of nice homes, and not a few shacks. Streets were either muddy or dusty, depending on the weather, and always busy. Carpenters labored overtime to raise new structures, stonecutters operated nearby quarries, and trade goods moved constantly into and out of storehouses. Sailors, servants, merchants, farmers, laborers—all mingled in a stew of humanity. Ocean-going trading ships tied up at the wharf, passing Ferry Farm to get there. For the Washington children, the exciting bustle of the port itself was magnified by the ever-entertaining ferry crossing right in front of their house. It offered a kaleidoscope of activity, with horses straining to control loaded wagons, lone riders galloping off on missions mysterious, toughs looking for work or trouble, whole families en route to a new beginning in the hinterland. All in all, it was an eye-opening experience for a small country boy.

Every boy in that era learned field and forest lore, of course, and how to handle a gun, while horseback riding was simply a part of everyday life. On the Rappahannock, George also learned about water—how to fish and swim and how to handle a small boat. Despite the persistent myths perpetuated after he became famous, portraying him as some kind of superior being even as a child, he was really an ordinary boy, perhaps more athletic than others his age, but certainly not too good a kid to be true. Like most of his young friends around Fredericksburg he was active and curious, and impatient to grow up.

During those years on the Rappahannock George also began his education, such as it was. Basically, George Washington was home-schooled, but not by his parents. His mother, Mary, did not have the time, the inclination, or the education to take on that task, while Augustine was too consumed by work and travel to be a very effective teacher. The family employed a tutor when one could be found. In a colony with few schools, this is how an education was normally obtained. Lawrence, himself fresh from school and a stint at tutoring, was around to help at first, and there is some indication that a local school of sorts may have been available for a while. The subjects were simple, focusing on the basics of reading, writing, and arithmetic. George was an apt student. He did well in writing, eventually developing a clear, strong hand that stayed with him all his life. Arithmetic was perhaps his best subject, but reading came easily as well. However, because his lessons were sporadic at best, his development remained spotty. For instance, his spelling remained "inventive" all his life. The lad's parents were not especially concerned, because they expected that he would eventually go to England to receive a thorough education. The Appleby School, they were confident, would smooth out all their son's rough edges, as it had done for Washington boys as long as anyone could remember.

Quite the most thrilling event in George's boyhood occurred while he lived at Ferry Farm. Lawrence, his hero, went off to war.

England and Spain were warring over trade in the New World. Carrying the improbable name of the War of Jenkins' Ear, the fighting sprawled across the Atlantic to America, spilling into the Caribbean Sea. England, forever needing manpower, recruited Americans to bolster a British force being sent to attack Spain's possessions in the Caribbean. Virginia was tasked to provide troops to accompany General Thomas Wentworth, sailing under the command of Admiral Edward Vernon. Lawrence received a commission as a captain and left with his unit in the fall of 1740.

To eight-year-old George, Lawrence looked positively smashing in his brilliant new uniform, and his departure for war left a lasting impression on the boy.

Lawrence was away for two years, and his family received only occasional, suspenseful news of casualties and fighting. As it happened, the largest battle involving the Virginians ended ingloriously, when Spanish forces repulsed a British attempt to capture the fortress of Cartagena, on the coast of today's Colombia. To Lawrence and his colleagues, that galling defeat was the result of sheer ineptitude by their British commander, General Wentworth, whose opinion of colonial troops was so low that he did not even deploy most of them from their ships during the fighting. Nevertheless, back at Ferry Farm, Lawrence's tales of life at sea, faraway places, and armed adventures mesmerized his ten-year-old brother. George was thereafter enraptured by thoughts of military service, and Lawrence became still more an object of veneration in his eyes.

With the exception of Lawrence's wartime absence—and a fire that destroyed the family home, requiring a temporary return to the future Mount Vernon—life along the Rappahannock was generally tranquil. George was eager to take his turn at The Appleby School in England, from which Augustine (nicknamed Austin to distinguish him from his father) had returned. But shortly after George turned eleven, death abruptly claimed his father and shattered George's plans.

Augustine's will divided his considerable estate among many heirs. To Lawrence went the plantation near Little Hunting Creek, which he promptly named Mount Vernon, after the respected British admiral he had served under in the Cartagena expedition. Augustine, next oldest, received the farm farther south along the Potomac, where George had been born. George, third in line, inherited Ferry Farm and some other parcels of land. He also became the owner of ten slaves. On the surface it may seem as if the boy had been transformed overnight into a prosperous landowner, but that was far from the truth. His mother would retain control of his inheritance until he came of age. (Even then, when he reached twenty-one, Mary did not relinquish her hold on his properties—it was not in her nature to turn loose of anything once she got her hands on it.)

The first major consequence of Gus's untimely death was the scrapping of plans for George to be educated abroad. In fact, under the revised circumstances, with the once imposing estate broken up into pieces (and with Mary proving to be less than able to manage her portion profitably), money was unavailable for any significant schooling even in Virginia. The homeschooling would have to continue, largely under the tutelage of George's two well-educated half-brothers. Moreover, George would now need to learn a trade in order to support himself. It was quite a fall in actual and perceived status for an eleven-year-old.

The second serious result was the sad disintegration of George's situation at home. Contrary to the normal practice for young widows, Mary did not remarry, nor did she exhibit any inclination to do so, appearing to be intent on running things on her own. She had reputedly always been a demanding, hard-to-take, self-centered woman. Under new pressures as a single mother, and in the absence of her husband's calming influence, her worst traits hardened. Crabby and controlling, she earned a fiery reputation that spread beyond her own domicile. One of George's boyhood friends later recalled that he "was ten times more afraid" of Mary than of his own parents. George, verging on adolescence, was particularly affected. And torn. He had been raised to obey his parents and to respect them, yet he found it increasingly difficult to tolerate so oppressive an environment with such a domineering mother. Accordingly, he spent as much time as possible away from her, living with relatives, especially his grown brothers. There, conveniently, he could rationalize his absence from home as a need to continue his studies. His half-brothers had not really known their stepmother until they were themselves young adults, and so usually shrugged off her irascibility and were quite sympathetic to George's plight. That sympathy led to George's first attempt to escape.

Lawrence, perhaps reflecting on the enjoyable life he had experienced under Admiral Vernon, concluded that becoming a midshipman might be just the answer to his young brother's dilemma. Going to sea in that apprentice status—sailing before the mast, as it was termed—would provide George an honorable and immediate release from an unhappy situation as well as the possibility of a long-term career as a naval officer. Pulling some strings, Lawrence made the necessary arrangements after obtaining George's agreement. But he hadn't reckoned on the stubborn strength of Mary Ball Washington. Only fourteen, George needed his mother's permission to ship out, permission which that determined lady was not about to grant, despite strenuous attempts to persuade her.[1]

Benedict Arnold grew up in an established Connecticut town as an eldest son. He was followed by Hannah, Mary, Absalom, and Elizabeth, in approximate two-year intervals. Benedict was eight when Elizabeth was born.

---

[1]   It is tempting to second-guess history in this case. What if Mary had not objected? Would George Washington have ended up as Admiral Washington of the Royal Navy?

For an active young boy, Benedict's first eight or nine years had to be close to idyllic. His earliest memories would have been of the elegant Arnold home, full of nooks and passages and stairs, and with extensive grounds to accommodate childhood games. His family lacked for nothing to make life pleasant. There were servants to keep the house running smoothly and to attend to Benedict's whims.[2] As he grew old enough to explore, he found beckoning in one direction the irresistible bustle of a busy seaport, with ships he could play on because his father owned them. In the other direction from the road running past his front gate stood the town center and the village green. Nearby was the Leffingwell Inn, whose guests, traveling from all over, added color and a touch of intrigue. As the scion of a prominent family, Benedict had access to businesses and homes wherever his meanderings carried him.

Nature vied with man-made points of interest. A short walk from the boy's home the Yantic River cascaded in a roar of white water down a boulder-strewn gorge to fill the deep pool of the port, an irresistible playground for an active youngster. Ponds and streams provided swimming in summer and skating in winter, while local woods held a special allure year-round. That was particularly exciting because numerous Indians still inhabited the area, descendants of the original owners of the land. Unlike most Eastern tribes, the Mohegans had remained friendly with the whites and had managed to live side by side with them while retaining their own culture. With all of that stimulation in his daily environment, Benedict's spirit of adventure blossomed quite naturally, and it could only have been sharpened by his father's tales of trading trips to the Caribbean, London, Canada, and other

---

[2]   Connecticut was then a slave-holding colony, and some of the servants were black slaves.

colonies. All in all, Norwich in the 1740s was a grand place for an Arnold boy to grow up. Life was good.

But the War of Jenkins' Ear disrupted colonial trading patterns, endangering vessels sailing to the West Indies. Money was still to be made, lots of it in some cases, but the risks were increased, threatening Captain Arnold's previously solid financial footing. If the war had been limited to England and Spain, he likely would not have been much affected, but a second and much larger war erupted, a dynastic clash called the War of the Austrian Succession. It engulfed Europe in a swirling melee lasting from 1740 to 1748. Americans, ever practical, saw it primarily as a war with France, which controlled Canada, and as the continuation of fighting with Spain to the south. Not overly interested in which claimant occupied the Austrian throne, colonists called the conflict King George's War. That prolonged period of disruption did not destroy the Arnold shipping enterprises, but it undermined and weakened their very basis, starting a downward spiral that would prove difficult to reverse.

Benedict, too young to grasp the long-term impact of the hostilities on his father's business, spent his first seven years immersed in an environment colored by constant talk of war. No fighting took place around Norwich, but numerous false alarms of French and Indian incursions from the north kept residents nervous, while the real threat of Spanish raiders at sea added an aura of danger to each of his father's journeys. The most stirring moment in the war for Benedict came when he was four. He watched entranced as the town's militiamen, including a number of his own relatives, formed up on the green and marched off to battle. They joined other New Englanders in an assault on the powerful French fortress at Louisburg, guarding the Atlantic entrance to the St. Lawrence River. Triumphant in that effort, perhaps somewhat to their own surprise, the veterans of the Louisburg campaign remained ever after supremely proud of their single achievement. But success was to have a bitter aftertaste. The peace treaty terminating the war three years later returned the fortress to France, to the consternation and immense disgust of the colonists.

Religious conflict strained the civil fabric of Norwich even more severely than did the war; it lasted longer, struck more directly at the townspeople, and fostered an attitude of rebelliousness.

Founded in the previous century by Puritans (although the passage of time had diluted the original founding fervor), Norwich had retained an official one-church policy common throughout Connecticut. That policy was challenged when a wave of revivalism—called the Great Awakening—swept the colony. Igniting emotions and splitting Norwich into two snarling camps, the revival movement rolled into town about the time Benedict IV and Hannah King married. The so-called "New Lights" tried to break away to form their own congregation while the "Old Lights" were determined to maintain the religious status quo. The Arnolds avoided the feuding as well as they could, but the mutual animosity persisted for decades.

Nevertheless, despite unease raised by war worries and religious infighting, Benedict's early life was on the whole a full and enjoyable one. He had the run of the town and port area, mingled with Indians and travelers, and engaged in all of the pleasures open to an outgoing and active boy. He didn't know boredom or loneliness, for there were lots of other youngsters around. Indeed, being intense and aggressive by nature, Benedict became a leader in the gang of kids he ran with. Endowed with superior athleticism and driven by a sense of bravado, he was something of a show-off. Whether out-skating his friends on the ice in winter, swimming riskily under mill pond waterwheels in summer, or swinging hand over hand through a ship's rigging any time at all, he was a noted daredevil bent on besting and impressing his contemporaries. At the same time, he was getting an educational foundation to prepare him for finishing school and a university, probably Yale. He was a sharp student, clear in penmanship and strong in math. In those years, too, his father exposed him to life aboard ship, taking him first on short cruises and then eventually on longer journeys. Benedict never lost his love for the sea. And with a sharp eye on her son's religious growth, his mother saw to it that he attended church regularly, where the family had a reserved front-row pew, a mark of community respect.

But then came a disastrous period that led to the virtual dissolution of the family. It started just before Benedict's tenth birthday, when three-year-old Absalom suddenly died. Three years later, Elizabeth and Mary died within days of one another, victims of an epidemic that swept Norwich. Debts and losses began to catch up with the shipping business, and, whether cause or effect, alcohol abuse began to catch up with Benedict IV. Hannah had apparently detected evidence of his alcoholism early. She took increasing responsibility to hold their finances together and hew to the plans they had made. Key in those plans was to send Benedict away to school to prepare him for a university.

So when Benedict turned eleven, his mother contacted the Reverend James Cogswell, a relative who operated a small boarding school in the town of Canterbury, fifteen miles away. He agreed to accept the boy as a student, and Hannah packed young Benedict off with strict admonitions to do well. She pointedly instructed the headmaster, "Pray don't spare ye rod and spoil ye child." Benedict spent more than two years studying under the Reverend Cogswell. He demonstrated not only academic prowess and university potential, but also continued to exhibit an irrepressible penchant for derring-do, much to the horror of the good Dr. Cogswell. The headmaster informed Hannah, in the spring of Benedict's second year, that, although her son was a good student, he was too "full of pranks and plays" for his own good. As an example, Cogswell cited an instance when the boy had foolishly entered a burning barn, climbed above the flames to the top, and walked along the ridgepole from end to end. Whether that became an occasion for not sparing ye rod we don't know.

For years Hannah Arnold battled valiantly to stave off the continuing collapse of her husband's business. There is strong evidence that she even tried to sail with him, hoping to keep him sober enough to trade profitably. But Captain Arnold had fallen too far. His case became hopeless. With her husband drunk most of the time, with creditors clamoring to throw him into debtors' prison, and with no feasible source of income other than charity from sympathetic relatives, Hannah finally reached the end of what she could conceivably do alone. Her destitute family had nothing left but the huge house, the fancy furnishings, and a mountain of debt. Through the long descent she had desperately attempted to sustain her son's education, scrimping to send him money even as the coils of bankruptcy tightened. But now she had no choice but to withdraw him from school. Benedict was fourteen, with no foreseeable chance for further education and no reliable means of earning a living. Worst of all, he was ashamed of his family's poverty and mortified by a derelict father who had become the town joke. Not surprisingly, the boy reacted by rebelling and becoming increasingly rowdy. Hannah took the only course remaining open to her. She approached relatives who owned a pharmacy business and asked them to take the lad in as an apprentice, teaching him their trade and, in essence, raising him until he reached adulthood. They agreed to do so.

Although Hannah was not technically a single mother, she was in effect just that. Both of Benedict's parents would die before he completed his apprenticeship, his mother first, of a broken heart; his father later, simply broken by alcoholism. Hannah's relatives saw to the details of her burial, placing her in Norwich's cemetery alongside her already deceased children. The inscription on her headstone reads: "In memory of Hannah, the well beloved wife of Capt Benedict Arnold & daughter of Mr John and Elizabeth Waterman (She was a pattern of Piety Patience and Virtue) who died August 15th 1759." When Captain Arnold himself died two years later, having long been the embarrassing town drunk, his son, nearly of age, had the responsibility of handling funeral arrangements. Curiously, no headstone for the captain stands today in the burying ground near the wife whose piety, patience, and virtue he had so grievously tested.

—————

Thus, before they were fifteen, both Benedict Arnold and George Washington found themselves essentially on their own. Death—actual or its alcoholic equivalent—had removed their fathers. Their mothers had attempted to carry on alone, but had been unable to do so. The boys' futures would depend on their own energy and ability.

There were differences in their individual circumstances, to be sure, but in many ways their experiences mirrored one another. Both had witnessed the cold touch of death on the face of siblings. Both had encountered the phenomenon of war at an early age, and had been stirred by martial mystique. Both had known the benefits of being born into a wealthy household, only to watch dreams and expectations wash away in financial reversals. Both had found themselves caught up in unhappy family circumstances from which some form of escape seemed necessary. Both were blessed by nature with good minds, strong bodies, and excellent health. Both had seen promises of higher education evaporate, replaced by the urgent need to learn a trade. Both had supportive relatives they could turn to, but each, in his early teens, stood inescapably responsible for his own future.

CHAPTER FOUR

SELF-MADE MEN

ANNAH ARNOLD CHOSE WISELY IN APPRENTICING HER
son. Her cousins, Daniel and Joshua Lathrop, graduates
of Yale and leading citizens of Norwich, were prosperous entrepreneurs. They owned a substantial pharmacy business
in town and also conducted a far-flung trading operation. Having
known the lad all his life, and acutely aware of the sad state of his
family's personal and financial affairs, they were happy to help by
taking him under their tutelage. Daniel's home, where young Benedict would live, was a stately structure across the street from the
pharmacy and an easy walk from the Arnold home.

By signing the apprenticeship papers, Benedict's parents committed him to servitude for seven years, ending when he reached
twenty-one. He was obligated to obey his new mentors, to do their
bidding without dissent, to follow their rules, to perform whatever
duties they directed. In return, he would receive room and board,
necessary clothing, and that degree of training adequate to prepare

him to become a druggist himself. Most important, under this arrangement the headstrong youngster would also receive the discipline and structure his own family could no longer provide.

Moreover, the contract came with a bonus. Daniel and his wife, Jerusha, having lost all three of their own children in an epidemic some years before, had ever since made a practice of taking in young people down on their luck, serving almost as foster parents to many of them. Eager to learn and fully appreciative of the opportunity, Benedict thrived in his new situation. It was a good fit. Daniel provided a firm male hand and the expertise to direct the boy's workaday education, while Jerusha provided a velvet touch to oversee his social growth. Daniel would show Benedict how to make his way in the world; she would show him how to behave in it as a gentleman. Both elements were necessary.

Jerusha's schoolroom was the parlor of her elegant home. There, surrounded by fine furnishings and good books, she could impart social graces and literary breadth. Young Benedict, having acquired a rather good classical foundation while at the Reverend Cogswell's academy, proved to be a most receptive pupil. After seven years of Jerusha's gentle shaping, he would be a cultured man.

Meanwhile, Daniel supervised the practical side of Benedict's development. The boy learned every part of the business by doing it, from the most basic forms of hard labor to the actual buying and selling. Children of the eighteenth century had to grow up fast. Teenagers approached life and learning with the maturity of adults. Dependable, intelligent, hardworking, quick to learn—Benedict soon took on more and more responsibility. Impressed, Daniel started taking him along on trading trips, both southward to the sea and northward into the interior of the country. Those overland visits included treks to the Lake Champlain area in New York, where

Benedict would later win fame in combat. By the final years of the apprenticeship, he was conducting such expeditions on his own. Serving as a trusted agent, he handled a good part of the Lathrops' business abroad. That fact reflects the remarkable esteem the men had for their ward's abilities. Between his own intense spirit of application and the Lathrops' careful nurturing, the apprentice flourished as he grew to manhood. It would be hard to imagine anyone who got more from an apprenticeship than Benedict Arnold. At its end he was fully ready to strike out confidently on his own.

Benedict suffered a hard blow, however, with the death of his mother when he was eighteen. Because he remained tied to the terms of his apprenticeship, he could not take on the burden of supporting his family. (His father was by then suffering from alcohol-induced dementia.) Responsibility for the family passed to his younger sister, his mother's namesake. Young Hannah, helped by handouts from relatives, kept the large house going and cared as best she could for the sodden shadow that was all that was left of Captain Arnold. Not until he succumbed, only months before his son reached legal manhood, was the family released from its mortification. Overwhelming debts left their home encumbered as collateral. Benedict Arnold's abiding sense of shame and resentment made him determined to succeed in life.

———•◦•———

Hostilities exploded between French and English forces in North America around the time Benedict Arnold began his apprenticeship. (That conflict, the French and Indian War, was triggered in the western woods by a brash young Virginian named George Washington.) The opposing sides tangled every year from 1755 through 1760, until English and colonial forces finally evicted the

French from the continent. The war itself formally ended with a treaty signed in Paris in 1763, but it was over, as far as Americans were concerned, with the capture of Montreal in September 1760. Benedict was nineteen.

Despite stories told after his treason—tales of repeated enlistments to collect bonuses, followed quickly by desertions—it appears that Benedict actually shouldered arms only once. In the third year of the war, French columns drove from Canada deep into New York, threatening western New England. Connecticut militia units mustered to march north. Arnold, just old enough to serve at sixteen, went with the contingent from Norwich with the approval of Daniel Lathrop. He saw no fighting, as the French withdrew before the troops from Norwich reached the scene of action. No further incursions seriously threatened Connecticut, and existing records indicate no further major mobilizations. Like all able-bodied men of his era, Benedict had the rudimentary training needed to bear arms. And he was willing to engage in combat if called upon. Indeed, it is quite probable that he enjoyed his time in uniform. But he was neither an experienced warrior, nor, at that time, a particularly eager one. The driven teenager's ultimate aim in life was to make money. Lots of money.

Toward that end, he could not have had better benefactors than the Lathrop brothers. Their commercial influence reached well beyond their base in Norwich, and they wanted to stretch it still further. That offered possibilities for Benedict and other young men like him to become junior partners in the expanding business. When it became clear that Benedict would leave the town of his birth as soon as he could, intent on escaping the stigma of his father's failure, the brothers pointed him westward to New Haven. In that busy port, already the third-largest town in Connecticut and growing rapidly, he would open another pharmacy linked to the one in Norwich. In a way, the Lathrops' scheme for growth represents one of the earliest examples of franchising in America.

For a venture of this magnitude, the impoverished intern needed capital. That, too, was forthcoming. The Lathrops provided an extremely generous amount of money and sent Benedict to London to make contacts and to purchase provisions for his new store. Arnold set up shop in New Haven in a rented storefront on Chapel Street. He raised a sign, proudly announcing himself as a druggist and bookseller, among other things. His upscale shop, brimming with London products, received a warm reception in the burgeoning city. Articulate, learned, polished, and hardworking, Benedict soon gained a loyal clientele. Twice in rapid succession he had to relocate to larger shops. The Lathrops' investment in him had paid off splendidly. Then, with his reputation made and his retail operation thriving, he decided to imitate the Lathrops by branching out into trading. Potential profits were immeasurably greater, and the prospect of going to sea was imminently more appealing to the active young man than selling beauty aids to town matrons and books to Yale students.

First, though, was the matter of closing completely that chapter of his life related to Norwich. Some time earlier, creditors had secured a lien on the Arnold home in order to cover the family's debts. Flush with funds from his flourishing business, Benedict returned to the site of his birth and purchased the old home place. Then, to the surprise of his former townsmen, he turned around and resold the house and property for a handsome profit. In that one act he signaled his monetary success, his business sense, and his utter disdain for the town where he had grown up. He brought his sister Hannah back to New Haven to help with his enterprises.

With a local partner in New Haven, Arnold bought a forty-ton sloop in 1764 and launched his trading career. He named the vessel *Fortune*. In another two years, at the age of twenty-five, he owned a total of three ships and was a rising figure in his adopted city. He was his own man, young, surprisingly successful, and poised to enter the tumultuous decade leading to the Revolutionary War.

———•·•———

George Washington's academic tutoring by his brother—and some sporadic formal schooling—faded away. He needed a trade, and at fifteen turned to surveying. From earlier experience at Ferry Farm, he knew he was adept with surveying instruments (he had practiced with his father's), and it was a trade that suited his taste for mathematics and precision. Moreover, with a vast, uncharted wilderness beckoning settlers westward over the Blue Ridge Mountains into the valley of the Shenandoah and beyond, surveyors were in heavy demand. He would be assured of work.

In the spring of George's sixteenth year, he accompanied a group on a surveying trip over the mountains, carefully observing the techniques of the experienced crew. That summer he took his first formal job, assisting in the laying out of the town of Alexandria, not far upriver from Mount Vernon. His work there was excellent, even a touch artistic. In following years, after obtaining an appointment to survey on his own, he crossed and re-crossed the mountains, mapping the far reaches of Virginia, marking boundaries for new farms, and acquiring a reputation for reliability. The teenager began to save and invest his earnings in land. He made his first major purchase at the age of eighteen, buying nearly 1,500 acres along a stream flowing into the Shenandoah River. He was officially a landowner. That was a heady feeling for an ambitious youth. He had taken the first step toward becoming one of his colony's wealthiest men.

Meanwhile, good fortune had entered the picture, presenting George an entry into the social scene of upper-crust Virginia society. It came in the person of William Fairfax. He conducted the American affairs of an English relative, Lord Thomas Fairfax, who held title to vast tracts of Virginia territory. William lived at Belvoir, a magnificent mansion for that time and place. It was constructed in the Georgian style and furnished exquisitely, including a prominent bust of William Shakespeare. Boasting a circular drive and an elaborate courtyard, the two-story brick structure overshadowed in splendor and size the neighboring Mount Vernon. Lawrence Washington married William's daughter, Anne, thus linking the Washingtons to the most powerful family in the Northern Neck. George, who spent a great deal of his time with Lawrence at Mount Vernon, became more than an occasional visitor at Belvoir. There he was exposed to a life far more sophisticated than he had seen at either Ferry Farm or Mount Vernon.

Four people entered George's life as a result of Lawrence's advantageous marriage, each of whom had a lasting influence on the shy but appealing lad. William Fairfax, who welcomed him into his home almost as a son. George William Fairfax, William's son, who, despite being eight years older than Washington and rather effete, became for a while his closest friend. Sally Fairfax, George William's wife, who as an eighteen-year-old bride completely captivated sixteen-year-old George Washington. And Lord Fairfax himself, who, upon making his home in America, promptly took a sponsor's liking to the energetic and dependable boy.

In fact, Lord Fairfax became something between a mentor and an exemplar to the unpolished lad, providing him lessons we can only guess at. One we do know of, and certainly among the most significant, had to do with a personality quirk exhibited early by the youngster. He had a free-wheeling temper. "I wish I could say that he governs his temper," Lord Fairfax wrote to George's mother at one point, identifying the flaw but maybe not suspecting that the son might well have inherited the undesirable trait from her. Exactly how he counseled the teenager is unknown, but it is known that George struggled for the rest of his life in a generally successful effort to keep his temper under control.

Related by marriage, respected for his strength of character, admired for his physical grace, George fit comfortably into the Fairfax world. Carefully patterning his behavior on the *Rules of Civility*, a lengthy listing of guidelines he had diligently copied in his schoolboy days and had worked ever since to internalize, he was unfailingly polite and diffident. He was good company. And he became a constant beneficiary of Fairfax largesse. Lord Fairfax and William gave him steady surveying work, George William gave him companionship, and Sally and the other ladies at Belvoir gave him the ability to banter easily, even flirtatiously, with women. He was almost as much at home at Belvoir as he was at Mount Vernon. At Belvoir he acquired a lifelong taste for such aristocratic pursuits as fox hunting, dancing, and theater. Here he gained the polish that would make him always welcome at balls and in drawing rooms. Here he also learned how to contain his emotions, to keep, as the English say, "a stiff upper lip." And here he whetted his appetite to excel in life. The Fairfaxes played the same role for George Washington that Jerusha Lathrop did for Benedict Arnold, imparting the sheen of a cultured gentleman.

Still, a huge gulf separated the young man from his Fairfax friends. They possessed vast inherited wealth; he had to work for a living. As a result, he lived two lives: one as a hanger-on in the lace-lined world of the landed gentry, and another as the rough-hewn surveyor toiling in the western wilds. As he approached his twenties, that gulf brought him to realize that he needed to do more to enhance his financial standing. Merely earning wages as a surveyor was too slow a path to the position in life he hungered for. Impatient, he had to find other ways to expand his prospects. Opportunity finally came, but on the back of tragedy.

Lawrence Washington seemed to have everything that his brother George did not. He was master of the Mount Vernon plantation. He had a thorough English education. He was a member of the House of Burgesses. He had an appointment as adjutant of Virginia's militia forces. He had a royal commission in the British army that gave him the security of half pay for life. He had high office in a consortium of speculators in western lands. He had a wife whose family wielded considerable influence. He also had tuberculosis.

Unless it could be treated early, tuberculosis—or consumption, as it was then called—was essentially a death warrant. Lawrence went to England seeking medical care, but the coughing persisted. George dropped his surveying work and took his ailing brother to visit naturally hot and supposedly therapeutic springs he knew in the west, but to no avail. In the fall of 1751 George accompanied Lawrence to the tropical island of Barbados, where the steadily weakening invalid could bask in warm Caribbean breezes while avoiding the chill winds of the Virginia winter. It would be the only time the future president would ever leave North America.

The Barbados adventure left lasting marks on the nineteen-year-old, literally as well as figuratively. The stormy voyage itself, thirty-seven long days at sea, may well have made him thankful that his attempt to become a midshipman five years before had failed. The brothers stayed seven weeks, living in a handsome house on the outskirts of Bridgetown overlooking the bay. For George it was a full and exciting period, punctuated by a serious illness of his own. Stricken with smallpox, he remained bedridden for three weeks. That episode left permanent pockmarks on his face, but also gave him immunity when the virulent disease later stalked the camps of the Continental Army. In the healthy weeks of his stay, George toured farming operations, examined the island's extensive defensive fortifications up close, attended the theater, dined with prominent families, and generally enjoyed the stimulation of the exotic setting. The young provincial, who had never before been far from his birthplace, gained a broadening glimpse of the wider world. Perhaps an echo of the abiding impact of his visit exists today in Mount Vernon itself. When George later revised and enlarged the mansion house, his design for the side facing away from the Potomac bore a marked resemblance to the landward side of his fondly remembered Barbados lodging. There was yet another important result of the trip, a fateful one for George Washington and for America. His thoughts turned to soldiering. For the first time in his life, he wrote about military matters.

The brothers were realists who recognized the odds against Lawrence's recovery. After his death, the position of adjutant in the Virginia militia would be vacant—and therein perhaps lay an opening for George. Given the flare of interest the younger man showed in the island's fortifications, it seems certain that the two spent some of the scores of quiet hours they had together discussing the possibilities of his succeeding Lawrence as adjutant. When Lawrence decided to go to Bermuda to try the air there, George took passage back to Virginia. Upon landing in January 1752, he went directly to Williamsburg to call on the new governor, Robert Dinwiddie, and deliver letters from Dinwiddie's acquaintances in Barbados. Dinwiddie had the power to appoint George adjutant should Lawrence not find a cure in Bermuda, and George wanted to make an impression. Dinwiddie, however, had already decided to create several such positions. The adjutant's primary responsibility was to assure that local militia units were properly trained, and the growing colony needed more than one person to cover all the different sectors. That spring, George began actively seeking an appointment to one of the new positions. He was only twenty and had no military experience, but he possessed boundless self-confidence and ambition and had a solid reputation for trustworthiness. Furthermore, he had connections through his brother and the Fairfaxes.

Lawrence returned that summer, resigned to an early grave. He wrote his last will and testament, made his farewells, and died. Governor Dinwiddie appointed four adjutants to replace him. One was George Washington. Before his twenty-first birthday, George put on his uniform and took the oath as a major in the Virginia militia. With hardly a break, he wore it for the next six years straight.

The new soldier's first trial was one of endurance and perseverance. France and England were stumbling toward conflict in the Ohio Valley, with French trappers spilling south from Canada and English settlers flowing west from the middle colonies. French troops were known to be somewhere south of Lake Erie and appeared to be preparing to penetrate farther yet. The apparent point of collision was the forks of the Ohio River, the site of today's Pittsburgh, where the Monongahela and Allegheny rivers join to form the Ohio. Late in 1753 King George II ordered Governor Dinwiddie to send a warning message to the French commander telling him to turn his troops around and return to Canada. The journey, in the deep of winter, over hundreds of miles of roadless forest, across swollen rivers, and through regions inhabited by hostile tribes, would be hazardous in the extreme. Chances were strong that the messenger would never return. Who should be sent? Major Washington knew some of the route already, and he was young and hardy from years of surveying. He volunteered for the mission. Dinwiddie gave it to him.

Washington's journey in dreadful weather over horrific terrain was epic. He nearly drowned, came close to death from exposure, and barely escaped being killed by a rogue Indian. But he found the French commander, delivered the letter, surreptitiously gathered intelligence on enemy dispositions and strengths, and dragged himself back to Williamsburg with the French response. A less determined man would not have made it. Dinwiddie published Washington's report of the two-month journey. Its wide distribution in both Britain and America gave the young officer his first taste of fame.

The French continued southward toward the forks of the Ohio, where they intended to erect a fort. Following the king's directive, Virginia mobilized a regiment to preempt the French plan. Dinwiddie appointed George Washington to be the deputy commander of the regiment and promoted him to lieutenant colonel. While the commander recruited more troops, Washington rushed westward in April 1754 with the forces available to him. The French reached the area first, but Washington pressed on, cutting a road for supplies. He assumed that the regimental commander would catch up to the column and bring new orders. Orders did not come—and neither did the colonel.

At the end of May, Washington ran into a group of French soldiers and immediately attacked. The Virginians inflicted heavy casualties on the surprised Frenchmen, killing ten, including the commander. One American was lost. It was Washington's first battle, and he was exhilarated by the experience. "I heard the bullets whistle," he wrote, "and believe me there was something charming in the sound." As all soldiers who have been under fire know, it is indeed pleasing to hear that sound, because it means that the deadly little missiles have missed.

Realizing that a larger body of Frenchmen and Indians would soon bear down on him, Washington withdrew to what appeared, to his inexperienced eye, to be more defensible terrain. In a large, low clearing dominated by tree-covered higher ground, he erected a hasty fortification. Calling it Fort Necessity, he estimated that it would permit him to fend off five hundred attackers. Actually, as he soon learned in blood and mortification, he had erected a death trap.

Reinforcements arrived, raising the Virginians' strength to about three hundred men. They brought word that the regimental commander had died—and that George Washington had been appointed to replace him. The new colonel found himself tested at once. Some six hundred French soldiers reached the clearing on July 3. Seeking revenge for Washington's earlier assault on their comrades, and supported by a hundred or more Indians, they attacked at once. A driving rainstorm transformed Fort Necessity into a mushy quagmire—and the mud quickly turned red. Musketeers firing from higher ground killed thirty Virginians by nightfall and wounded another seventy. The Frenchmen suffered three deaths. Distraught and humiliated, Washington accepted an offer to surrender. In a touch of martial gallantry, the victorious French commander permitted his opponents to keep their weapons if they would agree to go home. At dawn the next morning the surviving Virginians filed out of their woeful fort and headed east.

To say the very least, provincial officials were not pleased with the young colonel. Nor was Washington happy when he learned of a plan to disband his regiment and replace it with independent companies commanded by captains. As a colonial colonel, he was already in the galling situation of being subordinate to any officer holding a commission from the king. That rankled him no end, and the new arrangement would only make matters worse. Submitting to the change, he later wrote, would have been simply "too degrading." Angrily declining to take one of the companies and the accompanying demotion in rank, he resigned his commission. He took up residence at Mount Vernon, leasing it from Lawrence's widow, who had remarried and moved away. The new responsibilities of running a plantation tugged powerfully at his attention, but soldiering remained foremost in his heart despite the unfavorable turn of events. "My inclinations are strongly bent to arms," he stated, obviously hoping to find some role that would allow him to remain in uniform. His second chance came sooner than anyone might have predicted, for his forest clashes had ignited a war between France and England.

Major General Edward Braddock arrived with two regiments of British regulars and more artillery than had ever been seen in Virginia early in 1755. He had orders to settle the French and Indian issue. He planned to do so by marching straight to the forks of the Ohio, where the French had erected a bastion they named Fort Duquesne. There Braddock expected simply to overwhelm the defenders.

Besides bringing George a chance to don his uniform again, the advent of actual war and the arrival of British troops opened the possibility of earning the much-desired prize of a royal commission. To have any sort of security and to advance in the military profession it was essential to hold an appointment from London rather than merely a colonial militia position. Washington wrote Braddock at once, volunteering to accompany him as an aide. He added that he hoped "to attain a small degree of knowledge in the military art" by serving the general in that role. In the campaign to come, Braddock would do virtually everything wrong, but in this instance he made a good decision. He accepted the Virginian's offer.

A lightning move was not in Braddock's vocabulary. June was upon him before he was ready to march. He lurched west, following the rough road hacked out a year earlier by Washington, leading a massive column stretching some five miles from head to tail. It moved with agonizing slowness. Covering its own length in a day was considered good time. Washington fretted at the slow pace—they were giving the French too much time to prepare. Braddock split his forces and pushed ahead with a lighter element, but the advance was barely swifter. Weeks passed. French reinforcements arrived while the English column crawled slowly toward the forks of the Ohio.

Finally, on July 9, about a day's march from Fort Duquesne, Braddock felt that victory was at hand. He had with him more than a dozen artillery pieces and some 1,200 soldiers, mostly regulars. He started out that morning assuming he would besiege the fort by nightfall. Washington, recovering from a violent bout of dysentery, rode at his side on a padded saddle.

Contrary to Braddock's expectations, however, the French commander chose not to wait passively behind his walls. He marched out the same morning, planning to ambush the snake-like British column. To their mutual surprise, the two forces ran into each other in the forest. Braddock attempted to form his units into a line of battle according to conventional European tactics. The French and Indian fighters, on the other hand, raced immediately for protection in the trees along both sides of the road and began flanking the milling Englishmen. At close range from protected positions in the woods, they were able to pour devastating musket fire into the densely clustered groups of redcoats, turning confusion into chaos.

Panic took over. Formerly proud regulars fled to the rear, many dropping their weapons as they ran. Indians chased down and scalped the slower ones. Scores more were shot, often by their own comrades, in the smoke and bedlam. Leaders were swept along with the terror-stricken mob.

George Washington was one of the rare bright spots on the English side that day. Battle galvanized him. Fearless and dynamic, he seemed to be everywhere. Exposed constantly to fire, riding from unit to unit carrying orders, calming frightened soldiers, coordinating actions, he had much to do with bringing some sense of order to the melee. Four times musket balls ripped through his clothing. One bullet carried his hat away. Two horses were shot beneath him. By all accounts, he was the most active and visible person on the battlefield. When a marksman dropped Braddock, Washington and a few other officers stabilized the situation by establishing a defensive position to the rear where the disorganized survivors could rally. The French, satisfied with the punishment they had already inflicted, pulled back to Fort Duquesne. The British, badly bloodied and thoroughly beaten, with over half their men dead or wounded, retreated hastily, leaving French and Indian forces firmly in control of the battlefield. Laurels went only to the young Virginia volunteer, for the disaster would have been far worse without his extraordinary bravery and leadership.

Word of Washington's remarkable steadiness under the most trying of circumstances spread rapidly through the colony and beyond. Governor Dinwiddie, reassessing his earlier unflattering opinion of the young officer, placed him in command of all Virginia's military forces, with the mission of defending the frontier.

The new position, however, did not come with a regular commission. The overall commander in chief alone had the power to grant that. Washington campaigned hard for the appointment.

Twice he made long trips to plead his case in person, once in early 1756 going all the way to Boston to call on the senior British commander, and a year later riding to Philadelphia to meet with his successor. Both men turned him down, and the second one humiliated him. The experience was devastating to the young officer; only his sense of duty kept him in uniform.

The new responsibility thrust upon the twenty-three-year-old was daunting. Braddock's defeat had emboldened the Indians and left the western settlements exposed to attack. Prodded by the French, hostile tribes seized the moment to launch raid after devastating raid. For three terrible years Washington's undermanned and outmatched units waged a largely futile defensive campaign. The bloody edge of British civilization retreated inexorably eastward, as Virginians managed at best a valiant rear-guard action. The only way to stop the marauders, Washington came to realize, was to strike at the source of the enemy's power: Fort Duquesne. However, his pleas to do so were not heeded—Britain's overall strategy placed the priority of operations in the Canadian theater. The bloodletting dragged grimly on. Washington somehow kept his inadequate units in the field, more sieve than shield, waiting for the British to turn their attention to the southern theater once again.

The day of deliverance finally arrived in 1758, when Brigadier General John Forbes launched an expedition from Philadelphia to the forks of the Ohio. Colonel Washington, at the head of the colonial forces from Virginia, marched with him. It was the young officer's fourth trip to that strategic place, and it turned out to be all but anti-climactic. The French commander, isolated at the far end of a long and exposed line of communications, elected not to fight. He burned everything he couldn't carry and withdrew to Canada. General Forbes occupied the site and renamed it Fort Pitt. The war in Virginia was over.

Victory, however, was not much of a balm for Virginia's first soldier. He had been campaigning almost constantly for six years in brutal conditions, and was worn down both physically and emotionally. Worse, his abiding desire to gain a royal commission had come to naught. Despite all his service and sacrifices, British officials continued to spurn him. A renowned hero he might have been, but in their eyes Washington remained a provincial. Bone-tired and sorely disappointed, and with the scene of war having shifted away from his colony, he decided to hang up his uniform and concentrate on farming. He was twenty-seven years old.

CHAPTER FIVE

RADICALS

WHEN BENEDICT ARNOLD OPENED SHOP IN NEW Haven, the long, disruptive French and Indian War was all but over. England stood supreme on the North American continent from the Atlantic coast to the banks of the Mississippi. For a new businessman, a bountiful era of prosperity seemed imminent, but actions taken by Parliament turned financial promise into economic depression.

With France gone from North America, British regiments now had to occupy posts in the vast area north and west of the thirteen colonies. They had in particular to reduce friction between Indian tribes—some still on a war footing to protect their hunting grounds—and land-hungry Americans eager to push westward. Already burdened by a huge war debt, and now obliged to find additional funds to meet its new responsibilities, the government in London decided to raise money in the colonies. On the face of it that was not an illogical step. New World economies were doing well and the colonists themselves had not been overly taxed to support the war effort. Indeed, not a few had found the war to be a good occasion for profiteering. Besides, if redcoats were to be stationed in America for the purpose of protecting Americans, it seemed only fair that those reaping the benefits should help defray the costs.

Of course, that is not how things looked on the other side of the Atlantic. Colonials were not at all interested in taxes levied under any circumstances whatsoever, and could not see how Indians alone posed more of a threat than had the French and Indians combined. Resentment simmered. And it didn't help that the government implemented its postwar fiscal policy with an inept and heavy hand. Just as Arnold's ventures were flourishing, a jumble of new regulations abruptly altered the mercantile environment in the colonies. Those rules imposed a revised slate of taxes on consumer products, created a long list of items banned from international trade, and prohibited the import of many non-British goods, including such basic staples as rum and wine. Perhaps most infuriating to the merchants, however, was London's firm intent that the new mandates would be strictly enforced. Worse yet, they would be enforced by the Royal Navy, not local officials who could usually be depended upon to be indifferent about collecting levies. Taxes of one kind or another had been on the books for as long as memory stretched—and had been largely circumvented for just as long. Smuggling had become an accepted and upright way of life, especially for New Englanders, but Parliament's changed stance threatened that time-honored tradition.

Trading patterns established over decades began to unravel. Ever-resourceful Yankee merchants tried at first to find ways around the most onerous restrictions, but were overwhelmed when still more transatlantic bolts struck them. London ended the practice of permitting individual colonies to issue money, precipitating a crisis because of the resulting severe shortage of currency. Cash-strapped businessmen, sitting on large inventories that they could neither pay for nor sell, began to lurch toward bankruptcy. Recession struck and slid rapidly into depression. Then, exhibiting incredible insensitivity, the king and his ministers stoked higher the flames of resentment by directing that civilians could be forced to house soldiers where barracks were unavailable. That was a step sure to be seen by Englishmen anywhere as an arrogant slap in the face. Finally, apparently blind to the worsening negative impact of the stream of ill-advised acts, Parliament passed the Stamp Act. That law required tax stamps to be affixed to virtually every kind of paper product, from newspapers to licenses to playing cards. It was one act too far—igniting spontaneous and often violent resistance throughout the American colonies.

Uniting in opposition to the series of oppressive laws, the separate colonies began tentatively to coordinate their official positions. Nine of them sent delegates to a gathering—called the Stamp Act Congress—in New York, where they prepared petitions to George III and Parliament and adopted a declaration of rights and liberties. Meanwhile, a rowdy underground movement called the Sons of Liberty gained adherents by the thousands and devoted its considerable muscle to intimidating officials who attempted to enforce the provisions of the Stamp Act. In the face of such evidence of spreading anarchy, London rescinded the hated Stamp Act in 1766, ushering in a short cooling-off period.

Benedict Arnold had been in the thick of the unrest in Connecticut. London's restrictions and the accompanying economic turbulence had hammered his ventures. Like other merchants, he found himself floundering in debt and scrambling to avert bankruptcy. He joined the Sons of Liberty to agitate against the implementation of the injurious laws and quickly became a stalwart in that radical body. At the same time he sought to diversify his business by developing additional routes and clients. Increasingly, he investigated North American possibilities, carrying cargoes to ports along the coast as well as up the Hudson River to Albany and sailing along the St. Lawrence River to Quebec and Montreal. That astute expansion, coupled with a good degree of successful smuggling, carried him through the darkest days of the depression and left him in a relatively strong position when better times returned.

Meanwhile, Arnold had not neglected the imperative of gaining social standing. He craved community respect and was slowly earning it. Some had already taken to calling him "Dr. Arnold" in deference to his skills as a druggist, while others often referred to him as "Captain Arnold" for his exploits of seamanship. But as a recent immigrant from another town, he did not receive automatic acceptance into the aloof ranks of New Haven's old-line families. Although highly charming and successful he was nevertheless an outsider. For Arnold, whose bitter memories of his impoverished and belittled years in Norwich were ever-present, winning status stood on a par with making money. Among the steps he took to establish respectability was to join the Masons. Freemasonry was new to America, but it attracted many leading citizens, including Benjamin Franklin and George Washington. In Benedict's case, being a member helped him climb up the social scale by widening his circle of influential intimates. Doors previously closed began to open. One fellow lodge member, Samuel Mansfield, the county sheriff and also a well-to-do merchant, took a special liking to the bright newcomer and struck up a business partnership with him. As luck would have it, Mansfield had an eligible daughter.

Not only did Margaret Mansfield offer the possibility of quick access to the upper rungs of New Haven society, but it appears that

Benedict fell genuinely in love with her. Never one to hesitate when opportunity or passion arose, he launched a persistent and ultimately triumphant courtship of the doubly desirable young woman. They were married in February 1767, when she was twenty-two and he twenty-six.

Their first five years of marriage were turbulent both for them and for the country. After rescinding the Stamp Act in 1766, a petulant Parliament waited only a year before issuing yet another scheme of colonial taxation. Resistance was immediate and widespread, with the Sons of Liberty and others resorting to violence. The king in turn ordered troops to Boston, setting the stage for later bloodshed. The renewed tumult did not help the economy recover. Arnold spent much time at sea struggling to keep his staggering business going while his wife and sister handled affairs in New Haven. Those two competent women kept the home base of the Arnold enterprises intact, permitting Arnold himself to range farther and longer in search of remunerative cargoes. Running the complex ventures and the large home kept the Arnold ladies quite busy. There were employees to manage, books to keep, customers to satisfy, servants and household slaves to supervise, and children to raise. Margaret gave birth to Benedict VI a year after the wedding, and two more boys followed, in 1769 and 1772. Well before the third arrived, redcoats and civilians had clashed in Boston. The "Boston Massacre" became a rallying cry for radicals and prompted a temporarily subdued Parliament to drop all taxes in an effort to pacify the agitated colonists. All taxes, that is, except the one on tea.

Arnold's hard work and shrewd endeavors, not to mention his willingness to take considerable risks in his ventures, paid off handsomely. He transported a remarkably wide assortment of freight— horses one way, lumber another, wool to cool climes, rum nearly everywhere, merchandise of all kinds to meet every demand. By the early 1770s he had broken free of the financial thickets and was one of the richest men in New Haven. Some reckoned him to be the wealthiest. He enjoyed an enviable reputation as a bold trader, a courageous sea captain, and an astute businessman. People knew him also as a man not to be crossed, for he had amassed a formidable record as a duelist and a vigilante.

Arnold's first major clash with New Haven authorities came in early 1766. After learning that one of his sailors had attempted to earn a bounty by reporting him for smuggling, Benedict confronted the would-be informer and, in his own words, "gave him a little chastisement" to encourage him to leave New Haven. Failing to gauge adequately the fury of the pugnacious sea captain, the sailor stopped at a local tavern instead of leaving. That ignited Arnold's wrath. Rounding up several crew members to help, he went to the tavern, dragged the fellow out, tied him to the town's whipping post, flogged him roundly, and chased him out of town.

That prompt and forceful action met with full approbation from ships' crews, dockhands, and other blue-collar workers in New Haven. But it bothered some of the town's more cautious leaders, who were still hoping to avoid internal conflict. Arnold had to appear before justice of the peace Roger Sherman for taking matters into his own hands. Sherman assessed him a small fine. He paid it, but, unapologetic, defiantly led bonfire protests against those he portrayed as too meek to stand up to British insults. Then he excoriated those same supine leaders in a scathing newspaper column. Thereafter, Benedict Arnold wore the mantle of the champion of ordinary citizens in the area. (Sherman, a later signer of both the Declaration of Independence and the Constitution, would not forget the encounter. It would echo in his mind eleven years later when he was a member of the Congress considering Benedict Arnold for promotion in the Continental Army.)

Just as the feisty trader would tolerate no threat to his person or business, neither would he give an inch in the brawling, free-wheeling ports of call he frequented on his long voyages. To maintain control over contentious seamen and to avoid chiseling by unscrupulous agents, a ship captain had to be combative. Arnold was. Quick to take offense and owning a hair-trigger temper, he called a number of individuals—no one knows how many—to duels over what he considered slights to his sense of honor. Icily cool when facing an opponent's pistol at twenty paces, and a confident marksman himself, he never lost one of the deadly contests, and was apparently never even wounded.

A widely reported instance of one of his duels in the Caribbean illustrates his deadly seriousness in such encounters. His opponent, being the challenged party, had the right to shoot first. He missed. Arnold then fired, but hit the man's arm. According to the arcane code of dueling, that should have sufficed to satisfy whatever affront there had been to initiate the clash. But not so with Arnold. Indicating that they should reload, he snarled, "I give you notice—if you miss this time I shall kill you." Shaken and fearing for his life, the wounded foe apologized to end the duel. Word got around that young Arnold was not to be trifled with.

The fiercely competitive world of seafaring traders was sure to be contentious in the best of times. A difficult economy deepened rivalries as ship captains vied for the more prized cargoes. Despite his relative youth, Arnold's cleverness in deal-making and his willingness to work longer and harder than anyone else made him more successful than most, sparking a degree of jealousy. Moreover, the upstart's direct, unbending manner tended to alienate many of his fellow captains. That combination of envy and antipathy among his peers made Arnold a ripe target for petty retaliation. Although his detractors shrank from outright confrontation, they were not above whispering behind his back. Suggestions of whoring and venereal disease surfaced back home in New Haven, causing some understandable consternation in his family and threatening his standing in the community. Attacking the rumors head-on by obtaining depositions refuting them and by lodging lawsuits, Arnold apparently cleared his name to the satisfaction of his wife and those fellow citizens he cared about. He undoubtedly learned from that episode the imperative of turning to aggressive action in the defense of reputation. At home or abroad, Benedict Arnold was indeed a man to be taken seriously.

A leading force in opposition to British taxation policies and a surging star in Connecticut, the prosperous merchant had risen far in the decade or so since he had been a mere apprentice apothecary. It was time, he decided, to signal his success. Much as his father had done long ago in Norwich, Benedict designed a resplendent home reflecting his eminent stature in New Haven. Located on three choice acres along Water Street, replete with formal gardens and outlying structures for a coach and horses, the stately residence was nothing short of imposing, inside as well as out. Its spacious interior was richly appointed, including imported mahogany paneling and luxurious furnishings. The mansion made a clear statement in grandiosity that the Arnold name had returned to prominence.

The paint could hardly have dried on the new home's white picket fence before King George III and his ministers prodded slumbering colonial animosity again, this time by shipping to America large consignments of tea for which full duty was to be collected. Protests erupted in ports from Charleston to Boston, blocking the unloading of the tea. Goaded by Samuel Adams, radicals in Boston went an aggressive step further. On a mid-December night in 1773, a boisterous gang dressed as Indians clambered aboard the anchored ships and threw the tea into the harbor. An outraged London reacted to the "Boston Tea Party" by passing a number of punitive acts, notably closing the port of Boston and withdrawing rights of self-rule from Massachusetts. London also reinstated the Quartering Act and placed lands north and west of the Ohio River in the domain of the province of Quebec. Those laws assured that Americans everywhere would be riled, not just tea merchants and their supporters along the Atlantic seaboard. Capping a busy spring, the king sent General Thomas Gage to Boston as both governor of the colony and military commander in chief in North America. Accompanied by an occupying force of more than three thousand soldiers, Gage reached the sullen city in May 1774 and took up his duties. In less than a year the Revolutionary War would begin, and Benedict Arnold would have scant time to enjoy his new home or savor the other fruits of his wealth.

As the fighting in the French and Indian War shifted to other theaters, and with his uniform put away, George Washington turned wholly to civilian activities. High among them were his Mount Vernon plantation, Virginia politics, and the alluring west. But first came marriage. Maintaining the Washington family tradition of marrying advantageously, he wed Martha Custis in January 1759, the same month he resigned his commission.

When George had first met Martha she was married. Other women over the years had caught his eye, including an imposing member of an influential New York family, but nothing came of those possibilities. For one thing, his military duties often kept him out of circulation. Further, as various fathers realistically assessed the young man's potential, he did not appear to be the best of bets for their daughters. However, by the time Martha's husband died, George Washington had become a celebrity because of his battlefield heroics, and he was a major landowner. For her part, besides being attractive and available, Martha was one of the richest women in Virginia.

George waited a decent interval before calling on the winsome widow in March 1758, but the courtship itself was a fast one, indicating that the idea of marrying may not have been a new one to either of them. Only a month after that first visit, the two were poised to announce their engagement. George began at once to expand Mount Vernon. Time was short—he had to lead his regiment in the final effort against Fort Duquesne—so he simply added another floor to the house he had known since childhood, making it two and a half stories high. For the time being it would be a practical rather than a grand home. Workers completed most of the renovation while Washington was campaigning, and it was ready in time to accommodate his bride.

A few months older than her new husband, Martha was the mother of two small children from her previous marriage, which had lasted seven years. To her new marriage, Martha brought maturity and warmth. George brought high energy and renown— he won election to the House of Burgesses shortly before the wedding. And combining their two considerable estates put them among Virginia's foremost families.

Having formerly been a soldier who happened also to farm, Washington transformed himself wholeheartedly into a full-time planter. Land was his source of wealth, and he set out to harness the possibilities of his extensive holdings. Willing to experiment, in fact eager to do so, he found novel ways to make his acres more productive. Tobacco for export to English markets had from the earliest days of settlement been Virginia's traditional cash crop, and Mount Vernon fields had always grown it. But when it became apparent to Washington that his soil was less than ideal for tobacco, he turned with little hesitation to wheat and corn for local sale. Soon he was producing 15,000 to 20,000 bushels annually. And that was but one initiative among many. The Potomac brimmed with fish—Washington started a major fishing operation. People needed meat—Washington raised hogs, providing tons of pork a year. The climate favored fruit trees—Washington grew orchard upon orchard of cherries, apples, and other fruit. Grain needed grinding—Washington became a miller. Virtually everyone deemed liquor to be a necessity—and Washington eventually became a distiller. Innovative in products, he also sought improved means. His inventive activities ranged from designing a better plow to the grafting of fruit trees to exploring new uses for animals. Attempting to tame buffalo was one such effort. In all these efforts, success did not come at once, easily, or without setbacks. Dogged at times by debt, strapped for cash (for many of the same reasons that plagued New England merchants), at the mercy—as farmers always are—of bad weather, he faced any number of challenges in his early years. But he persevered. By the time he had been at the plantation's helm for a decade, Mount Vernon was a model of the sort of self-sufficient economy that America itself could become. Had he never risen to such awesome eminence for his military and political accomplishments, George Washington might well be better remembered today as one of our nation's preeminent leaders in husbandry.

Securing a seat in Virginia's House of Burgesses had long been a dream of his. The ambitious young man had first run when he was only twenty-three, but had lost. Next time around he organized more effectively, and won. Among other campaigning tactics he served up more than 150 gallons of alcoholic beverages, a very generous amount considering that there were fewer than 400 voters to consume it. At every subsequent election he spent just as freely, usually hosting a party afterwards. He won reelection every time.

After the wedding the newlyweds traveled to Williamsburg for George's initial appearance as a member of the colonial government, where his fellow members applauded him with a resolution of appreciation for his outstanding military service. That praise notwithstanding, and despite having attained his goal of becoming a representative, Washington never made any concerted effort to take a major role in the assembly. For the most part he sat quietly through sessions, rarely weighing in on issues, and compiling an altogether rather poor record of attendance. During the first dozen years or so of his service in that body, the focus of his attention was simply elsewhere. On Mount Vernon, of course, which had become legally his by inheritance in 1761, and on community activities such as Masonic events, service in local offices, and family affairs. And on the ever-beckoning lands beyond the mountains.

From his earliest surveying trips Washington's eyes had been fixed on the western horizon. As a soldier he had crossed the mountains four times and had spent years fending off danger in those dense, dark woods. He knew that an immense, uncharted wilderness stretched off toward the faraway Mississippi River, and he also knew that Virginians and others lusted to open the area to settlement. It isn't at all surprising, then, that he acted to grab a share for himself as soon as France ceded possession to England. He joined a group of fellow speculators seeking to gain a grant from the king for two and a half million acres. Although that effort was thwarted by London's 1763 decision to bar white settlement beyond the mountains, Washington continued to explore the area surreptitiously, betting that the ban would be lifted before long. He employed a surveyor to hunt for the most valuable lands, cautioning the man to keep "this whole matter a profound secret" lest it attract either censure or competition. Circumventing the king's rules to get acreage in the west was lawbreaking not too unlike smuggling in New England to avoid taxes on imports. It was a temptation too strong to resist.

When the ban on settlement was lifted in 1768, Washington was ready to leap. Former governor Robert Dinwiddie had promised to those who had served against the French at the forks of the Ohio in 1754 that they could have land over the mountains. A more recent royal proclamation authorized grants of western land to veterans of the French and Indian War. Colonel Washington considered himself qualified on both counts and applied at once. He also began buying up the rights of others who did not share his burning desire to acquire property in the west. In the autumn of 1770, eager to find and lay claim to the best tracts, he once more traveled his old trail to the forks of the Ohio. Then, with a small party in two canoes, he paddled some 250 miles down the Ohio to its intersection with the Great Kanawha River. There he made his claim by marking boundary trees around a fertile area fronting the Ohio for about fifteen miles and reaching some fifty miles deep. For the rest of his life he remained enthusiastic about developing the western interior.

In this pursuit, as in farming, Washington was innovative. Among many ideas he pondered, for instance, was one calling for the opening of the frontier to water transport by establishing a network of rivers and canals, a prescient concept but one in which he was a bit ahead of his time. Eight years of war followed by eight more as president were to prevent him from exploiting his interests in the far forests as he would have preferred. But even in the midst of those dramatic events, George Washington's vision of an inland empire never faded. It stayed with him all his life and was ever a guiding objective, in times of war and of peace.

Although the relative isolation and independence of plantation life shielded him to some degree from the vicissitudes of London's colonial policies after 1763, Washington could not escape them. He had quit military service with bitterness over the demeaning way British officials had rebuffed his efforts to gain a regular commission in the army, and he wanted nothing much more than to be left alone. But that was not to be. Slowly, act by act and year by year, George III and his ministers goaded Washington toward rebellion.

Right at the outset London's decision to block English immigration into the former French territories struck an especially raw nerve among all those who had cast covetous eyes westward. Then, when Parliament also put a stop to local printing of paper currency, Washington and other planters suffered along with coastal merchants because they could no longer generate enough cash to do business. Angry, he wrote that the matter might "set the whole country in flames." He watched ruefully as the waves of ill-timed and ill-considered taxation measures washed over the colonies. While disapproving of the violence perpetrated by partisan groups such as the Sons of Liberty, he nonetheless sensed a widening gulf between the values of the New World and those of the Old. He began to assume a more strident position in the Burgesses as that body took steps to resist. Growing increasingly resentful, he had by 1769 reached a point of frustration serious enough to cause him to write for the first time of the possibility of a resort to arms.

When the artist Charles Willson Peale came to Mount Vernon in 1772 to paint portraits, Washington chose to have his done wearing his militia uniform. He is seen in the painting armed with both a sword and a rifle.

By 1774 relations between Britain and America were approaching a crisis. British punitive reactions to the "Boston Tea Party" hit all colonies hard. Vital liberties appeared to be threatened everywhere, not only in New England. Moreover, for Washington himself the Quebec Act of that same year struck directly at his personal aspirations in the west, a blow painfully compounded when the British secretary of state ruled that western land grants for veterans of the French and Indian War applied only to regulars. Not only did that ruling wipe out the Virginian's claim to thousands of acres, it tore the scab off the sore of his old resentment at having been so brusquely refused a regular commission. Enough was enough. A line between Great Britain and the colonies "ought to be drawn," he proclaimed.

The man who rode away from Mount Vernon to attend the First Continental Congress in September 1774 bore none of the external trappings of a revolutionary. Gentlemanly, even courtly, he was by no means a firebrand. Civil and extraordinarily self-controlled, he had never fought a duel in spite of occasional serious provocations. A very wealthy landowner, he had much to lose by upsetting the economic system under which he had prospered. A much respected and admired member of society, he stood to gain little by disrupting the social system that accorded him eminence. And yet, and yet...freedom itself was at stake. If London could so lightly take away the rights of citizens of Massachusetts, Americans were safe nowhere. If Boston could be occupied, so could Williamsburg. General Gage's imposition of martial rule in that northern city, Washington wrote, provided Americans "unexampled testimony of the most despotic system of tyranny that ever was practiced in a free government." The Virginia planter was ready to take a stand.

George Washington had made plans in the early 1770s to enlarge Mount Vernon. Like Benedict Arnold, he wanted his home to reflect his prominence. Workmen began in 1774 to extend both ends of the structure and later erected a high-columned piazza across the entire side facing the river. But, also like Arnold, Washington was fated to have far fewer opportunities to enjoy his mansion than he ever could have anticipated.

Both were fed up with ministerial meddling in colonial affairs and stood ready to act if necessary to correct matters. Both felt that their individual and collective liberties were endangered. And both had come to think of themselves and their neighbors primarily as Americans rather than Englishmen. They were radicals ready to draw a line between colonial America and Great Britain.

CHAPTER SIX

WAR CLOUDS

————◆◆◆◆————

AFTER THE FIRST CONTINENTAL CONGRESS IN 1774, militiamen began drilling with newfound earnestness. Some peremptorily seized royal munitions. New units formed. Officials started stockpiling supplies.

King George III concluded that his New England subjects were in "a state of rebellion." On that score he was surely correct, but opposition boiled not only in New England. It was pervasive in other colonies as well, particularly in powerful Virginia. The exasperated monarch sounded a trumpet call to war against the rebels, declaring that "blows must decide whether they are to be subject to this country or independent." For their part, Americans were not yet prepared to declare independence, but they had obviously decided that it was time to stand up for their rights.

————◆◆————

Returning to New Haven from the Congress, Benedict Arnold plunged headlong into a leading role in the Sons of Liberty. That vigilante organization beat the drums of defiance and chastised supporters of the British. Records provide no full accounting of the intimidating activities of the Sons in New Haven, but they were undeniably harsh, and apparently effective. One victim wrote later that citizens dared not stand up to "the mobs of Colonel [David] Wooster and Dr. Benedict Arnold." Colonial supporters of the British—calling themselves loyalists but labeled as Tories by others— had a choice between retreating into silence or leaving altogether.

Men flocked to arms all across Connecticut as the colony worked to raise a respectable force, which wasn't as easy to do as it might sound. Militia units of long standing were often closed to new volunteers, serving almost as private clubs for cronies who clung to membership for its social aspects. Nor were all members certifiably radical enough for current circumstances. Many patriots, as they styled themselves, were obliged to form their own organizations from scratch. Benedict Arnold and sixty-four others, described as "gentlemen of influence and high respectability," banded together in the final month of 1774 to create a militia company. Each participant agreed to furnish his own weapon, purchase his own uniform, and find his own equipment. None of them had any particular military expertise, so they hired a knowledgeable person to instruct them. Drilling at least once a week, learning to fire and march first by squads and then as an entity, acquiring basic field survival skills, the new company considered itself ready for battle only three months after forming. Connecticut officials apparently agreed, for they chartered the unit as the Governor's Second Company of Foot Guards and authorized the men to elect officers. Second Company held its election on March 15, choosing as its captain Benedict Arnold.

That selection was no surprise. Arnold was well known among local radicals, he was an inspiring leader with much experience both as a ship master and in the Sons of Liberty, and he had been a key instigator in the founding of the company from the outset. Besides, he was independently wealthy and had quite likely helped many of the men procure their equipment, either with loans or outright grants. Arnold was eager to serve—selection as a militia commander certainly solidified his status and boosted his influence in New Haven.

The new captain did not have long to wait before hearing the war tocsin sounded. Early on April 19 a British column marched out of Boston to destroy patriot munitions stored at Concord, a few miles to the west. A small group of Americans made a hesitant, ineffectual stand at the village of Lexington along the way, losing eight killed but providing for posterity a beginning point for the Revolutionary War. Pushing on quickly to Concord, the raiders found not a supply depot, for the stores had mostly been removed, but instead a growing and soon overpowering mass of swarming militiamen. Retreating redcoats ran a bloody gauntlet all the way back to the safety of their lines at Boston, suffering severely in killed, wounded, and captured, and narrowly escaping annihilation. The war had started! Galloping riders spread out to alert other towns and colonies even before the fighting ended that day. A horseman brought the electrifying news to New Haven on Friday, April 21. Arnold gathered his men at once and urged them to join their compatriots outside of Boston. They resolved to march the very next morning.

The unit assembled early on April 22, strengthened by the late addition of several enthusiastic Yale University students and cheered on by a boisterous throng of well-wishers. However, not all of New Haven's citizens were supportive of an immediate move. Some of the more cautious leaders wanted to delay until they had a clearer picture of what had happened at Lexington and Concord. They were meeting that morning in a nearby tavern to discuss the matter, and had refused to open the town's powder magazine for Arnold's company. In a high state of agitation, he marched his troops to the tavern and demanded the keys to the magazine. Aware of Arnold's temper, the men inside sent out Colonel David Wooster, a colleague of the irate captain and a fellow radical. The town leaders, Wooster duly reported, would neither give the militia company access to the powder nor authorize it to depart for Boston.

Arnold's reaction to that was altogether predictable. "None but Almighty God shall prevent my marching!" he reportedly shouted. Moreover, he told Wooster, if he did not get the keys in the next five minutes he would order his men to break into the powder magazine and take what they needed anyway. No one who knew him doubted that he would do just that. They turned over the keys.

After supplying themselves amply, the militiamen set off amidst roaring shouts of approval from hundreds of excited townsmen. Riding jauntily at their head was Benedict Arnold, resplendent and proud in his new uniform, an eager if neophyte warrior off to adventures unknown. A patriot destined for fame—and infamy.

———

Although Virginia didn't have the coalescing presence of an occupying army, its fervor for armed resistance rivaled New England's. Even while the First Continental Congress had been in session, strident voices had stirred the populace, prompting action. George Washington returned to learn that his Fairfax County neighbors had already formed a militia company, proclaiming their hope "to excite others by our example." They elected Washington as their commander. That winter other counties did indeed follow the radical example of their Fairfax brothers, with unit after unit selecting the colonel from Mount Vernon to be their own senior officer. A governor still loyal to London continued to sit in Williamsburg, so all of that martial activity was unofficial and outside the law, but that fact slowed the patriots not at all. The colony rapidly assumed a war footing. Washington ordered one hundred muskets and several books on military training from a Philadelphia supplier.

The flurry of preparations bespoke a people feeling pushed to fight. Virginians would stand to arms, that much was clear. But to what end? To remove British officials ... to defend against an occupation like the one in Boston ... to go to the aid of other colonies? No one quite knew, but everyone understood that a competent soldiery would be needed, whatever the mission might be. Washington was a busy man that winter and spring.

Having previously been content as a back-bencher in the Burgesses, the colonel now strode to the forefront. It took the scent of gunpowder in the air to drive the old soldier to become a leading voice in the assembly. Delving into matters of military readiness, he huddled with other members to determine what steps were needed to assure that the colony reached a reasonable state of defense. Beyond those representational duties a spate of other responsibilities filled his days. He drilled militia companies, imparting knowledge gained from active service years before and from active reading more recently. He spent much time in consultation, either in correspondence or in personal meetings.

Charles Lee and Horatio Gates, among others, journeyed to Mount Vernon to confer with him. Both were British professional soldiers and long-ago participants with Washington in the ill-fated Braddock campaign. After retiring from military service they had settled in Virginia. The two had voluminous advice to offer their receptive host and former comrade. (Both would play key roles in the coming war, and each would end up as a less than friendly competitor to Washington.)

On March 25, his colleagues in the legislature overwhelmingly elected Colonel Washington to represent Virginia in the Second Continental Congress. That very day he wrote to his brother John, commending him for his work in training an independent militia company, agreeing to command the unit if it were "drawn out," and declaring that "it is my full intention to devote my life and fortune in the cause we are engaged in."

Readiness was one thing, an actual resort to arms another. Washington worked diligently to achieve the former, but, having long since grown out of his youthful hot-headedness, he remained reluctant to take the first overt, hostile step in rebellion against what he had known all his life as the mother country. Be prepared, yes. Defend if attacked, certainly. But to bear arms offensively against king and country, that was an irretrievable act from which there could be no turning back. It was an act to be taken only after the fullest deliberation.

In April the governor placed the gunpowder in Williamsburg's magazine aboard a British warship, seeking to remove it from rebel reach. Furious militia leaders across the colony wanted to retrieve it at the point of a bayonet. Washington counseled calm, hoping to give patriot political leaders time to convince the governor to return the powder. They were successful in doing so, but some Virginians marched anyway, showing disdain for Washington's go-slow approach, and showing also how very close Virginia was to outright revolution.

It took eight days for word of the fighting at Lexington and Concord to reach Mount Vernon. A rider brought the news on April 27, just a week before Washington left to attend the Second Continental Congress. Those tidings changed everything. The line had been crossed. Great Britain had signaled beyond any lingering doubt that its armed might would be thrown against colonial rebels; Americans had demonstrated a willingness to counter armed suppression. The only question was how far the conflagration would reach—would New England resist alone or would other colonies join in the battle? That was the most momentous question Americans had ever faced. It would have to be answered in the Congress due to assemble in Philadelphia on May 10, 1775.

May 4 dawned hot and sweaty for that time of year in Virginia. A south wind brought humid air to Mount Vernon's fields. A feeling of foreboding cloaked Washington's departure. His coach, its four horses hitched and ready, waited near the front door. A fellow delegate, Richard Henry Lee, was there to go along. Lee was one of the colony's most incendiary rabble-rousers. The journey to Philadelphia was sure to be anything but calm with Lee along. The two men mounted and rode away into history. Looking back to wave at Martha as the carriage disappeared down the drive, Washington had the last sight of his beloved Mount Vernon that he was to enjoy for over six years.

Perhaps the colonel had a premonition of things to come—he had packed his military uniform, intending to wear it at sessions of the Congress.

CHAPTER SEVEN

TO WAR

W HAT A DIFFERENCE SIX MONTHS CAN MAKE. BEFORE adjourning in October 1774, members of the First Continental Congress had voted to meet again the next spring to see what effect their united appeals to the king might have had. Surely, they hoped, a benevolent monarch would recognize the seriousness of their plight and would rein in his iniquitous Parliament. If not, delegates to the Second Continental Congress would contemplate further steps to make the colonies' case. But the sobered representatives gathering in Philadelphia in May 1775, charged primarily to address economic issues, found themselves instead confronting matters of war and peace.

Resentment had exploded into rebellion. After the bloody events of April 19, mobs of militiamen from the four New England colonies had penned up General Thomas Gage and his troops inside Boston. There the two sides still sat a fortnight later, glowering at one another across Boston Neck but not quite knowing what to do next. Americans had neither the weapons nor the know-how to breach the enemy's barricades, while the British, with painful lessons of Lexington and Concord fresh in mind, dared not venture beyond their defenses.

What to do about that situation was the unavoidable and terrible question the Second Continental Congress had to deal with. Would the delegates opt for war or reconciliation?

With eleven colonies present, the Congress convened as scheduled on Wednesday, May 10. Whereas the First Continental Congress had held its meetings in a union hall, the Second sat in Philadelphia's State House, a sign of the greatly changed circumstances. Members elected Peyton Randolph of Virginia president, prudently agreed to open all sessions with prayer, and adjourned until ten o'clock the next morning. They needed time to talk things over before confronting so momentous an issue as waging war.

Thursday came hot and humid. Deciding that all sessions would be conducted in secret, delegates closed doors and windows, sentencing themselves to swelter in the sultry chamber. They consumed most of that day listening to descriptions of the fighting in Massachusetts. They met again Friday, only to adjourn immediately. More delegates were on the way, and it had become apparent that the assembly was breaking apart into two camps, a war party headed by Massachusetts representatives, and a more cautious faction comprised mostly of members from middle and southern colonies who hoped against hope that colonial grievances could be addressed short of total conflagration. In the next few days delegates from Georgia and Rhode Island reported in, and more arrived from pivotal New York. Only Canada, the hoped-for fourteenth colony, remained unrepresented.

The newly arrived New Yorkers, fearing (correctly, as it turned out) that their colony stood at high risk of invasion if the conflict should spread from Boston, requested advice. Reflecting its internal split, the Congress answered equivocally. Act passively, it said, even to the extent of letting British soldiers occupy barracks in New York City, but remove military stores for safekeeping and be prepared to "repel force by force." As the New Yorkers were unclear just how they might accomplish that last suggestion, the Congress further resolved "that a committee be appointed to consider what posts are necessary to be occupied in the Colony of New York, and by what number of troops it will be necessary they should be guarded." For a committee chairman, delegates turned to the only person in their midst wearing a uniform: Colonel George Washington of Virginia.

Except for that single action, which was arguably more precautionary than hostile, the Congress made little headway in coming to grips with the vexing question of whether to go to war. New Englanders grumbled at the lack of progress, but could not budge their less bellicose colleagues. In fairness to those reluctant members, it must be said that few of them had specific guidance from leaders in their respective colonies, and rebellion itself was a very frightening prospect. Rebels faced hanging. On May 17, the delegates met at noon after attending graduation services at the College, later the University, of Pennsylvania. The Congress voted to curtail exports to other British possessions in America and then adjourned for the day. As the representatives scattered to taverns and lodgings, electrifying news arrived.

Hundreds of miles from Philadelphia, on the shores of Lake Champlain in northern New York, Americans had stormed and seized Fort Ticonderoga, capturing its entire garrison of British soldiers. That bastion, famed for its pivotal and bloody role in the French and Indian War, guarded the only well-traveled route into Canada and was a major storehouse of military materiel. Suddenly, the central issue the delegates had been wrestling with for the past week had been taken largely out of their hands. The fighting had already spread—and patriots had started it. Attacking a royal post in the northern woods of New York could hardly be justified as a defensive measure to stop redcoat forays from the port of Boston. The momentum of conflict was outpacing the ability of delegates to contain it.

The assault on Fort Ticonderoga had occurred on the very day the Congress had convened, May 10. The leader of that audacious strike was none other than Benedict Arnold.

The Congress reacted quickly to try to stem events. Fort Ticonderoga should be given back to British forces forthwith, the delegates resolved, while the captured artillery pieces should be removed and safeguarded until they could be returned after "restoration of the former harmony between Great Britain and these colonies so ardently wished for by the latter." But the moment had passed.

Washington, quiet as usual, nevertheless favored taking an aggressive stance. He seized on the opening his committee assignment gave him to sway others to his thinking. That night and the next he kept his committee up late, pouring over maps of New York. It was at once obvious that the Hudson River was the most strategically significant geographical feature in New York, if not in all of the thirteen colonies. It must be held. That would require acting decisively—and promptly. Exactly one month to the day after Lexington and Concord, Colonel Washington delivered his committee's strong report to the Congress.

Obliged to face up to the circumstances thrust upon them, the delegates heatedly discussed the report's unblinking recommendations for five days before finally reaching a shaky consensus for vigorous action. Gradually, the radicals prevailed, with one of their number, John Hancock of Massachusetts, becoming the new president of the Congress. On May 25, the representatives passed a slate of six resolutions concerning the defense of New York, warning New York's newly minted Provincial Congress to be energetic in establishing defenses because it was "very uncertain whether the earnest endeavors" for reconciliation any longer had a real hope of success.

During the debates, George Washington had spent each night alone in his room. But after these resolutions passed and the colonies appeared to be moving toward a war footing, he relaxed in City Tavern two nights in a row. "Unhappy... it is to reflect," he wrote in a letter that month, "that a brother's sword has been sheathed in a brother's breast, and that the once happy and peaceful plains of America are either to be drenched with blood or inhabited by slaves. Sad alternative! But can a virtuous man hesitate in his choice?"

That same fateful May 25, 1775, a thirty-two-gun frigate, *Cerberus*, fresh from London, dropped anchor in Boston Harbor. Aboard were three members of Parliament who also happened to be major generals in the British Army—John Burgoyne, Henry Clinton, and William Howe. In a coincidence almost too delicious to be true, the ship was named for the three-headed dog guarding the gates of hell in Greek mythology. All three generals were destined to command forces that would meet failure in one way or another at the hands of George Washington and Benedict Arnold.

Also on that day, a message from a commander in the northern reaches of New York was on its way down the Hudson to the colony's patriot leaders. The name of the writer was becoming rapidly familiar: Colonel Benedict Arnold. That intrepid officer had not stopped with the conquest of Ticonderoga. He had continued attacking British forces scattered along the northern lakes and waterways that provided the major linkage between Canada and colonies to the south. By May 25, he was in general control of that strategically vital area, but he fully expected the British to react forcefully.

A month earlier, Captain Arnold had marched his company from New Haven to join American forces investing Boston. How had he, in a month's time, managed to become a colonel and make himself master of the northern lakes? The story all but defies belief.

From New Haven to Boston was a march of nearly 150 hilly miles. Arnold's well-drilled Second Company of Foot Guards, averaging about twenty miles a day, entered the American lines on April 29 and pitched camp on the estate of the colony's former lieutenant governor. Their active-minded commander, though, was already pondering an idea far more exciting than merely participating in the ongoing military standoff in Massachusetts.

On the march from New Haven, Arnold had met a fellow Connecticut patriot, Samuel Parsons, who was returning from a visit to the American positions at Cambridge, outside Boston. Describing the situation there, Parsons explained that the militiamen could do little to break the stalemate because of their lack of artillery. Arnold listened intently. He knew where big guns could be found. Lots of them. During his many trading journeys in Canada he had learned that military arms, including "a great number of brass cannons," were stored in weakly defended arsenals on Lake Champlain, far north of Albany. They could be seized in a bold raid, he told Parsons. By the time he reached Cambridge, the aggressive captain of New Haven's Foot Guards had constructed a plan to capture Fort Ticonderoga. A day after arriving he met with several senior Massachusetts leaders to present his proposal. The Lake Champlain bastion held some 130 pieces of artillery, he said. Moreover, it was in serious disrepair and guarded only by a small garrison of second-rate soldiers. The fort "could not hold out an hour against a vigorous onset," he boldly claimed. Intrigued, the men from Massachusetts heard him out. Arnold, always the consummate trader, sold them.

Two days later, the Committee of Safety, charged with coordinating the colony's military activities, approved an expedition. It made Arnold a Massachusetts colonel, provided him supplies and equipment, gave him a little money and a line of credit, authorized him to recruit up to four hundred men in the western part of the colony, and directed him to capture "the cannons, mortars, stores, etc., upon the lake" and bring back to Cambridge those that were serviceable. By any standards of any time, that decision was made exceedingly rapidly, especially when considering that the Massachusetts rebels were commissioning a Connecticut patriot to attack a British post in their neighboring colony of New York.

Responding just as rapidly, the new colonel said farewell to the men of the Foot Guards, deputized a handful of compatriots to command companies in the regiment yet to be raised, and sped west on May 3.

Meanwhile, other men in other places had also focused on Lake Champlain and the prizes of war to be found there. And they were moving even faster. Samuel Parsons, his imagination stimulated by Arnold's description of the value and vulnerability of Fort Ticonderoga, hurried on to Hartford. There he huddled with some influential patriots, telling them what he had learned. Among them was congressman Silas Deane, a seemingly omnipresent figure in the story of the rise of Benedict Arnold. Knowing Arnold well, Deane placed full credence in the intelligence his friend had provided. At once, and on their own authority, Deane and his colleagues decided to launch a raid to seize the British arms stored in the old stronghold in the New York wilderness. They designated Captain Edward Mott to lead the expedition.

Wasting no time at all, Mott sped north with a small party on the very day that Benedict Arnold reached Cambridge at the head of his company. The impulsive group in Hartford also sent an envoy galloping northward to try to enlist the assistance of Ethan Allen. Allen, a former citizen of Connecticut, was the leader of the Green Mountain Boys, a loose band of renegades operating in disputed territory between New York and New Hampshire. (The area would one day become Vermont.) The Boys held sway in the general vicinity of Fort Ticonderoga and were already casting covetous eyes at the loot there. They needed no convincing. Mott and Allen, meeting in Bennington the same day Arnold started west from Cambridge, promptly put in motion a plan of attack.

With three very different outfits converging on the old fort, confusion was all but inevitable. Mott, accompanied by just a handful of men, rode under very unofficial Connecticut orders. Arnold carried a proper Massachusetts commission, but had no soldiers until he could enlist them along the way. Allen, possessing merely an informal invitation from Connecticut, could nevertheless count on plenty of eager men to back him up. However, the three shared a desire to strike Fort Ticonderoga as soon as possible.

While recruiting in northwestern Massachusetts, Arnold learned of the impending raid by Mott and Allen. He was thunderstruck. The interlopers, as he saw them, were usurping his responsibility—and threatening his glory! Leaving his captains behind to complete their recruiting, he frantically spurred forward alone to intercept his competitors. A mad dash on muddy backwoods roads brought him during the night of May 8 to the final rendezvous spot of Mott and Allen, a tavern in Castleton. He was too late.

After agreeing on organizational arrangements, Allen and his Boys had departed earlier that day, marching to the planned jump-off point on the eastern side of the lake across from Fort Ticonderoga. Although Mott's strength had grown since his departure from Hartford, mostly with the addition of forty or fifty militiamen from the vicinity of Pittsfield in western Massachusetts, he had readily conceded command to Allen, as the Boys would follow the orders of no one else. Mott himself would chair an overarching military committee.

Arnold ate a hasty meal, slept some, and raced on the next morning. When he galloped into the encampment of the attackers, he found them making preparations to begin the assault that very night. Flourishing his Massachusetts commission, the colonel imperiously announced that he was there to take command.

Consternation followed. Even, according to some reports, pandemonium. There was no denying the validity of Arnold's commission, especially in consideration of the shaky legitimacy of the Mott-Allen forces. But Arnold had no troops at all, while Allen controlled a couple of hundred and Mott had a few dozen more. Muddying matters further, most of Mott's men were Massachusetts militia—should they now honor their own colony's orders or continue to support the Connecticut effort they had volunteered for? Their leaders were James Easton and John Brown, two names fated to appear, unhappily, time and time again in the saga of Benedict Arnold. Disliking the idea of Arnold's intervention, the two were nonetheless unsure of their ground. They equivocated. Ethan Allen was particularly perplexed. An outlaw on whose head New York authorities already had a price, he did not want to end up being an enemy of Massachusetts as well. Perhaps a joint command could be arranged? That idea went nowhere—the Boys themselves would have none of it. Their allegiance was to Allen alone. In fact, they threatened to pack up and go home before they would follow the little pouter pigeon strutting around in a red uniform, claiming to be in charge.

To the frustrated Arnold it became clear that without Allen in the lead there would be no attack that night. Worse yet, the large assemblage of troops almost under the shadow of Fort Ticonderoga could not go undetected more than a day or so. To wait for his own recruits would surely forfeit the advantage of surprise. Benedict had come too far to let everything collapse at that point. He saw no alternative other than to compromise. So, after some further discussion, he agreed to march with Allen, acting as titular leader of Massachusetts troops but not in command of any Green Mountain Boys. Seeing their own status thus diminished, Easton and Brown went along with the arrangement, but resented it deeply—a harbinger of difficulties to come.

The story of the actual storming of Fort Ticonderoga is easily told. In many ways it was more farce than feat. The assaulting force, some 250 men strong, moved quietly to the crossing site, a spot opposite the objective where the lake was about a mile wide. Oarsmen began rowing the troops across in the middle of the night, but a shortage of boats and a howling rainstorm seriously slowed the operation. Hours passed. Dawn approached. Arnold and Allen, on the verge of losing the cover of darkness, decided to push on with just a third of the raiders, leaving the rest to continue crossing and catch up as fast as they could. As the first subtle hints of daylight touched the eastern sky, the small column approached the gate of the looming fortress. All was quiet inside.

Locked away in wilderness isolation, the garrison's commander, Captain William Delaplace, was blissfully unaware of his imminent rendezvous with history. Remaining incompletely informed of the clash of arms around Boston and having failed to take seriously some earlier warnings from his higher command in Canada, Delaplace had not placed his men on alert. Except for a token guard or two, everyone in the fortress was sound asleep.

With a rush, Arnold and Allen, followed closely by about eighty men, burst through the rickety gate and into the courtyard, shouting for the surrender of the garrison. Rubbing sleep from his eyes, a partly dressed officer, holding his pants in his hands, appeared at the door of a second-floor room. Looking in disbelief at the hubbub below, he tartly demanded to know in whose name the rude action was being taken. The towering Allen, dressed in Green Mountain garb, and the diminutive Arnold, conspicuous in his red uniform, strode over to the stairs together. Assuming the pantless officer to be the commander, Allen reputedly roared that the attack was made "in the name of the Great Jehovah and the Continental Congress." Since the Congress was not due to open until later that same day, and Allen was not noted for being particularly religious, what he probably said was more akin to another version: "Come down here, you damned old rat!" Arnold was a bit more civilized in responding, but the message was the same. A stunned Captain Delaplace emerged, sized up the situation, and capitulated. The fort had been seized in less than ten minutes, without bloodshed. More than forty redcoats became prisoners, along with a number of women and children.

As soon as the enemy soldiers had all been rounded up and secured, Allen turned his men loose to plunder. They were very good at that, and right away located the liquor stores. In no time the fort was awash with drunken troops. Arnold, aghast, attempted to halt the carousing, only to be ignored by Allen and scornfully derided by the revelers themselves. Some even took potshots at him. Fuming with anger, he nevertheless recognized his inability to control events so long as the bulk of the soldiery backed Allen.

The rowdies were running amok like drunken sailors, a type he knew only too well. He figured that the Boys would drift away and go back to their farms once they had sated their appetite for booze and loot. He bided his time, waiting for his own men to arrive.

May 11 was a day for report writing. Arnold prepared a message for his superiors, the Massachusetts Committee of Safety that had commissioned him. Allen, not so constrained by a formal chain of command, wrote dispatches to patriot bodies in both Massachusetts and New York. Mott addressed a letter to Connecticut authorities.

Not surprisingly, Arnold portrayed himself as having had the dominant role in the attack, but he did give a nod to Allen's participation. Allen didn't so much as mention Arnold in his missive to Massachusetts leaders, while lionizing his own role and giving high praise to James Easton and John Brown. However, to authorities in New York, where he was considered more a hoodlum than a hero and thus needed to show that he was not freelancing, he carefully stated that he and Arnold had entered the fortress "side by side." Mott, wielding a malicious poison pen, praised Allen and his cohorts but scathingly castigated Arnold. Allen shrewdly sent his messages via Easton to Massachusetts and Brown to Philadelphia, where the two were to make sure in briefings to show Arnold in a poor light in comparison with the others. That scheme worked in Massachusetts, where Easton showed up five days before Arnold's report arrived, but not in Philadelphia. When Brown brought the explosive news of the seizing of Ticonderoga to the Continental Congress on May 17, he perceived rather quickly that many delegates were more horrified than pleased. Without hesitation he altered his instructions, slyly thrusting Arnold forward as the leader of the assault while downplaying the role of Allen and others. Arnold was damned by full praise. In those various reports were sown mischievous seeds of dissension and confusion that would sorely trouble affairs in the Lake Champlain region for weeks to come.

The clash of egos and ambitions would have been bad enough had it been the only problem injecting chaos into affairs at Ticonderoga. But other factors contributed as well. First was the practical matter of time and distance. In the best of conditions, diligent couriers might reach the environs of Boston in four days, Philadelphia in seven. Adding some time for consultation and decision-making, the turnaround time for an answer to be received was measured more in weeks than days. In a fast-moving situation, communications were doomed to be out of date as soon as they arrived. Still, such delays were a fact of colonial life and could have been accommodated had there been one central authority in control of operations and policy. But that was not the case in May 1775. Each colony acted independently, the Continental Congress saw its role primarily as advisory, and no overall military command existed. The mix of confusing relationships, unclear responsibilities, and warring personalities, all bubbling in a pot of slow communications and stirred by too many cooks, was indeed a witches' brew.

While waiting for his own officers to arrive with enough troops to tilt the scales and permit him to assume command, Benedict Arnold turned his attention to the basic reason for the attack in the first place: gathering and inventorying serviceable cannon. Meanwhile, boatloads of the more sober Green Mountain Boys had pushed against heavy winds to Crown Point, twelve miles farther north along the lake, where they seized and ransacked a second unready fort. In the two places combined Arnold counted more than two hundred pieces of artillery. The expedition had been a huge success, considerably more so than he had anticipated back in Cambridge. But his ever-active imagination could not let things end there—he conjured up still more possibilities.

Standing on a rampart of the newly captured fort at Crown Point, he looked out across glistening waters stretching away to the north as far as he could see. A narrow pencil of a lake, studded with islands, Champlain was over a hundred miles long, reaching from well south of Ticonderoga all the way into Canada. It was the major north-south highway in the region, flanked for most of its length on both sides by mountain ranges and nearly trackless forests. It was obvious to the most amateur eye that any military force wanting to move either north or south between the Hudson and St. Lawrence rivers needed to use the waterway. Patriot control of the lake would secure Ticonderoga from the threat of counterattack more effectively than anything else that could be done.

The seasoned sea captain quickly took stock of available watercraft. In addition to numerous bateaux of the sort Allen had rounded up to use in the attack of Ticonderoga, two large vessels plied the lake. One, a schooner owned by a loyalist living at the southern end of Lake Champlain, was already in patriot hands. Enemy forces held the second, a seventy-ton sloop of war docked at the settlement of St. Johns near the other end. If in a rapid raid he could capture or destroy everything floating there, Arnold reasoned, he would be able to control the lake. To him the time from idea to action was always short. He resolved to attack—never mind that such a raid would carry him more than twenty miles inside Canada, expanding the war still farther.

The means came soon to hand when his own men began arriving in good numbers, fortuitously including several who could handle large sailing ships. Renaming the captured schooner *Liberty*, Arnold armed it with four small cannons and six swivel guns from the fort. Trailing a string of smaller boats, he set sail for St. Johns on May 16 and reached the Canadian border late the next day. When uncooperative winds stalled him there he unhesitatingly put thirty-five men in two bateaux and rowed all night to reach his objective. (Even as the irrepressible warrior was projecting the war into Canada, displeased congressional delegates were resolving that Fort Ticonderoga should be returned to His Majesty's troops. How disconcerting it would have been if they had known how rapidly events were outracing their resolutions.)

About six o'clock Thursday morning, May 18, the raiders surprised the dozen soldiers posted at St. Johns, taking them prisoner. They then quickly climbed aboard the sloop and overpowered its unsuspecting crew of seven. In addition to the warship, the Americans found nine bateaux. They manned five and burned the others. Gathering all weapons in sight, including two brass cannons, Arnold and his men departed as swiftly as they had come. Reaching the armed schooner *Liberty* by noon, he pointed his flotilla south toward Crown Point and Ticonderoga. He was master of the lake.

For a while quiet settled in. Easton and Brown had not yet returned from their missions of slander, and Allen was subdued after the departure of a majority of his men. Arnold, for the moment unchallenged as commander, devoted himself to training new units, preparing artillery pieces for transfer to Boston, and repairing the land defenses as best he could with limited resources. He also outfitted the captured sloop, which he christened *Intrepid.* With *Liberty, Intrepid,* and a fleet of lightly armed bateaux, the former sea captain had in a sense become America's first naval commander. According to one of his officers, Arnold's concept was to "cruise the lake, and defend our frontiers, until men, provisions, and ammunition are furnished to carry on the war." He was thinking ahead to launching further operations as soon as patriot strength permitted. In the meantime, he could enjoy the lull in activities.

But the plot was thickening elsewhere. In Philadelphia, the Continental Congress debated George Washington's recommendations for defending New York. New Yorkers, meanwhile, established a body to coordinate their own defensive efforts, sent supplies northward to support Arnold's activities, and urged the Congress to assist also. Governor Jonathan Trumbull of Connecticut, an avid patriot himself, was busy organizing military elements to reinforce American positions at Ticonderoga. Massachusetts leaders, watching New York and Connecticut becoming more and more involved in the Lake Champlain region, saw an opportunity to disentangle themselves, which would in turn improve their capacity to concentrate on the Boston area and, not insignificantly, to reduce costs. It would also leave Benedict Arnold in limbo, for his authority sprang only from Massachusetts. One can imagine the welter of messages crossing and re-crossing one another as weary couriers rode back and forth over the web of roads connecting Philadelphia, Boston, New York, Hartford, and Ticonderoga.

It isn't at all surprising that things soon began to come unglued. Arnold learned on May 29 of the Congress's eleven-day-old order to evacuate the fortress. Convinced of the utter folly in giving back the vital position, he poured himself into composing an emotional appeal for the overturn of that decision. But, as was so often the case, before his message got very far along the road to Philadelphia it was overtaken by events. The Congress reversed itself on May 31, voting to hold the strategic posts on Lake Champlain after all. Then, the very next day, still trying to find a handle on the constantly shifting situation, the representatives agreed to place a ban on any military "expedition or incursion" into Canada. But even as that last message was making its way to Arnold, he was in fact devising a plan to do that exact thing.[1]

Curious to know how Guy Carleton, the governor and commanding general in Canada, was reacting to his conquests, and wanting intelligence on which to base future actions, Arnold personally led an armed reconnaissance mission northward in early June. With his two warships and several bateaux, he cruised the lake for nearly a week, gathering information from Indians and others in the area. He sailed almost to St. Johns, finding it defended by almost half of the seven hundred regulars Carleton had in Quebec province. (Among them was John André, whose star was destined to one day cross Arnold's in the most dramatic of ways. But that was in the future; at the moment, André probably agreed with General Carleton's disdainful dismissal of Colonel Arnold as a mere "horse-jockey." That derogatory term, in the parlance of the time, connoted a shifty, dishonest horse dealer, similar to "used-car salesman" now.) Arnold learned that the enemy in Canada was weaker in both number and capability than the Americans had assumed. Still more encouraging, Indian tribes and French inhabitants were not particularly disposed to help the British. He returned brimming with excitement. Canada was vulnerable. A rapid strike now, before

---

[1] Terms used in the late eighteenth century can be confusing to modern readers. "Canada" is one example. While the word broadly identified those vast, mostly unpopulated, and largely unexplored reaches north of the other thirteen colonies, in common practice it often merely meant Quebec province, where most of the inhabitants lived. That province extended right and left of the St. Lawrence River and stretched from the Atlantic vaguely westward toward the Great Lakes. When Americans said they hoped to make Canada the fourteenth colony, they were generally thinking of Quebec province. The two terms were used more or less interchangeably and almost always imprecisely.

reinforcements could reach the redcoats, would be highly likely to succeed. He sat down to prepare a plan.

Militarily, Quebec province was a barbell, two defended areas around Montreal and Quebec City connected by the long rod of the St. Lawrence River. General Carleton had insufficient strength to protect either place against a determined push. Montreal's defenses, Arnold thought, could be easily overrun by troops moving swiftly north from Lake Champlain. Then an isolated Quebec City, which would be defended mostly by surviving remnants of enemy forces, could be invested and taken. Canada would become the fourteenth colony by conquest. Speed was essential, however. The attack should be launched "without loss of time." Never one for subtlety, the enterprising colonel stated that he was prepared to lead the expedition and "answer for the success of it." Realizing that such an escalation of the war would require higher approval than that of any single province, and probably despairing of cutting through the morass of conflicting lines of authority among the various colonies, he sent his plan straight to the Continental Congress itself.

As Benedict Arnold contemplated a wider war, the Continental Congress was taking the extraordinary step of creating an army of its own. Unable under current circumstances to control the expanding hostilities—caused in no small part by Arnold's extemporaneous exploits—and sensing that it could never do so as long as each colony acted separately, the Congress had concluded that it needed a military force answerable to it alone. On that conservatives and radicals could agree. The former saw such a step as a way to help curb adventurism; the latter saw it as a way to wage war more effectively.

The Continental Army was born on June 14, 1775, when the Congress adopted the milling horde of militiamen around Boston and called up six companies of riflemen from the Pennsylvania, Maryland, and Virginia frontiers. But an army needs a head. The next day, the delegates selected George Washington to be commander in chief "of all the Continental forces raised or to be raised in the defense of American liberty."

For the representatives toiling in Philadelphia's State House, the three weeks from their May 25 passage of resolutions for the defense of New York to the founding of the Continental Army had been anything but easy. Faced with the unavoidable fact of Arnold's control of the entire Lake Champlain region, and battered by appeals from New York and New England, they had backed down from their initial stance that Fort Ticonderoga should be returned to the British. Despite struggling to contain the fighting, the Congress had been preempted by the impulsive capture of Fort Ticonderoga and by Arnold's subsequent raid into Canada, not to mention the constant and provocative posturing of militiamen around Boston. And the resolution prohibiting any incursion into Canada had loosed a drumfire of shrill voices favoring invasion. Still of two minds concerning war and peace, the Congress had nevertheless found itself pulled by both politics and prudence to think more and more about warlike measures. And with actions elsewhere driving policy, the members came to realize the need to try to lead events rather than merely react to them.

Several committees explored martial issues. Washington served on all of them. John Adams recorded that "by his great experience and abilities in military matters" the colonel was "of much service to us." Other delegates became accustomed to turning to the tall warrior with questions regarding armed conflict. He continued to wear the blue and buff uniform of a Virginia militiaman, a reminder that he was both a soldier and a southerner—the latter being an especially important distinction since virtually all armed forces then mobilized were from New England, and the patriots wanted an army drawn from all the colonies.

The Congress did not actually vote to go to war. Rather, it established its army for the protection of American freedoms. At that point patriots thought primarily of redress, not permanent rupture. If the king did what was right for his American subjects—and surely he would—there would be no further fighting.

The new commander in chief had about him an air, a presence, that made men trust him. Pronouncing himself inadequate for the task, he had been a reluctant candidate for the job, which of course made him all the more desirable in the eyes of his fellow congressmen. Many, if not most, of them harbored a gut fear of an ambitious general, a man on horseback who might aspire to become a dictator. However, they did not detect any indication of that trait in their diffident colleague from Mount Vernon. Eliphalet Dyer of Connecticut wrote approvingly: "He seems discreet and virtuous, no harum-scarum, ranting, swearing fellow, but sober, steady, and calm." Washington accepted the appointment but told his colleagues that he felt "great distress from a consciousness that my abilities and military experience may not be equal to the extensive and important trust."

Distressing, too, was the necessity of leaving Martha behind at Mount Vernon. Dreading to tell her, he hesitated two days after accepting the post of commander in chief to break the news in as agonizing a letter as he ever penned. "It was utterly out of my power to refuse this appointment," he wrote. Then, noting that "life is always uncertain," he enclosed a newly drafted will for her to keep. He knew from personal experience that warfare was a high-risk pursuit.

The Congress also appointed four major generals: Artemas Ward, who was already nominally leading the besieging forces around Boston; Israel Putnam, an old soldier with experience in the French and Indian War; Philip Schuyler, a wealthy and influential New Yorker who had vast landholdings in the Albany area; and Charles Lee, a retired British officer who had recently settled in America. Politics, geography, and military considerations drove those selections. Few considered Ward to be a truly effective leader, but he was already in place and was a citizen of Massachusetts. Putnam, although quite fat and perhaps too elderly for field duty in that era, had a reputation for bravery, and was from Connecticut. Schuyler brought administrative and logistical rather than soldierly skills to the position, but his service in the French and Indian War had been in the strategic region of northern New York. Lee was the only one chosen solely for his professional background. He was thought by some, including himself, to be a military genius.

The Congress then named nine men as brigadier generals, including Horatio Gates, another former British officer who had retired to America. Washington had requested him by name to serve as adjutant general, the top staff position in the army. The commander in chief convinced Joseph Reed to go along as his military secretary and chose Thomas Mifflin to be his aide-de-camp. Both Reed and Mifflin were bright young Pennsylvania politicians.

The selections over, the ceremonies completed, General Washington set himself immediately to tackling the myriad details of preparing for war. He had only a few days before it was time to go. On June 20, the Congress gave the new commander of the Continental Army his charge: "You are to repair with all expedition to the Colony of Massachusetts Bay, and take charge of the army of the United Colonies." Three days later Washington left Philadelphia, accompanied by Lee, Schuyler, Gates, Reed, and Mifflin. (In an interesting quirk of fate, Washington, Lee, and Gates had been comrades in the long-ago and ill-fated Braddock campaign, along with another young officer, Thomas Gage, now the British commander they were riding to oppose.) The six men departed amidst great fanfare. Bands played, flags flew, people cheered. Members of the Congress accompanied them a short distance along the road before stopping for a final salute. In that entourage rode John Adams. The plump congressman was excited that other colonies were at long last joining the fight in Massachusetts, but he could not help being envious of the honors paid the departing soldiers. Describing the ceremonies to his wife, he wrote: "I, poor creature, worn out with scribbling...must leave others to wear the laurels which I have sown." Washington himself was sober rather than jubilant; he understood that he was taking a path into an unknown future that could more easily bring failure than fame. "I can answer for but three things," he said, "a firm belief in the justice of our cause, close attention in the prosecution of it, and the strictest integrity." The last of those three traits would set him apart from a good number of his contemporaries.

As dust and distance removed the cheering well-wishers from view, Washington and his five companions settled down for the long trip. Of those five, all but Schuyler would become an enemy of the commander in chief. Two of them would also become bitter internecine foes of Benedict Arnold.

Meanwhile, in upper New York, circumstances had deteriorated even as the Congress was attempting to stabilize the overall situation. On the same day George Washington left Philadelphia on his journey to Boston to take command, Benedict Arnold angrily resigned his commission.

The month of June had started out well enough. Arnold's water and land forces dominated Lake Champlain and held the northern forts. Canada itself was tantalizingly ripe for the picking. Massachusetts leaders, striving to elicit additional support from other colonies, had highly praised Colonel Arnold, their commander on the scene. And that satisfied officer thought he had finally ridded himself of the infuriating James Easton.

Easton had from the very outset been openly antagonistic toward Arnold. A failed tavern keeper, he had sought military position as a way to rejuvenate his personal fortunes. Arnold considered him to be an incompetent and a coward, as well as a malevolent conspirator, and refused to second his aspirations for rank. Tension between the two built until it spilled out into the open. When Easton acted in a surly manner toward Arnold on June 11, it was one time too many. The combative nature of the former shipmaster burst loose. In a rage, he lashed out physically at his longtime detractor, admitting later, "I took the liberty of breaking his head." Noting that the cowering innkeeper carried both a sword and loaded pistols, Arnold challenged him to a duel. Then and there. He dared his foe to take his choice of weapons and "draw like a gentleman!" Easton backed down. Not to be deterred, Arnold continued to berate him, "kicked him very heartily," and ordered him to get out of his sight and stay out. The publicly humiliated man and his followers left quickly. Arnold, pleased with himself, believed he had heard the last of their intramural bickering. He hadn't. Not then, not later.

After just a few days the commander's sense of satisfaction was shattered. Benjamin Hinman, a colonel from Connecticut, arrived at the head of a thousand troops and announced that he had been sent to take charge of the Champlain theater of operations. Arnold refused to relinquish his position, claiming (correctly from what he knew) that Massachusetts had just reconfirmed his status. Hinman made no fuss. He calmly accepted the status quo in the belief that the confusion would shortly be cleared up. Instead, the situation worsened. Massachusetts leaders had empanelled a committee to investigate command matters at Ticonderoga and to resolve funding issues. That group arrived on June 23, six days after the bloody Battle of Bunker Hill had further lessened any likelihood of reconciliation with the mother country.

The Massachusetts Committee of Safety had initially provided Arnold only a very small amount of cash. He had been covering many of the burgeoning expenses of operations by dipping into his own resources. Now he was confronted by a committee charged with investigating his conduct and examining his account books. Worse yet, the committee informed him that Colonel Hinman was indeed to assume the overall command. Arnold would revert to being merely the commander of his original regiment.

He was mortified. He had been leading at the Lake Champlain post for six weeks. He had endured insults and gunshots. He had persevered in the face of near-constant squabbles over command arrangements. He had weathered a spate of contradictory instructions from all sides. He had dug deeply into his personal finances to underwrite operations, while Massachusetts had provided precious little support, monetary or otherwise. In spite all of that, he had managed to conquer and hold the militarily vital area. Now, notice of his replacement as overall commander and the lack of trust implied by the arrival of an investigating committee proved to be more than he could stomach. Indignant, he quit. "I have resigned my commission," he wrote in his memorandum book, "not being able to hold it longer with honor."

If Arnold had been upset upon learning that Colonel Hinman would supplant him as senior officer in the region, he was absolutely devastated when he heard that his replacement as commander of Massachusetts troops would be a citizen of that colony...none other than "Colonel" James Easton! Adding salt to the wound, John Brown became the regiment's major.

At the lowest point on the emotional roller coaster he had been riding in recent weeks, the distraught merchant from New Haven handed over command and shifted his attention to tying up loose ends. First was the matter of his wounded pride. Preparing a long newspaper column under the name "Veritas," he lashed out defiantly, telling readers what a dishonest and cowardly miscreant James Easton was. Perhaps that made him feel better. Second was balancing his books. That would not be simple, for he had contracted numerous "small and unavoidable debts" in his own name in order to cover day-to-day expenses of his unit and ships. He felt he could not leave honorably with such bills remaining open, so he had to send home for funds to "discharge those debts out of my private purse." He would square accounts with Massachusetts later. Third, he remained in the vicinity in hopes of hearing from Philadelphia regarding his offer to lead an eruption into Canada.

That last reason evaporated early in July when he learned that the Congress had authorized the expedition but had designated to lead it one of the Continental Army's new major generals, Philip Schuyler. Ironically, Arnold's message containing a rationale for the invasion and providing a workable campaign plan had been a key document in persuading the Congress to order an incursion into Canada less than a month after it had expressly forbidden any such thing. With nothing left to hold him longer in the Lake Champlain region, a crestfallen Arnold departed on July 4. It was a bitterly disappointing end to an adventure he had begun just two months earlier.

Much had changed in America in that brief period of time, and Benedict Arnold had been one of the leading agents of that change.

Heading to Albany on his way back to New Haven, once more a simple patriot without a role of any kind, Arnold resolved to call on General Schuyler, who had just arrived to take command. He did not know what sort of reception he would receive from the patrician New Yorker, who had been a member of the Continental Congress until his appointment in the Continental Army, but his sense of responsibility would not permit him to quit the area without seeking a meeting to discuss the forthcoming Canadian campaign. After all, he possessed an enormous amount of knowledge, both from his recent activities and from connections previously made as a merchant trading in the valley of the St. Lawrence. This knowledge would be very helpful to the commanding general of the newly designated Northern Department.

As it happened, the two hit it off well. Schuyler had already formed a favorable opinion of Arnold. He had received glowing reports from New Yorkers in the Lake Champlain region who understood and fully appreciated what the daring and energetic leader had accomplished. Moreover, before leaving Philadelphia, the new general had been privately briefed on the situation at the lake and forts by Silas Deane, a fellow member of the Congress who not only knew Arnold personally and well but was quite aware of the whole background to the initiative to seize the northern posts.

Deane had been involved in that project from the beginning, and his brother had reported to him on what he had found during a visit to the region in late May. "Col Arnold has been greatly abused and misrepresented by designing persons, some of which were from Connecticut. Had it not been for him, everything here would have been in the utmost confusion and disorder; people would have been plundered of their private property, and no man's person would be safe that was not of the Green Mountain party."

Schuyler, charged with responsibility for the Northern Department, understood the value of the former colonel's experience. Wanting Arnold to take a key position on his staff, he asked Silas Deane to inquire quietly to see if the Congress would make that appointment. It was an offer highly flattering to the younger man, who at that moment was suffering the pangs of rejection. And it held unusual promise. With Schuyler's patronage, he might very well redeem his reputation.

Once again, though, fate intervened. A much-delayed letter from Hannah Arnold finally caught up with her brother, probably having traveled up to Ticonderoga and Crown Point first. It brought sad news. His wife had died suddenly some three weeks before. He would have to return home at once.

Before leaving Arnold assured General Schuyler of his genuine interest in an assignment to the Northern Department, and wrote to inform Deane that regardless of all setbacks he intended to continue serving in uniform one way or another. He vowed to return to active support of the patriot cause as soon as he could take care of family matters and clear his account with Massachusetts, for "an idle life under my present circumstances would be but a lingering death."

Readers could surely be pardoned for wondering if they weren't sensing the hand of a mad or malevolent novelist in the pen strokes of the unfolding story of Benedict Arnold's military career. Especially since this phase of the tale ends with still another blow to that beleaguered individual. On top of everything else, Arnold came down with gout, a painfully debilitating illness that would reoccur periodically for the rest of his life.

CHAPTER EIGHT

TAKING
THE OFFENSIVE

———◦❖◦———

NEW YORK OFFICIALS WERE IN A DITHER. HAVING STRUGGLED for months to placate both radicals and loyalists, wanting to support patriots while at the same time striving to avoid a clear break with the Crown, they had been pacing a nervous path between the two sides. It was a course fraught with mischance, if not with outright peril. As time passed, the more tenuous their two-faced policy became. And now, in late June 1775, their worst nightmare seemed to be coming true.

The commander in chief of the Continental Army was set to reach New York City on his way to Boston on the same day that the royal governor of the colony was scheduled to resume his duties after more than a year's absence in England. General George Washington was approaching overland from New Jersey while Governor William Tryon was preparing to debark from a British warship anchored in the harbor. Timorous notables in the city cringed, worried lest they offend either party. Or, worse yet, afraid that rioting would erupt between partisan crowds.

As it turned out, their fears were for naught. Washington crossed the Hudson River several hours before Tryon came ashore, cautiously landing north of and beyond the reach of British naval forces in the bay. Relieved officials had time to welcome the general before breathlessly rushing off to greet the governor. Both Washington and Tryon studiously ignored the other's presence.

Actually, the American generals had more on their minds than tiptoeing around an awkward protocol problem. New York City was where they were to split, with Philip Schuyler heading up the Hudson River to Albany to organize the Northern Department while the others continued to Boston. It was also where they first heard of the bloody fighting at Bunker Hill, further evidence that the war was escalating beyond the control of the Continental Congress. They could not tarry.

Washington issued his first major military directive. He left Major General Schuyler in command of New York, with instructions to watch Tryon and to be ready to intervene should the governor take actions hostile to the colony's defense. Schuyler was particularly charged with overseeing activities in the Lake Champlain region, where he was expected to implement the Congress's instructions to bring Canada into the revolutionary fold.

After just one fretful day in New York, Washington and his entourage spurred on toward Boston. On Sunday, July 2, the group reached Watertown, the seat of the Massachusetts Provincial Congress. After a minimum of discussion with Bay Colony leaders, Washington rode the remaining few miles to Cambridge, where his headquarters would initially be established in the handsome home of Samuel Langdon, Harvard's president. Arriving without fanfare, as befitted New England's custom for keeping the Sabbath free of non-religious activities, the commander in chief made preparations to formally take command the next day, July 3. The date cast long shadows in Washington's memory. Twenty-one years ago that very day, his first military campaign had ended in ignominious surrender at Fort Necessity.

The armed host now calling itself the Continental Army assembled for its new commander in chief that warm July Monday. But the atmosphere was anything but welcoming. General Artemas Ward, the former overall commander, was incensed at being replaced, and by a southerner at that. At least he showed up for the ceremony—some others absented themselves to avoid what they deemed to be personal and regional humiliation. Nor were the soldiers themselves in a much more receptive mood than their leaders. The concept of a united effort among all colonies strained their parochial powers of comprehension, and they resented the arrival of this stranger from outside New England. After all, had they not done quite well on their own? Had they needed outside help to repulse the redcoats at Lexington and Concord? Had not they bloodied the British at Bunker Hill? Were not their defensive works keeping General Gage penned up inside Boston? Besides, this new general brought no troops of his own with which to reinforce them. Continental the army might be, happy it was not. In truth, at that moment the Continental Army was neither continental nor really an army.

Straightaway, Washington addressed the fact that the soldiers were all New Englanders. In his first set of general orders, issued on July 4, one year to the day before the United States would declare itself independent, the commander in chief spoke grandly of an "American Army" and proclaimed that the soldiers were "now the Troops of the UNITED PROVINCES of North America."

Then he turned his attention to determining just how capable was the assemblage of armed elements he headed. One ride through the encampments was enough to reveal the woeful answer: not very. The men lived in sprawling shantytowns scattered willy-nilly across the countryside. The telltale stench of open latrines raised questions about hygiene and discipline. Officers were often indistinguishable from their men in either appearance or behavior, and many were patently incompetent. Training was done as an afterthought, if at all. As for numbers, no one had a credible count of how many soldiers there were. At any given time perhaps fifteen thousand would be available for a fight. The defensive works, thrown up hastily with scant engineering expertise, gave testimony to the lack of fortification skills. Significantly, the patriots had virtually no artillery. Most immediately worrisome, gunpowder was in extremely short supply, with stores on hand providing no more than a handful of shots per man. Washington led an unready throng.

Did General Gage realize how unprepared the Americans were? A British attack at that moment, Washington feared, would in all likelihood scatter his units disastrously. It was painfully obvious to the new commander that he had to conceal his army's weaknesses even as he strove to repair them.

He dove in immediately, energetically attacking the distressing array of shortcomings in order to mold the motley units into an effective fighting force as rapidly as possible. Ultimately he succeeded in sharpening the army into something approaching competence, but it was neither quick nor easy. In the first few weeks he remained constantly on edge, fearful that the British would take advantage of the evident American vulnerabilities. Seeing how "fatigued and worried" the commander in chief was, James Warren, the president of the Massachusetts Provincial Congress, wrote, "I pity our good general, who has a greater burden on his shoulders and more difficulties to struggle with than I think should fall to the share of so good a man."

Gradually that summer the Continental Army was born. Washington managed to transform the individualistic Yankee units into the semblance of a unified force, one with improved leadership and firmer discipline. Importantly, the sense of surliness that had greeted the Virginian's arrival dissipated as New Englanders had time to take his measure and to feel the stamp of his leadership. He enforced rules strictly, punishing violators and ruthlessly cashiering officers who could not or would not shape up. One chaplain observed, "There is great overturning in the camp as to order and regularity. New lords, new laws." Washington rode the lines daily, a present and visible leader sowing inspiration wherever he went. Henry Knox, himself fated to play a major role in the war, said about his charismatic new commander, "General Washington fills his place with vast ease and dignity, and dispenses happiness around him." Supply officers procured adequate amounts of gunpowder for muskets, relieving concern on that matter. Money remained scarce, as it would all the years of the war, but, bolstered by plentiful food and comfortable weather, morale soared. The men were eager for action.

The arrival late in July of troops from other colonies created a stir in camp. Tales spread quickly about the remarkable new soldiers, frontiersmen armed with rifles, some of whom had marched six hundred miles in three weeks to get there. They were impressive in size and physical prowess, matchless in marksmanship, and seemingly addicted to brawling. Their very presence stiffened the army—and signified that it was indeed continental.

All in all, by the time August arrived Washington was feeling better about the organization he commanded. He could turn his attention to wielding it.

Flatly stated, revolutionaries must be offensive-minded. Theirs is the task of seizing power, of overthrowing those in control. Only by acting aggressively can they remove constituted authority. They must snatch the initiative. Rashness, even recklessness, becomes their watchword. And that is precisely how patriots behaved in the opening months of the war, lashing out with an almost instinctive impetuosity. Benedict Arnold's headlong exploits in the Lake Champlain area are a case in point.

A lull had settled in following the Battle of Bunker Hill. It took time for Americans to create a more normal military establishment, to ready it for offensive operations, and to achieve a consensus on the need to carry the conflict to the British.

Just a month after taking command, General Washington was ready to end that lull, and sought ways to assail the enemy. Although the Continental Army still had serious shortcomings—it was underfunded, ill-trained, inadequately equipped, and burdened with inexperienced leaders—it nevertheless enjoyed major advantages over its foe. As had already been amply demonstrated, the redcoats bottled up in Boston did not have the staying power to survive if they left their defenses. Nor were the meager garrisons in Canada and elsewhere any better off. Widely separated and unable to support one another, those garrisons were ripe to be picked off one by one. Although Americans had no counter to the mighty Royal Navy, warships were of scant help in battles fought away from the coast. On the other hand, England had the capability to alter the balance of power almost overnight by shipping reinforcements across the Atlantic. Washington recognized that his comparatively favorable circumstances were unlikely to remain that way for long. Waiting would not improve his relative strength; instead, it could diminish it. The danger of inactivity far outweighed the hazards of boldness. Audacity became an imperative. Writing on August 4, 1775, he proclaimed, "We are in a situation which requires us to run all risques."

But how to do that? Recognizing the requirement was one thing, achieving it another. Having neither artillery nor a fleet, an American assault on Boston was hardly feasible. Employing privateers to harass enemy shipping would inflict some pain on British interests. Likewise, encouraging pressure against pockets of royal authority throughout the colonies would strengthen patriot control and weaken loyalist resolve. But those and other such actions could not of themselves be decisive. There had to be something else. Canada was the answer. Adding the weight of that vast territory to the other thirteen rebellious colonies would be a major gain. Furthermore, the Continental Congress had already approved an invasion and General Schuyler had been charged with conducting it.

There was just one problem. Schuyler was proving to be exceedingly cautious. Weeks had passed since he had taken charge of the Northern Department, but preparations for the incursion into Canada were stalled. More a logistician than a leader, Schuyler saw obstacles rather than opportunities. He dallied, complaining that his numbers were insufficient, that he needed more tents, that his troops lacked discipline. He wanted everything to be in order before pushing north. Some who knew him well had wondered at the time of his selection as general officer whether he had the "strong nerves" needed in a battle leader. An exasperated George Washington, able only to urge haste on his hesitant commander, fumed in frustration. Time was precious, and it was being wasted. While he himself had full resolve to run all risks, Washington was discovering that not all of his generals possessed the same warrior spirit.

At that crucial moment an officer appeared at headquarters requesting an audience with the commander in chief. The face and name were familiar to Washington, but it was the visitor's reputation for extraordinary audacity that made him especially welcome. No one doubted the daring or dash of Benedict Arnold.

———•·•———

Arnold's days after leaving Albany were among the worst he had ever experienced. Homecoming for the new widower had been especially hard. Not only was his wife gone, but so was his father-in-law, who had died shortly after. His three boys were all right, secure under Hannah's care, but Arnold's own normally sturdy health had deserted him. Gout, magnified by grief, forced him to bed for several days. He was emotionally and physically drained.

But the world would not wait. His business matters were in disarray because of his lengthy absence and the hostilities with England. Moreover, he had to resolve his former command's fiscal accounts. Still worse, the war continued without him. He willed himself out of bed.

Building on arrangements Hannah had enterprisingly set in motion, Benedict reverted momentarily to the role of bold merchant trader. He engaged again in sending ships on risky business voyages. He located crews and loaded cargoes and issued instructions to captains. He worried particularly about the status of one ship, a brigantine named *Peggy* after his wife. Carrying a load of rum, *Peggy* had sailed for Quebec City, a destination he knew could take it right into the teeth of the gathering conflict. His worry was not misplaced, as he would discover months later in a nearly incredible coincidence.

Arnold also spent long hours preparing and reconciling documents for the accounting session he would have with Massachusetts officials. In about a fortnight he had regained his strength and put his affairs into rough order. Leaving his boys, his home, and his business in the hands of his devoted sister, Benedict Arnold left New Haven on the road to Boston. Some three months earlier he had started down the same road as a proud captain in command of a militia company. Now he rode alone.

On Tuesday, August 1, 1775, the former Massachusetts colonel reported to the Provincial Congress to settle his accounts. A committee was appointed to review his records. Once again the touch of a whimsical author might be suspected in the unfolding tale of Benedict Arnold's military career. The committee chairman was Dr. Benjamin Church, a leading congressman later discovered to be a British spy.

For two long weeks, members of the Church committee haggled with Arnold over expenses. He laid out his claims, they disputed them. He presented receipts, they asked for further documentation. He described his actions, they questioned his motives. The contentious bickering cast both sides in an unflattering light, but neither would bend. Finally, on August 14, Church submitted his committee's recommendations, denying well over half of Arnold's requests for reimbursement. So far as the Provincial Congress was concerned, if the man it had commissioned to retrieve cannons from Ticonderoga had spent his own money exceeding his orders, it was not a Massachusetts responsibility. Rather than appeal further, an embittered Arnold ended the dispute by accepting the money offered. (Through his friend Silas Deane, he applied to the Continental Congress for the balance—and received it five months later.)

It was out of character for Arnold to accept so meekly what he deemed to be an unpardonable affront to his pocketbook and honor. He had fought duels over less. But just then he had more exciting matters to deal with. By mid-August he was deeply involved in what would turn out to be one of his greatest feats and would add an epic campaign to the annals of American arms: the march to Quebec.

It was during a break in his squabbles with the Church committee that Arnold rode to Washington's headquarters to call on the commander in chief. That meeting turned out to be a fateful one not only for both men but for the very future of the United States. Washington was looking for boldness. Arnold was seeking opportunity. Both were thinking of Canada.

Arnold briefed the general on the military supplies captured in his raids near Lake Champlain, especially the scores of artillery pieces he had found. He told Washington that he thought the British were weak in Canada, and reported what he had seen in his trading voyages along the St. Lawrence River. He laid out his proposal, which he had written in mid-June, for a northern offensive. Soon the two men were talking of the need to move quickly before Governor Guy Carleton could strengthen his defenses—and before the onset of the Canadian winter.

Both Arnold and Washington had heard of a route leading to Quebec through the Maine wilderness going up the Kennebec and Dead rivers, over an arduous portage, and then down the Chaudière River to the St. Lawrence. An oft-traveled Indian track, it had been traversed by small military detachments, but never by major combat forces. If a thousand soldiers or more could work their way over it to appear suddenly outside the walls of Quebec, the surprised city might succumb with little or no resistance. Carleton's meager military forces in Canada, trapped between patriots in Quebec and General Schuyler's troops in the vicinity of Montreal, would then face surrender or destruction.

Many officers in headquarters thought the idea was preposterous. A march of that many men that far, over such difficult terrain, carrying the huge amount of supplies they would need to fight once they reached the St. Lawrence, was not in the books. Not ordinary books, anyway. But George Washington harkened back to his own long-ago experiences on wilderness campaigns to Fort Duquesne. He thought it might be done. Moreover, he was quite willing "to run all risques." So was Arnold. He volunteered to lead the expedition.

The concept appealed to Washington, partly because it was so bold that the enemy would hardly expect it. Washington said he would think about it while Arnold completed his work with the Church committee. So Arnold returned to Watertown to terminate that unhappy affair—and began writing an operational plan for a campaign to Canada.

Within days, after carefully reviewing the risks and possibilities, General Washington resolved to send a column through Maine. Writing to Schuyler on August 20, the commander in chief told him about the plan for "an expedition, which has engrossed my thoughts for several days." He envisioned sending up to 1,200 men who would "make a diversion that would distract Carleton" from Schuyler's own attack. Should the British commander break away to protect Quebec, Montreal would be easy prey; if he stayed at Montreal, Quebec would fall. Either way, the outcome would be decisive. The new plan served as a prod to the commander of the Northern Department. He could no longer delay. Success depended on attacking both Quebec and Montreal simultaneously. Speed would be essential, Washington warned, therefore "not a moment's time is to be lost in the preparation for this enterprise." He also informed Schuyler that he was considering appointing Benedict Arnold to command the expedition.

The crucial element of command could not wait for a response. Preparations must begin at once. Arnold was available, was eager to do it, and had impressed Washington favorably. Besides, he knew the valley of the St. Lawrence from firsthand experience. But the controversies surrounding his command in the Lake Champlain region raised question marks. Was the Connecticut firebrand temperamentally suited for so important a position?

Enter Silas Deane. The Continental Congress had adjourned, allowing Deane and other members to visit the army. The Connecticut congressman told Washington what a splendid job Arnold had done in northern New York, how shoddily he had been treated, and that Schuyler wanted him to return to Albany to serve on his staff. Deane's recommendation tipped the scales. Washington informed Benedict Arnold that he would lead the march to Quebec, and instructed him to begin at once making the necessary arrangements.

Ships had to be found to transport the expedition by sea to a forward assembly area in Maine. Orders had to be placed with a boatyard on the Kennebec for two hundred bateaux, many of which would have to be built on the spot. A workable organization had to be designed. Supplies had to be gathered. And on and on. A flurry of planning and coordination filled the final days of August.

On September 2, word arrived from General Schuyler. He was very pleased with the new plan, telling Washington that he "only wished that the thought had struck you sooner." He seemed at long last to be energized enough to kick off his own languishing campaign. While concurring in Arnold's selection as commander of the thrust through Maine, Schuyler cautioned that the fiery and independent-minded leader must understand that he would be the subordinate commander when the two columns met in Canada. With the overall effort thus as synchronized as was possible in that era of slow communications, Washington was set to go. He appointed Benedict Arnold to the rank of colonel in the Continental Army and directed him to put their jointly devised plan of operations into execution.

In general orders on September 5, the commander in chief called for volunteers "to go on command with Colonel Arnold of Connecticut." Men wishing to join must be "active woodsmen, and well acquainted with bateaux." What the mission might entail, or even the destination, was mysteriously left unstated. That intriguing call attracted flocks of soldiers. They had no idea what they were in for, but it sounded exciting—and far superior to the boredom of camp. Arnold, assisted by Horatio Gates, walked through the packed throng of volunteers and personally selected nearly eight hundred officers and men who appeared strongest and hardiest. Some three hundred riflemen, under command of Captain Daniel Morgan, completed the force. Leading elements marched out of camp on September 11, heading toward Newburyport on the coast north of Boston, where they would load onto ships for the first leg of the journey. From framing the idea to starting the expedition had taken less than a month.

Wanting to keep the mission secret for as long as practical, and perhaps to avoid any last-minute irresolution on the part of some delegates, the commander in chief waited another ten days before sitting down to write a letter officially informing the Continental Congress of the plan.

Meanwhile, in northern New York, General Schuyler laid siege to General Guy Carleton's army at St. Johns. Though outnumbering the British defenders, Schuyler chose the route of caution. It took two months for patriot forces to shift behind Carleton and cut his supply line to Montreal, forcing his surrender. Most of Carleton's regulars became prisoners. (Among the prisoners was

Lieutenant John André. He and others were marched to prisoner-of-war camps in the interior of Pennsylvania to await their fate.) The officer who actually conquered St. Johns was Schuyler's deputy, Brigadier General Richard Montgomery. Schuyler himself, ill and indecisive, had returned to Albany on September 16, at the very time Arnold was readying his own men to board eleven sailing ships assembled at Newburyport.

After a rough passage in adverse weather, the seasick soldiers went ashore at the village of Gardiner near the head of navigation on the Kennebec. There they transferred supplies and equipment to waiting bateaux and started upriver. It was late September, and the leaves were already beginning to turn.

America was committed. The thirteen colonies were assuming the strategic offensive, with Colonel Benedict Arnold leading the charge.

CHAPTER NINE

WINNING INDEPENDENCE

W HEN THE CONTINENTAL CONGRESS DECLARED AMERICA'S independence on July 4, 1776, it was confirming in words what the Continental Army had won in deeds more than three months earlier. April arrived that year to find not a single redcoat stationed anywhere in the thirteen former colonies. Only a desperate few clung grimly to the fortified city of Quebec, keeping Canada from becoming the fourteenth state in the new union. It had been only half a year since the Americans had gone on the offensive. The two principal actors in fashioning that astonishing military outcome were George Washington and Benedict Arnold.

Along Maine's meandering waterways, the distance from Gardiner to Quebec City is three hundred miles or so, not counting any need to double back after taking a wrong fork. But the primitive and unreliable sketches Americans had to work with showed the wending route to be only about 180 miles. Therein lay the awful seeds of disaster. Arnold estimated that the journey would take three weeks, putting him on the St. Lawrence in mid-October, well before winter's full onset. As it turned out, though, the march would consume more than twice that much time. Survivors of the ordeal would encounter deep snow and freezing weather long before glimpsing the walls of Quebec.

Not far upriver from Gardiner stood a former army supply post known as Fort Western (the site of present-day Augusta), where Arnold assembled his force for final preparations. There he organized the expedition into four divisions. Captain Daniel Morgan and his riflemen were to be the advance guard. Lieutenant Colonel Christopher Greene would march next at the head of three musket companies, followed by Major Return J. Meigs leading four more companies of musketmen. Bringing up the rear was Lieutenant Colonel Roger Enos, in charge of three musket companies and a detachment of twenty boat builders to repair the bateaux as needed. Finally, selected soldiers augmented by a few local Indians served as swift-moving scouting teams. Their mission was to roam far ahead of the main column, probing the way and seeking information. Enthusiasm was at a peak. Anticipation of imminent adventure fired the men's imaginations.

Morgan's division departed on September 25, tasked with clearing the way. Scouts were already out. A day later Greene started, then Meigs. The troops took turns rowing the bateaux and walking alongside the river. Enos and the rear guard shoved off on September 29, followed by Arnold and his command group in canoes. Traveling lightly and rapidly, Arnold passed the elements of his column one by one, exchanging boisterous salutes with the high-spirited men and catching up to Morgan in less than four days at a place called Norridgewock Falls.[1]

Progress had been good, thanks in large part to the assistance of settlers along the way and to a very dry season that had left the river calm and the portages relatively easy. But some fifty miles into the journey, at the edge of uninhabited remoteness, came the first serious setback. Many of the bateaux, hastily constructed for a one-way trip, were coming apart. They could not be used again without major repairs. Carpentry work and re-caulking consumed the better part of a week. But the lost time was not the only or even necessarily the worst problem. Water sloshing around in the boats had ruined much of the hastily packed provisions. The originally generous forty-five-day supply had been cut to worrisome levels. Moreover, nighttime temperatures were already dropping to the frost point, and the constantly soaked soldiers were paying a price. Scores had fallen prey to upper respiratory diseases. In a report sent to General Washington, Arnold lamented the delay but praised the great "spirit and industry" of his soldiers, who, he said, spent so much time in water that they might have been mistaken "for amphibious animals."

The colonel remained confident. By his reckoning, based on the maps he carried, his little army had covered nearly a third of the distance to Quebec, and the amount of food remaining would be

---

[1]   If the reader is still on the watch for touches of a whimsical novelist, a glimpse can be seen here in the person of one of Arnold's aides. Nineteen-year-old Aaron Burr went along as a volunteer. In later life Burr would turn out to be a thoroughgoing scoundrel, eventually being tried for treason after serving as vice president of the young nation. Thus the two most notorious traitors in the history of the United States started side by side up the Kennebec on that beautiful fall day in 1775.

adequate—barely. Besides, hunters fanning out on the flanks of the column might be able to supplement the rations with wild game. Arnold sent Morgan and his rugged frontiersmen ahead with orders to find and mark the "Great Carrying Place," a twelve-mile route over a series of ponds connecting the Kennebec to the Dead River. By October 8 the rest of the column had pulled out of the camp at Norridgewock Falls. Almost as if on signal from a spiteful Providence, torrential rains began that day, ending the period of balmy weather. The men would not be dry or warm again.

Captain Morgan's division encountered little difficulty in locating the Great Carrying Place, three dozen or so miles farther up the Kennebec. A scouting team had already reconnoitered the route, reporting the trail to be bad, "but capable of being made good." However, the scouts had been there before drenching rains and rising waters had turned the naturally soft turf into muck. The road could not be "made good." There was nothing to do but wade straight into the quagmire. Wrestling with heavy loads—notably the cumbersome boats and bulky supply barrels—the men sank knee-deep in sucking mud, while concealed roots and fallen trees tore at shoes and shins. Then the weather worsened. Close behind the pounding rain came howling wind and driving snow. Trees toppled. One crushed a soldier to death. Men fell ill from exposure and exhaustion, and from drinking swamp water. So many, in fact, that Arnold had a log structure raised along the way to serve as a shelter for the seriously sick. That rudimentary hospital filled to overflowing as soon as it was built. Finally, on October 13, ten trying days after leaving Norridgewock Falls, Morgan's weary riflemen stood on the banks of the Dead River. The rest of the expedition did not manage to finish crossing the Great Carrying Place until October 20, a date by which Arnold had once hoped to be investing the citadel of Quebec.

With most of the column straining against the rushing torrent of the Dead River, the skies opened up again on October 19, raising the level of the swollen river another three feet and accelerating the already speeding current. Precious little headway could be made, and still more food and supplies were lost to the turbulent waters. The wastage of food was particularly galling, for Arnold had already been compelled to put everyone on half rations. Nevertheless, the morale of the soldiers remained surprisingly high, in good part due to their colonel's personal example and constant encouragement throughout every trial. Benedict Arnold's inspirational leadership was never more evident than in those dark days. The expedition rode out this deluge as it had the others.

Then, just when it seemed nothing worse could happen, it did. On October 21 a hurricane roared into Maine. Pelting rain, slung by gales strong enough to throw the already battered boats high onto the riverbanks, slashed the soldiers in stinging sheets. The river rapidly rose another eight feet, becoming a virtually featureless lake before the violent weather abated the next day.

Determination to proceed prevailed even after that shocking blow from Mother Nature. Grimly, the companies set out again, only to find navigation in the flooded region to be more difficult than ever. Arnold watched helplessly as swirling waters overturned several bateaux. The men swam to safety and somehow recovered the boats, but everything in them was lost. That was the final blow. It shook even the formerly indomitable Benedict Arnold. Mindful that General Washington had directed him to abort the mission rather than risk the loss of the entire force, he stopped the advance. It was time to take stock.

To say things looked bleak would be a grand understatement. The haggard men were close to the raw edge of endurance. Hunger was a constant. Very little food remained and the surging waters had essentially ended hopes for catching fish or game any-time soon. Major quantities of military supplies—including critical items such as gunpowder and musket balls—had been lost. There was no clothing for winter. In wilderness isolation, cut off from information about operations elsewhere, no one had any idea what the overall situation was. And scouting parties, reporting back after ranging ahead into Canada, had brought the sinking realization of how much farther it was to Quebec than anyone had thought.

Colonel Arnold assembled his officers within quick reach to a council of war. It was late in the day on Monday, October 23, almost a full month since the expedition had left in exuberance from Fort Western. The march to Quebec trembled at the point of failure.

Reasons for admitting defeat and turning back were many and evident. The logic for reversing course showed in the sunken faces and tattered clothes of the handful of leaders clustered around their commander. No one would ever blame them for quitting after all they had gone through. But the very idea of retreat revolted Bene-dict Arnold. Was there not a way to continue? After all, in another thirty miles or so they would leave the flooded rapids of the Dead River behind. Then, after one more challenging portage over the continental divide, known there as the "Height of Land," the way would be all downhill. They would reach expansive and calm Lake Megantic, which fed the Chaudière River, whose churning current would carry them swiftly downstream to the St. Lawrence. And most important, food could be found in French Canadian settle-ments along the Chaudière. As desperate as matters were, and despite the long odds against success, the importance of their mis-sion overrode all qualms, including the very real possibility of dying in the effort. The grimly determined officers chose to take the risk.

Emboldened by that stouthearted vote of confidence, Arnold issued orders to streamline his bedraggled column. With a small band of handpicked men, he himself would dash ahead to villages on the Chaudière River to obtain food to send back to the rest of the column. To lighten the main body, "sick and feeble" soldiers would be returned to civilization on the Kennebec. Hopeful cheers rang in Arnold's ears as he set out early on October 24 in a race against time. His men accurately saw their own salvation riding on their colonel's broad shoulders.

Even with a fast-moving group unencumbered by baggage, Arnold's task was anything but easy. Nor was it without danger. Deepening snow and brutal winds added misery, ice-covered portages were unusually hazardous, and the increasingly frigid waters posed constant peril. Bogs reminiscent of the Great Carrying Place prompted one soldier to name the Height of Land the "Terrible Carrying Place." Energized by the awful realization that the survival of the entire body of men depended upon finding help quickly, the group pushed on despite all obstacles.

After reaching Lake Megantic, Arnold took sixteen strong men and the four remaining serviceable bateaux for a rapid descent of the Chaudière. At that crucial moment, a scout brought heartening intelligence. Word out of Quebec was that the bulk of General Carleton's forces were massed near Montreal, leaving Quebec City itself weakly defended. Moreover, local inhabitants appeared to be friendly and quite willing to help. That good news was all the more welcome because there had been so little of it lately. The intrepid colonel found the settlement of Sartigan (today's St. Georges) on October 30 and began at once to buy food for his famished men. By next morning drovers were pushing a small herd of cattle along a riverside path while a flotilla of canoes laden with grain and meat splashed up the river itself. Hours could mean the difference between life and death for all too many of his men, Arnold feared. He was right, although the actual situation was worse than he imagined.

All of Arnold's principal subordinates had received his orders to continue the march. All but one obeyed. Lieutenant Colonel Roger Enos turned fainthearted. Commanding the rear guard and having barely advanced up the Dead River, he was tantalizingly close to safety in retreat. Claiming Arnold's plan to be foolhardy, he turned his element around and stampeded to the rear. He also took some three hundred men with him, depriving the expedition of combat power it would sorely need once it arrived in Quebec. That shameful performance earned the wrath of George Washington, who had Enos arrested and court-martialed for "quitting without leave." But the damage had been done.

The other commanders—Morgan, Meigs, and Greene—pushed on, expecting to perish if Arnold's plan to meet them with food did not work. And perish they almost did. Six more inches of snow fell as they started, another foreboding sign. They struggled for days in the wasteland at the Height of Land and meandered in abject frustration in the maze of bogs near Lake Megantic. They were reduced to eating candles and anything else even slightly edible, including items made of leather. Increasing numbers weakened and died. Their friends, having neither the energy nor the tools to bury them, merely covered the corpses with tree branches and left them where they dropped. Somehow, the skeletal survivors stumbled on. As the calendar turned to November, the last of them, except those lost or dying, finally reached the Chaudière. Not knowing what else to do, they kept walking. Most were numb with exhaustion, many were delirious, all shuffled zombie-like, gaunt ghosts driven primarily by the instinct for survival. The woeful column stretched twenty miles along the river. Next day, those up front saw what appeared to be a mirage—or a miracle. Cattle for slaughter. Arnold's desperate race had succeeded.

Feeding the emaciated men was the first step. Finding stragglers and nursing the sick back to health was the next. Then came procuring clothing and blankets, restoring a clear sense of military organization, obtaining intelligence, and reaching out to Indians and French Canadian settlers for allies. The expedition still had its mission: attack and seize the walled city of Quebec, another sixty miles away. Arnold kept his focus on that goal.

A head count showed that at most 650 men had made it to Canada, with a large percentage of them now incapacitated. More than 400 had failed to finish the trek, including the 300 Enos had spirited away.

Locals soon brought word that authorities in Quebec were wise to the presence of an American force on the Chaudière, so surprise was no longer a part of the equation. But they also reported that the British garrison was disorganized and essentially demoralized, which meant it could fall to a rapid thrust. Arnold began to shift his scarecrow army in slow stages farther down the Chaudière, letting the men regain strength as they went. He designated the village of St. Mary as the final assembly area and collected canoes and boats all along the way. He would need them to cross the St. Lawrence.

Arnold himself moved ahead to conduct a personal reconnaissance of the route and select a suitable crossing point. On November 9, standing in swirling snow on the south bank of the waterway he had sailed on so often as a merchant, he gazed across at the objective of his terrible journey. Looming high above the water atop steep cliffs sat Quebec City. All he had to do was ferry his soldiers a mile and a half to the other side and capture it.

All, indeed. He had found watercraft enough to transport the soldiers overnight in relays—that is, if winds did not whip up waves and if the moon stayed behind clouds. In any event, crossing would be risky in the extreme, for two British warships rode at anchor under the city walls, ready to scatter any attempt. Once across, Arnold's small army, lacking artillery, could anticipate facing a larger and better-armed force holding the city. All in all, a daunting prospect.

But, as Arnold knew instinctively, boldness magnifies might. Raw recruits, sailors, and shakily committed French Canadians were the heart of the defense in Quebec, and the senior leader was a nervous civilian bureaucrat who knew next to nothing about the military. If the Americans could get there quickly and confront the frightened garrison, it might very well be bluffed into capitulating. Ever-daring, the colonel resolved to make the attempt.

By November 10 Americans had closed on the river in numbers adequate to proceed. A crossing that night or the next seemed quite possible. But Providence intervened yet one more time. A fierce winter storm blew in from the northeast, churning the river and making it completely impassable to Arnold's small boats and canoes. Bitterly cursing what appeared to be a malevolent fate, the men hunkered down to wait for the storm to blow by.

That last bad break of weather may have saved the city of Quebec. Out of touch far upriver, but growing increasingly fearful for the unprotected fortress, General Guy Carleton sent Lieutenant Colonel Allan Maclean with a contingent of trained soldiers to reinforce the city. With his slow transports stopped short by the same storm that was holding Arnold on the south bank, Maclean learned of the American threat. Alarmed, he put his men ashore on the north bank and force-marched them to Quebec, entering the city gates a day before the winds abated. Maclean's troops added a dimension of quality to the defense that Arnold could not match, but, more important, Maclean himself injected a sorely needed degree of military know-how into the garrison. He would not be duped by a ragamuffin army.

Far to the west, Montreal fell to Richard Montgomery's forces on November 13, leaving Quebec City as the only major position left between the invading Americans and the conquest of Canada. That very day, at Quebec, weather conditions turned favorable for a crossing. The Americans made their move.

After nightfall, Arnold and Morgan shoved off in the lead canoe, aiming for Wolfe's Cove to the west of the town. A path there led up the cliff to a large, level plateau, the Plains of Abraham, where a British army had defeated French forces in a decisive battle of the Seven Years' War. The path had been left unguarded. The boats made the dangerous transit three times before dawn stopped the operation, leaving Arnold and perhaps five hundred soldiers ensconced on the historic battlefield, looking at the walls of Quebec. That city perched on a triangular promontory where the St. Charles River joined the St. Lawrence. With the wide rivers acting as moats on two of the town's three sides, the garrison could concentrate its attention on the third, the western wall threatened by the rabble that had emerged from the wilds of Maine.

Just getting that far was a remarkable accomplishment. Benedict Arnold's star shone brilliantly. Thomas Jefferson compared the march to Quebec with the most fabled military exploits in antiquity. James Warren, president of the Massachusetts Provincial Congress, proclaimed the Connecticut colonel to be nothing less than a genius for completing a campaign unequaled in modern history. Nor were Americans alone in their awe of the achievement. Major General Henry Clinton, who would later be deeply involved in the drama of Arnold's treason, described the march to Quebec as a feat "which for the boldness of the undertaking and the fortitude and perseverance with which the hardships and great difficulties of it were surmounted will ever rank high among military exploits."

When the Continental Congress addressed the subject later that winter, members said flatly that Arnold's performance rated with Hannibal's legendary crossing of the Alps. They promoted him to the rank of brigadier general.

But that was in the future. In mid-November 1775, America's Hannibal had Quebec in his grip; it remained to be seen whether he could crack it.

———•••———

That fall, while Benedict Arnold and Richard Montgomery led columns crashing into Canada in a far-flung pincers movement, George Washington was doing everything in his power to strike other royal forces anywhere he could get at them.

Great Britain had numerous small garrisons scattered throughout much of North America east of the Mississippi River. Some occupied bases in Florida. Several stood guard in Nova Scotia, the Bermudas, and in the islands of the West Indies. Others manned frontier forts in the Great Lakes area. Moreover, pockets of loyalists and a declining number of royal officials clung stubbornly to posts in the thirteen colonies. No possible target escaped the notice of the commander in chief. By year's end he had compiled a clear record of combativeness bordering on brazenness. Among his more notable actions were that he had: organized a raid on Bermuda; considered assaulting Nova Scotia in the face of the Royal Navy; urged southern colonies to launch an expedition aimed at St. Augustine; tried to foment unrest among inhabitants of the West Indies; assembled a swarming fleet of privateers to prey on British shipping; attempted to foster attacks by friendly tribes against redcoats stationed in wilderness forts; encouraged the removal everywhere of officials who remained loyal to George III; and, of course, launched the campaign to seize Canada.

Never once, though, did he take his eyes off the enemy troops bottled up in Boston. He continuously sought to harass the redcoats there, keeping pressure on them while looking for any opening to attack.

Bunker Hill had actually been a victory, Washington realized in retrospect, because of the unusually heavy casualties inflicted on the British army. Could it be repeated? That is, could he goad General Gage into making another foolish attack against dug-in Americans? He tried to do just that in late summer, placing troops in a threatening position on "a hill within point blank (cannon) shot of the enemy's lines" near Bunker Hill, hoping to initiate a fight. Gage would not bite, however, having been bled in that fashion once already and recognizing that the rebels' handful of cannons posed more of an annoyance than a real danger. Gage easily neutralized the patriot guns with the overwhelming weight of fire his warships could bring to bear.

Washington next contemplated an attack on Boston itself. He envisioned making a frontal attack supported by an amphibious flanking movement. Presenting that scheme to his generals on September 11, the very day Arnold's expedition left the Continental Army's encampment on its way to the Kennebec, he sought their concurrence. (The Continental Congress had directed the commander in chief to gain the approval of a council of war before launching any major engagements.) If the Americans could gain the benefit of surprise, Washington told the eight generals present, such a daring assault "did not appear impractical, though hazardous." A military rule of thumb has it that councils of war do not fight. That rule held in this instance. The generals unanimously disagreed with their aggressive commander in chief.

Rebuffed, Washington nevertheless kept the plan alive in his own thinking. As time passed and the standoff at Boston showed no signs of resolution, he remained convinced that the outcome of inaction would be worse than any result of action. Defeat would be fatal for the British, whereas a repulse for the Continental Army would be simply a setback. Winter's approach, coupled with the expiring enlistments of most of his men, made the general determined to try a bold stroke while he still could. In mid-October he convened the council of war again. To his chagrin, the generals remained unconvinced, although this time only five voted "no." Nathanael Greene sided with Washington, and two others equivocated. The Continental Army's notable weakness in big guns was the primary reason the senior leaders were opposed.

Clearly, Washington needed to create an artillery command. Enough weapons were available in the stacks of artillery pieces Benedict Arnold had gathered near Fort Ticonderoga. A good number of them had been sent north with the troops attacking toward Montreal, but there were plenty of big ones left to strengthen the main army outside Boston. Next was the matter of an organization to employ the cannons and mortars. The commander in chief established the Continental Regiment of Artillery, designating Henry Knox, a hulking young Boston bookseller, as its colonel.

In November Washington ordered Knox to go to northern New York to get the guns as quickly as he could. That was no easy mission. First of all the artillerist had to figure out how to haul the massive pieces across New England without becoming mired at each water crossing. Frozen ground and streams would solve that problem. Knox left for the Lake Champlain area as winter fell, intending to use huge oxen-drawn sleds to transport the heavy guns when the New England snow was deep enough to permit it.

Meanwhile, the commander in chief turned his attention to the dicey task of disbanding one army and replacing it with another yet to be raised, all under the observation of an alert enemy. That risky undertaking would consume the remaining weeks of the year. There could be no assault on Boston until early in 1776, when the "new" army would be ready and the Fort Ticonderoga cannon would be present.

For a few days after occupying positions on the Plains of Abraham, Arnold postured and probed, trying to make his little army appear stronger than it actually was and hoping against hope for an opening of some kind. But the defenders, their collective spine stiffened by the arrival of British reinforcements and a determined commander, ignored American taunts to come out and fight. Refusing even to read overtures to surrender, they responded defiantly with cannon fire. Having no artillery and almost no gunpowder, the patriots were too weak to do anything other than bluff. "Had I been ten days sooner," Arnold lamented in a letter to Washington, "Quebec must inevitably have fallen into our hands, as there was not a man there to oppose us." That assessment holds up well in the full light of history. Ten days. Maybe even fewer.

Thrilling news arrived on November 17. Brigadier General Richard Montgomery's forces had taken Montreal. Americans besieging Quebec could anticipate help soon, including the all-important addition of artillery. Even more exhilarating to the shivering soldiers, Montgomery's troops had found stacks and stacks of warm British uniforms to bring them. With his expedition reinforced, reclothed, and resupplied, Arnold would be able to mount an attack. However, until those reinforcements showed up, the Americans were vulnerable to an enemy sortie from the city, which the British might be tempted to try if they learned how weak their besiegers really were. The colonel prudently decided to move some twenty miles upriver to await the arrival of the conquerors of Montreal.

While Arnold was blustering unavailingly before Quebec, a semi-comic scene played itself out far up the St. Lawrence. Governor Guy Carleton, having nothing left but naval vessels after all his ground forces had been swallowed up in Montgomery's invasion, attempted to escape down the river to join the Quebec garrison. But his ships, stopped by the same storm that had initially delayed Arnold's assault crossing of the St. Lawrence, found themselves trapped by Americans. Coincidentally, the force included Benedict Arnold's former regiment. In desperation, Carleton disguised himself in the garb of a Frenchman and slipped away at night in a small boat. Rowing with the current, his oarsmen made it safely past American patrols to reach open water, where an armed British ship sighted them. On November 19, as Arnold's men tramped upriver toward their safe encampment, they watched curiously as the ship carrying the governor sped past going the other way to Quebec.

Carleton had slipped through to take command in the city, King George's last foothold in Canada. Inspecting the defenses there, he was utterly dismayed by the precarious situation he found. "I think our fate extremely doubtful," he reported gloomily to London.

He would have been less worried had he known the extent of the problems just then confronting General Montgomery. Ominously, ice chunks already floating in the St. Lawrence foreshadowed winter's imminent closing of the waterway. Winter warfare was not for the faint of heart. With a string of victories to brag about, New England troops were ready to call a halt to campaigning and head home. Many did, including James Easton, Arnold's nemesis from the previous summer. He and John Brown still led Arnold's original regiment. But Easton had had his fill of campaigning that year. After overrunning and looting stores of British equipment, he decamped with a large portion of the regiment, leaving John Brown in charge of some 160 men who remained ready to fight. From the other units of his army Montgomery was able to muster only about three hundred more soldiers willing to continue, all from New York. Putting his game but skimpy group aboard a hodge-podge of vessels, he linked up with Arnold early in December and assumed overall command. Montgomery's reinforcements, Arnold's veterans, a contingent of French Canadian volunteers, and a few dozen Indians brought the grand total of armed men on hand to attack Quebec to around 1,300, a number barely larger than the complement Arnold had started with in the first place. A pitifully small number for a mission so crucial to the thirteen united provinces, it spoke eloquently of the abject inefficiency of that neophyte nation's war-making ability.

Richard Montgomery and Benedict Arnold were kindred souls. Both knew full well that the strength they had managed to assemble outside Quebec was marginal, at best, for a successful assault. But both also recognized that waiting would not make things better. The replacement pipeline was empty. They needed to work with what they had. Moreover, the army's numbers would start to drop precipitously as enlistments expired at the end of the year, especially in the New England companies that had followed Arnold up the Kennebec. Carleton, on the other hand, would not lose men over the winter—they had nowhere to go. And he could surely anticipate reinforcements from England just as soon as ice on the river broke up in the spring, allowing the Royal Navy to sail to his rescue. Finally, even if no other reasons had existed to underscore the urgency to act, the health of the army did. It was brittle. Although the men now enjoyed better clothing, adequate food, and even limited shelter, the bone-crunching conditions of the Canadian winter brought soaring sickness rates. Of utmost concern, doctors reported seeing cases of smallpox, that terrible scourge of military camps in the eighteenth century. Something had to be done at once—before the army simply faded away. One way or another, Quebec had to be taken before the end of December.

By December 5, the combined American forces once more occupied positions on the Plains of Abraham. Quartermasters began building up supplies and equipment for the assault Montgomery felt sure would be necessary. In the meantime, though, he followed Arnold's earlier scheme of attempting to precipitate a collapse of will among the defenders. A capitulation would be unlikely, he knew, but it was worth a try to avoid the costs in casualties of an outright assault. Moving cannons and mortars into firing batteries, and placing riflemen into forward sites for sniping, Montgomery brought the city under fire. To protect his outgunned crews, and trying to deceive the defenders into thinking the Americans had mustered far larger forces than they had, he spread the firing positions from one end of the western wall to the other, and shifted them around often. The whole effort proved to be fruitless. The rifle fire was galling, forcing sentries on the wall to keep their heads down, but it was bearable. In the artillery duel, however, Carleton came out ahead. His larger guns outranged those the patriots could bring to bear. Offers from Montgomery to accept the garrison's surrender on good terms were peremptorily declined. For some two weeks a desultory exchange of fire and probes continued with little evident impact on the defending garrison, and with absolutely no effect on the ever-stubborn Guy Carleton.

If anything, it was the Americans who first began to show signs of cracking. The men themselves were not overly eager to face the hazards of charging defended walls so very near the end of their enlistments. Montgomery, aware of their mounting uneasiness, tried to inspire them to gird for one last grand effort. In addition to an appeal to their patriotic fervor he aimed at their sense of self-interest by offering them freedom to plunder once Quebec was taken. He won grudging acquiescence. But there was resistance among a number of the officers as well. Some of Arnold's company commanders, still pouting over previous chastisement from their forceful and abrupt colonel and stirred up by the ever-malicious John Brown, became balky as temperatures fell and snowdrifts deepened. Montgomery defused that problem while Arnold bit his lip in silent fury at the renewal of the feud with Brown. The nagging incident was symptomatic of the overall fragility of the deteriorating situation. As one young soldier remarked, summer's flaming patriotism "seemed almost extinguished" by winter's icy blast. Arnold and Montgomery reluctantly concluded that they had no choice but to gamble on a roll of the dice. They would have to storm the city.

Montgomery intended to force a penetration of the west wall at its center. He would break through using a concentration of infantry carrying scaling ladders while other troops jabbed at the flanks to draw Carleton's attention away from the main attack. Hoping to gain surprise by cloaking the movement of his troops, Montgomery decided that the assault would be made at night and under cover of falling snow. On Christmas Day orders went out. Every available soldier would remain in readiness to execute the plan upon the arrival of favorable conditions—meaning very bad weather. Units shifted forward when snow started falling on December 27, only to be halted as the snowstorm stopped suddenly and the clouds parted, silhouetting the attackers in a world of white. It was an agonizing setback. The days of December were passing all too rapidly. And each new dawn brought diminished chances of crowning the invasion of Canada with an ultimate victory.

Sensing that deserters and the false start had compromised his plan, Montgomery hastily revised it. Quebec consisted of two sections, an "upper town" sitting atop the cliffs and behind the high wall facing the Plains of Abraham, and a "lower town" nestled narrowly on the shelf of land between the riverbanks and the bottoms of the cliffs. In the new plan, instead of striking directly at the upper town, patriot columns would force an entry at both ends of the lower town, link up, and then turn to take the upper town from the rear. The two prongs would attack simultaneously. Arnold, on the north, would have his own men while Montgomery would lead the three hundred New Yorkers to hit the south end. To confuse the defenders, remaining troops would threaten the upper town with a diversionary effort against the west wall. Arnold and Montgomery resolved to lead their attacks personally to inspire the ranks. The troops took their places, a blizzard blew in, and Montgomery gave the order to go. The advance began in blinding snow at 4 a.m. on December 31, 1775—for hundreds of the soldiers, the last day of their enlistments.

Luck did not favor the bold that night. General Montgomery's New Yorkers, squeezed into a pencil-thin column by narrow ledges along the way, were delayed by blocks of river ice thrown up on shore and then encountered a series of man-made obstructions. They found the first barrier undefended. Soldiers with saws and axes quickly cut a passageway through it. No enemy guarded the next one either. It, too, was rapidly breached. Montgomery stepped through, followed by several others in the advance party.

Across an open area stood a wooden structure converted into a blockhouse. In the dim light it loomed ominously quiet as the attackers crept cautiously forward. Was it defended? If so, how strongly?

Already behind schedule, with his main body still strung out along the way, Montgomery decided to charge the blockhouse before anyone manning it had time to get ready. Waving his sword and yelling to those around him to follow, he ran forward. Unlike the first two obstacles, however, this one was occupied. Armed with muskets and small cannons, the men inside were ready. When the Americans got within easy range, the defenders opened up with everything they had. That first point-blank blast of fire stopped the charge in its tracks. Montgomery and several others were killed outright. A few shaken survivors stumbled back to the second obstacle about the time the main body arrived.

Colonel Donald Campbell, a noted blowhard, was now the senior officer present. He surveyed the bloody scene. The patriots had suffered only a handful of casualties, the main force had not yet been engaged, and the blockhouse itself could be outflanked. Despite the death of Montgomery, the situation was far from desperate. But, as are most braggarts, Campbell was a coward. He promptly lost his bluster. Abandoning the dead and wounded where they fell, he turned the entire column around and sent it scurrying back to the safety of its original position on the Plains of Abraham. That craven action also left Arnold and his men to fight alone on the other side of the lower town.

Snow and ice had hampered Arnold's force to a lesser extent than it had Montgomery's, although he too was obliged to advance in a strung-out column, actually progressing single-file at times. But the enemy situation was quite different. Arnold encountered resistance as soon as he reached the city, where the path to the first barrier wedged his column right underneath the walls of the upper town. Musket fire from the top of those parapets began to inflict casualties well before the Americans could bring their own arms to bear. More or less on schedule, but faced with a fight from the outset, Arnold's men pressed on, albeit with wavering motivation.

Colonel Arnold's order of march revealed his assessment of the fighting effectiveness of his units. The bravest and most reliable led the way. He himself went first, accompanied by twenty-five volunteers, called in the parlance of the day a "forlorn hope." Next came Captain John Lamb with the crew of a small, sled-mounted artillery piece. Behind the artillerists tromped Daniel Morgan and his riflemen. They would be the attack's mailed fist. Following them were musket companies filled with soldiers serving the final day of their enlistments, more riflemen, and a small number of Indians and Canadian volunteers. At the very rear were units led by the captains who had attempted to detach themselves from Arnold's control. If they broke and ran there would be no troops behind them to be caught up in the panic.

Peering intently into the blinding snow, ignoring the plunging fire from above, Arnold finally saw the dark shape of the first barrier looming ahead. Signaling the forlorn hope to halt, he sent word back for Lamb to bring the cannon forward where it could blast a hole in the wooden wall. At that moment a blaze of musket fire illuminated the darkness—and one lucky shot took Arnold out. A lead ball ricocheted off a stone wall or a large boulder to hit him in the left leg. Misshapen from whatever it struck first, the ball tore into Arnold's flesh slightly below the knee and cut a jagged path down through muscle, scraping along the bone and coming to rest near his Achilles tendon. Stunned and bleeding heavily, Arnold was unable to stand. Men nearby dragged him out of the line of fire. Adding to the chaos, the cannon had become stuck in the snow. The assault stood on the edge of being stopped even before being launched.

But up front with Arnold was Captain Daniel Morgan. Seeing his colonel incapacitated, he seized the moment. Ordering one of his riflemen and a chaplain to take the wounded commander to the rear, where a doctor might save his leg, or at least his life, Morgan took over personal leadership of the assault. Waving men with scaling ladders forward, he charged the wall and climbed the first ladder placed against it. As he poked his head over the top a volley of musketry blew him back. Miraculously, he was untouched and the snow softened his fall. Shaking himself off, he climbed the ladder a second time and leaped into the midst of the enemy soldiers, who were busy reloading. Riflemen and members of the forlorn hope were right with him. The astounded defenders, promptly losing their zeal to resist these wild Americans, surrendered meekly. After opening the gate to let the rest of the patriots in, Morgan and a few of his men fixed their attention on the second barrier.

What happened next has been obscured by the fog of war. Years later Morgan himself wrote that he raced on to the next barrier, walked through the passageway, and looked around. There was confusion aplenty, but no armed defenders could be seen. That part of the lower town seemed to be his for the taking. Hurrying back, he urged his comrades to move forward before the British could reinforce. But his fellow officers turned cautious. Unnerved by the loss of Arnold, worried about leaving a hundred or more prisoners in their rear, and concerned that nothing had been heard from General Montgomery's direction, they decided that staying put until more of their trailing companies could arrive was the best course of action. Reluctantly, Morgan acquiesced. Later he was to lament that by doing so, "I sacrificed my own opinion and lost the town."

Whether that was so must remain a secret of history. What happened thereafter, however, is sad fact. Darkness, horrible weather, the normal confusion of combat, the absence of Benedict Arnold's steadying hand—all contributed to a brief period of paralyzing chaos at the most crucial moment of the battle. Although historians have been unable to reconstruct the details of the melee, the result is clear: the American attack lost all momentum.

By the time enough patriots had passed the first barrier to permit the column to continue, British forces had occupied the second in strength. The Americans now had to assault the wall Morgan had walked through half an hour before. They did, led once again by the irrepressible frontiersman, but were repulsed with heavy losses. That was the high-water mark of the American attempt to conquer Canada.

The patriots' ineffectual feint against the west wall had not deceived General Guy Carleton. Seeing how the fight was progressing, he sent a strong force out of the upper town to cut off the retreat of Arnold's troops. Blocked front and back, unable to maneuver on the narrow way, bloodied and not knowing the fate of Montgomery's column, all but out of dry powder, the Americans surrendered. Daniel Morgan was among the last to hand over his sword; artillery captain John Lamb sustained a gruesome wound when grapeshot blew away much of one side of his face. In the future both would figure significantly in the saga of Benedict Arnold, but for now they were among the nearly five hundred patriot casualties—killed, wounded, or captured—suffered in the unsuccessful attack. Many of the men whose enlistments ended that day were fated to remain in Canada after all—as prisoners.

That same December found huge Henry Knox inspecting artillery pieces stored at Fort Ticonderoga. He selected some sixty of them, cannons and siege mortars capable of pounding the defenses of Boston and battering British ships in the harbor. Workmen quickly built forty-two sleds while assistants spread out over the countryside to gather eighty yoke of oxen. The late-December storms that hit Quebec also blanketed New York and New England with snow deep enough to support sleds laden with tons of the deadly brass and iron guns. His bulk belying his energy, Knox wasted no time in starting his journey back to Boston. As the strange convoy snaked its way past Albany before turning east to cross the Berkshire Mountains, Colonel Knox beamed in obvious pride. "A noble train of artillery," he called it. To General Washington's delight, that noble train arrived in late January. At last the commander in chief had the means to get at his foe in Boston.

———•••———

January did not start as well outside Quebec. From his hospital bed, Arnold directed his remaining men to prepare for the counterattack he was sure General Carleton would launch. He ordered even the wounded, starting with himself, to take up weapons. The chances of beating off a resolute enemy in such circumstances seemed remote, but the pugnacious leader, in deep pain and weak from loss of blood, considered no other option. Carleton chose not to test the colonel's will. He was no longer dismissive of Arnold as a "horse jockey."

Incapacitated himself, and with a depressingly large number of his officers lost, Arnold wrote urgently for assistance. With Montgomery dead, the senior American in Canada was Brigadier General David Wooster in Montreal. Wooster was the very same officer Arnold had faced down in New Haven the previous April, nearly nine months ago, to gain entry to the town's powderhouse. Arnold had little respect for his elderly and acerbic townsman, but his own condition left him no choice. Wooster's presence at Quebec was "absolutely necessary," he wrote. So were reinforcements. "For God's sake, order as many men down as you can possibly spare... and all the mortars, howitzers, and shells that you can possibly bring." But Wooster was not inclined to leave Montreal in January; instead he sent Colonel James Clinton, a competent New Yorker. Clinton relieved Arnold so he could recuperate from his wound.

The Continental Congress, moved by Arnold's renown and urged on by his benefactor Silas Deane, voted on January 10 to promote him to brigadier general. Not aware then of his serious wound, the delegates assumed that the intrepid warrior would remain in the thick of the fighting in Canada. Learning later that month of the repulse at Quebec, they began frantically casting about for troops to send northward to ameliorate the situation. They were months late.

By February, Arnold's wound was healing. Able to limp from room to room, he assumed command again and planned to attack Quebec as soon as he had the new soldiers promised by Wooster. Late March appeared possible, maybe April, but May would be too late, for British reinforcements were anticipated by then. One element of the attack would be to destroy ships and wharves by sending fire ships into the port area. One of those was his own *Peggy*, the vessel that had sailed from New Haven the previous summer with a load of rum. Soldiers gladly unloaded the rum for camp use and filled *Peggy* with flammable materials. Arnold was committed to do whatever it took to conquer Quebec. In a letter to his sister, penned as he lay wounded, he had pronounced, "I have no thoughts of leaving this proud town, until I first enter it in triumph." His gutsy determination won praise from his superiors. Washington saw it as "fresh proof of Arnold's ability and perseverance in the midst of difficulties." A few troops arrived in early February, not enough to permit action but enough to raise hopes that more might follow. Then, a month after his actual selection, Arnold learned that he was a general.

That was a high point. From then on things got worse. More men trickled in, others left to go home as their enlistments ended. Some of the newcomers, having joined for a term of just three months, had scant weeks left to serve by the time they reached the Plains of Abraham. Overall, American strength climbed, peaking at about 2,500 by the end of March, but the number of effectives was quite a different story. Smallpox had hit in December and was soon ravaging the ranks. From a quarter to a third of the soldiers were unfit for duty at any given time. On top of disease, the coldest winter in years added to the army's woes. Morale sank, with scores of formerly stalwart soldiers beginning to contemplate defeat. And finally the Americans ran out of hard money needed to purchase supplies locally. Far from being able to mount an assault in March, the patriots were merely holding on as that month ended. The major thread keeping the army intact was the perseverance of Benedict Arnold. But, as he himself put it, he was making bricks without straw.

Then, on April 1, David Wooster rode into camp. Haughtily, the senior general took command from Arnold, letting him know that his services would no longer be needed in Quebec. By the middle of April the dejected brigadier was in Montreal, responsible for defending the captured city from Indians and redcoats. His adventure in Quebec was over.

George Washington was ready to attack. Knox had brought artillery, the new soldiers would soon be assimilated, and ice in Boston Harbor would be thick enough for troops to cross. Moreover, a large detachment of British units had sailed south (to eventually attack Charleston), leaving fewer than five thousand defenders to face about twice as many Americans. Circumstances were unlikely to get any better. Yet one more time the commander in chief convened a council of war; he was "willing and desirous of making the assault." Yet once more his fellow generals voted "no." They believed the men were simply too green to carry off an attack against redcoats ensconced behind barricades. In his heart the Virginian suspected they might be right, that he was perhaps pushing "to put more to the hazard than was consistent with prudence." But this time he did not adjourn the council. Continued inaction was not an option, he told them. If not an outright attack, he asked, what else could be considered?

The group gradually developed a scheme of maneuver. A stretch of high ground called Dorchester Heights dominated both the city and much of the fleet's anchorage. Artillery placed there could inflict considerable damage, while enemy gunners would be unable to elevate their own cannon sufficiently to respond. British troops would be compelled to leave their defenses in order to silence the incoming fire. The American generals agreed to move field pieces to Dorchester Heights "with a view of drawing out the enemy," which would precipitate a battle in circumstances favorable to the patriots. Dorchester Heights could become another Bunker Hill.

In what amounted to a gleeful statement from the normally stoic Virginian, Washington wrote that fortifying Dorchester Heights would "bring on a rumpus between us and the enemy." But he did not intend that "rumpus" to be merely a repetition of Bunker Hill.

Moving quite beyond the guidance of the council of war, the general was envisioning a decisive battle, a fight to destroy the occupiers, not just to bleed them.

Major General William Howe had become the commander of British forces after London recalled Thomas Gage late in 1775. Having led bloody assaults at the Battle of Bunker Hill, Howe was hardly likely to underestimate the fighting strength of entrenched Americans. He would surely strike at Dorchester Heights with a force powerful enough to overrun the defenders quickly with a minimum of losses—which meant that Boston itself would be left temporarily vulnerable to an amphibious attack somewhere along its waterfront. Washington planned a trap, "a settled and concerted plan" to defeat the entire occupying force. Six thousand men—with boats to carry them—would wait in hidden positions until Howe's troops were committed at Dorchester Heights. Then they would pour into the city from the rear. To achieve his plan, Washington had to wait until the harbor was free of ice and he had sufficient stores of powder to sustain artillery barrages.

After dark on March 4, the Americans occupied Dorchester Heights, hauling prefabricated fortifications to emplace atop the ridge. All night they labored, their work sites illuminated by a bright moon but screened from the British by a wispy surface fog, the sound of their hammers and construction shrouded by the continuous shelling from Knox's artillery. Dawn revealed to Howe's startled sentries a formidable fortress on what at dusk had been a barren hilltop. British gunners tried at once to neutralize the patriot position, but the hill was too high. Cannonballs fell harmlessly short. Knox's guns, however, subjected enemy positions and ships to a galling shelling. The situation was intolerable. Howe had to either attack Dorchester Heights or evacuate Boston. He decided to attack that very night, March 5. He ordered troops to be ferried over to the base of Dorchester Heights. Washington watched in anticipation verging on wonderment—Howe was taking the bait. The trap was working.

Fate stood on edge. Howe was poised to land, and the Americans were ready to bend oars to rush into the mostly vacated town. It was a climactic moment, and, as historians have held ever since, the outcome was entirely unpredictable. George Washington himself was serene. He had long pressed for this moment. Howe, on the other hand, began having second thoughts. Perhaps memories of the carnage at Bunker Hill haunted him, perhaps he had learned of Washington's trap. Just then, as if unable to stand the suspense, Providence intervened, taking the decision out of human hands. A storm of near-hurricane force lashed the area for two days, preventing Howe's attack. By the time the winds abated, the British general, though sorely embarrassed at being outfoxed by a mere provincial, was grudgingly ready to admit defeat and leave Boston. The king's units loaded their ships and sailed away on March 17, 1776. Washington had won, but it was not the smashing military triumph he had sought. He acknowledged that he could "scarce forbear lamenting the disappointment."

Others saw it differently. Patriots everywhere rejoiced and lionized the Virginian. Harvard bestowed an honorary doctorate of laws on the commander in chief, and the Continental Congress voted to award him a gold medal. Forcing the British out of Boston followed a string of smaller victories elsewhere that winter—notably in the southernmost colonies. Patriots held sway throughout the thirteen colonies, with only the Canadian city of Quebec remaining in British hands.

Things were rapidly unraveling in Canada.

After surveying the situation in the vicinity of Montreal, Arnold gloomily informed General Schuyler, who was still hunkered down in Albany, that the lack of resources had brought everything to a standstill. Unless that could be remedied soon, he wrote, "our affairs in this country will be entirely ruined." He also expressed considerable bitterness that the Continental Congress could have been so shortsighted in its seemingly lackadaisical support of the Canadian campaign.

But, prodded by the frowning imminence of defeat, the Congress had in fact begun to exert itself. The delegates sent Major General John Thomas to replace the dead Montgomery and started another few thousand troops marching northward toward Lake Champlain. Unable to do much more than that, the men in Philadelphia dispatched a commission to assess the situation. That group, headed by seventy-year-old Benjamin Franklin, included two other members of the Congress, Charles Carroll and Samuel Chase.

Thomas had supervised the overnight construction of fortifications on Dorchester Heights and was a well-regarded officer. When he reached Quebec on May 1, he found utter chaos. Blustering David Wooster had accomplished next to nothing, and half the soldiers were sick with smallpox. Next day, word arrived that the long-anticipated British relief force was approaching up the St. Lawrence. There was nothing to do but gather the sick and start a retreat westward toward Montreal. Thomas, looking for some way to delay the enemy's pursuit, latched onto Arnold's plan to damage the city's harbor with fire ships. Only one vessel was rigged to go, Benedict Arnold's own brigantine, *Peggy*. Thomas committed the ship after nightfall on May 3, but watchmen detected the silently approaching dark form and alerted waiting artillery crews. Their fire was accurate. With cannon balls hulling her, *Peggy* exploded in a spectacular fireworks display just short of the harbor entrance, doing no damage. It was one more sacrifice Arnold made to the cause.

As soon as the first British reinforcements landed, Carleton pushed out to probe the rebel lines, causing pandemonium. Rather than beating an orderly retreat, the patriots raced away in panic, forsaking wounded and sick comrades. Carleton, still overly cautious, chose not to chase the fleeing Americans, and with that reprieve Thomas tried to restore order to his ranks. But then he, too, fell victim to smallpox.

In the rear, Benedict Arnold was in constant motion, despite a hampering limp from his still-healing wound. He worked to find and prepare defensible positions from which to retard the enemy advance from Quebec. He sent an element west from Montreal to intercept a body of Indians led by a small number of British soldiers—and then had to go personally to rescue the men after an incompetent officer blundered the group into ambush and captivity. He received and deployed American reinforcements as they arrived from Lake Champlain, but could provide them very little support. Recording the sad result of unpreparedness, he noted that at long last "men we have indeed, but almost every other requisite for war is [unavailable]."

To Arnold also fell the responsibility of hosting Franklin, Carroll, and Chase. He was appreciative of their presence even if they brought only advice, rather than the money and materiel he so sorely needed for waging war. To his mind it was evidence that politicians in Philadelphia finally recognized the importance of supporting operations in Canada. For their part, the three congressmen were much impressed by the storied American Hannibal. Maybe expecting to meet a rough, blunt battler in the mold of Daniel Morgan, they were pleasantly surprised to find a man of sophistication. "An officer bred up at Versailles could not have behaved with more delicacy, ease, and good breeding," reported Carroll. The lessons so long ago in Jerusha Lathrop's parlor in Norwich had been well learned.

While the crumbling situation in Canada became painfully clear to Benjamin Franklin and his colleagues, they could see firsthand that it was not caused by any lack of energy or leadership from the still convalescing Connecticut general. Noting approvingly that Arnold's "lameness does not prevent him from stirring about," they predicted that he would enjoy still greater success in the future. "Believe me, if this war continues, and Arnold should not [become a casualty] pretty early, he will turn out a great man. He has great vivacity, perseverance, resources, intrepidity, and a cool judgment."

Not everyone would have agreed. Arnold's hard-nosed and hard-charging attitude could weigh heavily on subordinates whose slowness or timidity often brought forth his anger. Most of them recognized the tongue-lashings for what they were—forceful outbursts made in the excitement of the moment, passionate outpourings to prod men to action. Some, however, with egos more susceptible to bruising, harbored a lingering resentment at such peremptory treatment. The longer Arnold remained in command, the longer grew the list of affronted officers. John Brown, an implacable adversary ever since the capture of Fort Ticonderoga in 1775, was a prime example. His feelings had hardened when Arnold accused him and James Easton of ransacking captured supplies for personal profit during the invasion of Canada. In the hectic final weeks of the Canadian invasion one Moses Hazen joined that list.

Hazen, an influential inhabitant of St. Johns, had at first supported Carleton's efforts to defend Canada, but had switched loyalties when patriot forces appeared to be gaining the upper hand in 1775. The Congress made him a colonel to command a regiment of Canadians fighting for the Americans. Upon reaching Montreal, Arnold replaced Hazen as the senior officer. At first the two got along well, but a shouting disagreement over tactics soon brought the colonel and the brigadier to an insulting exchange of verbal blows. Both crossed well beyond the line of behavior expected of men of their rank. Focused on the mission and the deteriorating situation, Arnold put the incident aside, but Hazen did not. He simmered. A short time later, when a still-brooding Colonel Hazen refused to follow instructions during the evacuation, Arnold upbraided him fiercely. Browbeaten into obeying, but enraged, Hazen vowed to demand a court of inquiry to clear his reputation and to demonstrate what a demeaning lout Benedict Arnold was. He would carry through with that intent, causing untold trouble at a crucial moment later in the year.

Learning that the royal relief force amounted to many thousands of British and German regulars under the command of Major General John Burgoyne, Arnold and the two remaining members of the congressional commission (Benjamin Franklin, ill and old, had returned early to Philadelphia) concluded that a fighting withdrawal was the only reasonable course of action. But back in Philadelphia an out-of-touch Congress issued a wholly impractical order: commanders in Canada were to "contest every foot of the ground." Such unfortunate thinking led to the final disaster in Canada. Major General John Sullivan, arriving just in time to replace the dying John Thomas, rashly engaged the British at a site along the St. Lawrence called Three Rivers. The conflict was short, brutal, and entirely one-sided. Burgoyne inflicted heavy casualties on the patriots. It was at last evident to everyone in the northern theater that Canada could not be held in the face of such overwhelming British strength. Arnold accurately assessed the situation, writing that any hope of joining "the Canadians with the colonies—an object which brought us into this country—is now at an end." Soon thereafter he received orders to wage a rear-guard action to gain time for the evacuation of all Americans and those Canadians who had supported them.

That turned out to be a relatively easy mission to accomplish. Arnold, who always thought aggressively, was surprised when Guy Carleton kept his fresh troops on a tight leash. The governor held Burgoyne to a methodical advance that permitted the battered American units more than enough time to escape. Burgoyne's large army of regulars consumed an enormous amount of supplies, which Carleton was hard-pressed to provide in a countryside already picked over by the invaders, who had occupied it for more than half a year. Moreover, Carleton did not want to be saddled with a host of hungry prisoners he would be obliged to feed and who would further strain his stretched supply lines. Accordingly, the powerful British army followed rather than pushed the patriots out of Canada.

By June 18, 1776, all troops except the rear guard under Arnold's direct control were safely making their way to rendezvous sites farther south. Occupying St. Johns, Arnold may have reflected on the coincidence of time and place. Almost exactly one year earlier, as master of the lake, he had reconnoitered Carleton's defenses in that area, found them weak, and strongly urged an American invasion then and there.

The retreating soldiers put much of St. Johns to the torch, including the home of Moses Hazen. Leaving nothing of value to the enemy, they pushed off in bateaux. Finally only one boat remained, and two mounted men—Benedict Arnold and his aide of two weeks, Captain James Wilkinson.

Wilkinson was then only nineteen years old. His future military service, destined to be several decades long, would be marked by dishonor, intrigue, and base disloyalty—if not outright treason. Like Aaron Burr, to whom he would later be a shady accomplice, James Wilkinson was to become one of America's greatest rogues. Arnold had started his invasion of Canada with Burr at his side; he was ending it nine months later with Wilkinson in the same role: bizarre bookends, those two, to the entire adventure.

Pensively, as if reluctant to call an end to the whole valiant, frustrating affair, Arnold rode back a short distance. He and his young aide quietly watched the approaching enemy for a few minutes. Then, wheeling their horses, they spurred quickly to the water's edge, where they removed their saddles and threw them into the waiting boat. They shot their horses, climbed aboard, and left Canada.

CHAPTER TEN

DEFENDING THE UNITED STATES, 1776

K ING GEORGE III AND HIS CABINET WERE ADAMANTLY resolved to quash the uprising in their colonies in 1776, at whatever cost. That year Great Britain sent across the Atlantic the largest expeditionary force it had ever sent anywhere: 35,000 soldiers to New York City and 13,000 to Canada, all backed by an enormous armada of over 500 ships. Lord George Germain, the minister for colonial affairs, was not speaking loosely when he stated that the mother country was "exerting the utmost force of this kingdom to finish the rebellion in one campaign."

Never in their most pessimistic moments had the Americans expected to face so formidable an adversary. Worse yet, by their own assessment, they needed at least a two-to-one superiority in numbers to overcome the stark advantage the enemy possessed in training, organization, and equipment. But the very most they could even remotely envision mustering was fewer than their opponent would field. In the end, 25,000 Americans squared off against an enemy 48,000 strong—a two-to-one ratio, just not in the patriots' favor.

The massive British reinforcements altered the strategic situation dramatically. Before then, American leaders could afford to take large risks, for even a serious defeat would probably not have proven fatal. The British had been simply too weak to capitalize on any victory they might have gained. That was obviously no longer the case. If royal forces were to overpower the Continental Army now, it could quite likely signal the death of the infant republic. The commander in chief was correct that July when he solemnly announced that the "peace and safety of our country depends (under God) solely on the success of our arms." The ultimate fate of the Revolution rested squarely on the performance of Washington's outmanned and outgunned army.

Surprisingly enough, the defense of the United States in 1776 defied the hard logic of numbers and military might. Against all odds, when that year's campaigning was over, London's forces had failed "to finish the rebellion." Instead, they sat frustrated about where they had started in July.

Two of the principal actors in fashioning that astounding military outcome were George Washington and Benedict Arnold.

———•·•———

British sails were not out of sight beyond Boston Harbor before George Washington began to contemplate next steps. His strategic thoughts shifted to the Hudson River. Washington recognized that retaining control of the Hudson was his foremost strategic imperative. So did British leaders.

Wide and tidal for most of its length, and navigable to oceangoing warships all the way from New York City to Albany, that waterway linked the Atlantic Ocean to the St. Lawrence Valley in

Canada. It was the only militarily significant avenue leading into the interior of the continent. All other locations, like Boston, went nowhere—they were strategic cul-de-sacs. British dominance of the unbridged and unfordable river would present a mighty barrier to any attempted east-west movement of the Continental Army. The Royal Navy could cruise the river virtually unmolested if British forces held both Albany and New York City. New England soldiers and supplies would be severed from the rest of the United States, cutting the nation into two roughly equal parts in terms of population and resources. With the Royal Navy already dominating the Atlantic Coast, at least one end of the river had to be held if the Americans were not going to lose the initiative to the enemy. Guessing that his opponent would probably center his operations on the Hudson River, Washington began shifting his army to New York. He personally took charge of the defense of New York City, trusting to Philip Schuyler to hold onto gains made in Canada.

Washington saw hostilities entering a new phase. In the conflict's first year, patriots and redcoats had mostly glowered at one another over barricades. Maneuver was the exception. But the Americans were obliged to defend their shores everywhere, while royal forces were free to attack anywhere. The Continental Army needed to become agile, able to move quickly to any endangered spot and to fight in the open. Washington himself would exercise command from a mobile headquarters. "After I have got into a tent," he informed the Congress, "I shall not soon quit it."

In consultation with the Continental Congress that May, Washington devised "a plan of military operations for the ensuing campaign." Not knowing that London would hire thousands of mercenaries from German principalities, the Americans calculated that Great Britain would be able to send no more than about 22,500 men across the Atlantic, with 10,000 of those going to

Canada. Wanting a two-to-one edge in manpower, the Americans decided to raise 20,000 troops for northern New York and 25,000 to defend southern New York, with another 10,000 held in a mobile reserve, called a "flying camp." They would rely on local militiamen to defend New England and the southern colonies.

On the capacity of each side to raise and deploy field armies, the planners were wildly off the mark. Americans eventually mobilized no more than 25,000 of the estimated 55,000 men, while the British and their Hessian cohorts numbered well beyond twice what the Americans expected. Washington was reasonably accurate regarding the strength of the British buildup in Canada, but was woefully wrong about British strength along the lower Hudson.

Having already outfoxed Howe once, the commander in chief was initially confident he could do so again. But it was not to be. The Virginian was about to learn how pitifully ineffective untrained patriot units were against European regulars in open combat. Reality began to set in when the vanguard of 35,000 British and German troops streamed ashore on Staten Island, across the bay from New York City, just as the Continental Congress was approving the Declaration of Independence. The new nation was in a new war.

By late August 1776 General Howe was ready to throw his huge army into battle. Americans had placed obstacles in the waters around New York City to disrupt movement by warships and had emplaced ground units to cover all likely areas of attack. Altogether, Washington had nearly twenty thousand men under arms, the largest army he would ever command. But a distressingly few were veterans. Most were militia and new recruits, scarcely trained and incompletely equipped. Over a year after establishing an army, the United States remained inept at raising and supporting one.

The largest concentration of defenders occupied positions at the western end of Long Island. There Howe decided to strike. After ferrying more than twenty thousand troops from Staten Island, he pointed them toward the patriot lines on August 27, 1776. The ensuing Battle of Long Island was a quick affair. Local commanders apparently assumed that the British would come straight at them. Instead, Howe sent a fast-moving column circling around the American left flank, which was neither defended nor watched. Startled to find enemy units behind them, the continentals bolted, scurrying back to the protection of entrenchments already prepared on Brooklyn Heights. Losses in killed, wounded, and captured were considerable. Howe followed cautiously.

Washington crossed over from Manhattan Island at about that point, bringing reinforcements and taking personal command. For a time he stood firm, daring Howe to assault. The new lines had no open flanks; this time the British would have to approach frontally. The American commander envisioned another Bunker Hill, with his foe obliged to "wade through much blood and slaughter" on the slopes in front of his entrenched troops. But Howe was not about to repeat that error. He started siege works, a slower but surer and safer method of attack. Frustrated, but seeing the futility of staying in place, Washington extricated his entire force on the night of August 29. A withdrawal from contact is one of the most difficult and hazardous maneuvers in warfare. But thanks to a friendly fog, outstanding work by his boatmen, and sterling leadership from George Washington himself, the Americans pulled it off. It was as brilliant an operation as was recorded in the war. The commander in chief shoved off in one of the last boats to leave.

There was a general feeling of relief that most of the survivors of the fighting, perhaps as many as ten thousand of them, had been safely returned to Manhattan Island. Still, there was no disguising the fact that the battle had ended in defeat. That was not what Americans had come to expect from their clashes with the king's units. For the first couple of weeks in September both sides paused to catch their breath, the patriots to prepare for further combat and the British to see if the rebels would listen to sense and agree to cease resistance.

————•—————

Earlier that same summer, while George Washington was positioning his army to defend New York City and the Congress was drafting the Declaration of Independence, Benedict Arnold was devising an operational concept for the defense of northern New York.

After leaving St. Johns just a rifle shot ahead of advancing redcoats, Arnold caught up with his commander, John Sullivan, at a rallying point near the northern end of Lake Champlain. Sullivan, still wringing his hands over his ignominious defeat at the hands of Burgoyne and the subsequent loss of Canada, and having no plans for recovery, sent the junior general to brief Philip Schuyler and ask for orders. Arnold, accompanied by Captain Wilkinson, pushed south on Lake Champlain, passing islands, inlets, and broad waters well known to him from his exploits a year before—and due shortly to become even more familiar.

Not finding Schuyler at Fort Ticonderoga, they continued to Albany, reaching the mansion of the commander of the Northern Department shortly before midnight on Monday, June 24. Right away, the two generals closeted themselves to discuss the tenuous situation and to settle on a course of action. They worked through the night. By the time dawn broke on Tuesday they had plans in place and had written implementing instructions. Waiting couriers galloped off with letters updating General Washington and telling General Sullivan to withdraw the remnants of his battered army to the vicinity of Fort Ticonderoga, where he was to establish new defensive positions. Arnold's impact on the normally sluggish Schuyler was evident. Decisiveness molded the plans and alacrity marked their implementation.

It was clear that Carleton intended to keep pushing south—the American leaders had learned that warships suited to fight on the lake had been prefabricated in England and shipped in pieces to Canada. It was a good bet that even at that moment workers were making preparations to assemble them at St. Johns.

The countering American strategy was bold but simple. Above all else, Fort Ticonderoga must be held. If the British captured that bastion they could advance to Albany and the Hudson River. Arnold and Schuyler did not delude themselves—if it came down to a clash between the ramshackle American units straggling in from Canada and Carleton's larger and rested regular army, the outcome could hardly be in doubt. It was imperative, then, not to await an attack but to strike first to prevent the enemy from ever reaching the south end of the long lake, or at least to delay them until they had sufficient defensive strength to withstand an assault. That meant confronting Carleton on Lake Champlain itself. At sea, so to speak.

The two generals saw at once the need for "a naval superiority on the lake," but the patriots' naval forces were essentially limited to the vessels Benedict Arnold had mustered the year before. That was entirely inadequate for so daring a mission. From his experiences in 1775, when he had been master of the lake, Arnold realized what power the British armada might wield. To stand a chance of countering it he reckoned that the American ships already available would need to be reinforced by "a large number (at least twenty or thirty) of gundolas, row galleys, and floating batteries." Fortunately, having foreseen the need for increased naval forces, Schuyler had already established a shipyard at the south end of the lake. The Americans would strive to put a fleet together before the British could complete theirs. A wilderness arms race was under way.

There would be a battle on the lake. That much seemed certain. The key question was when. Arnold calculated that the British would not be ready to attack for a couple of months. They would require at least that long, he reasoned, to gather supplies necessary to support ten thousand men in the forests of northern New York and to construct shipping adequate to move the force southward over the lake. Moreover, having had ample opportunity to take the measure of Carleton's generalship, Arnold felt sure that the Englishman was too conservative a commander to advance before everything was in readiness. So, all things considered, it seemed that the Americans would have until the end of summer before they would have to employ their "naval armament."

That, in turn, raised a tantalizing possibility. Delaying the approach of the enemy fleet until the onset of winter might be just as effective as defeating it outright.

During that long night Schuyler informed Arnold that the Congress had promoted Horatio Gates to major general and had ordered him to replace Sullivan as the commanding general of forces in Canada. He was expected to arrive in a few days.

Gates would be Arnold's fifth boss in just seven months. Richard Montgomery had been killed attacking Quebec. John Thomas had died of smallpox. David Wooster and now John Sullivan had been relieved.

Nevertheless, the news pleased Arnold, for the two had worked well together in readying the expedition up the Kennebec River, and earlier in the year Gates had extended high praise, writing that Benedict was "a most persevering hero." But in that appointment lay seeds due to sprout into bitterness. There were no forces left in Canada for anyone to command; Gates's assignment therefore placed him on a direct collision course with Schuyler. Arnold would eventually be caught between the two senior generals.

For the time being, however, amity ruled. When Gates arrived at the end of June and became apprised of the awkward command situation, he and Schuyler agreed at once that the army could not have two heads, that the Congress would have to sort out the confusion it had wrought. The Congress did act a week later, charging both generals to serve in harmony and saying that Schuyler would remain senior so long as "the troops should be on this side of Canada." With that understanding the two pulled in tandem during the summer and fall to try to repel the pending British invasion. Schuyler directed Gates to concentrate on the defenses of the Lake Champlain area, while he himself retained overall direction of the entire northern theater of war.

General Gates saw land and lake as two distinct operations. While he elected personally to focus on preparing land defenses and strengthening his ground forces, he felt less competent to deal directly with naval affairs. Accordingly, he recognized a need for someone to "give life and spirit to our dockyards" and for a subordinate officer "of firmness and approved courage" to command the fleet itself. Fortunately, he had right at hand the ideal person for both tasks: Benedict Arnold.

Indeed, no one else in the Continental Army was better prepared to serve as commodore of Lake Champlain's naval forces. He had the requisite nautical experience, he was a battle-tested leader, and he had excelled in a similar capacity the year before. Besides, he very much wanted the job. "Arnold (who is perfectly skilled in maritime affairs) has most nobly undertaken to command our fleet upon the lake," Gates happily reported to General Washington and the president of the Congress. "With infinite satisfaction, I have committed the whole of that department to his care, convinced he will thereby add to that brilliant reputation he has so deservedly acquired."

Arnold went immediately to inspect the shipyards, located at Skenesborough some thirty miles south of Fort Ticonderoga. Arriving on July 23, he was elated to find the construction going well. But there was still much to be done, and the weeks of summer were passing all too quickly. "I think we shall have a very formidable fleet" by the middle of August, he wrote, but gathering supplies and enlisting enough able-bodied seamen would take longer. The new commodore needed every ounce of his energy for the task. Nevertheless, at that anxiety-ridden juncture Benedict Arnold had to attend a court-martial.

The Revolutionary War thrust into leadership positions innumerable warriors whose service rendered them larger than life, many even with a tinge of greatness. It also cast up others small-minded and selfish, officers unable to see beyond personal pettiness to glimpse the greater good. A bevy of that latter sort surfaced in the summer of 1776 at a most inopportune moment.

The troubles began when the malevolent duo of James Easton and John Brown made their way to Philadelphia to complain to the Congress and to malign Arnold. They wanted a hearing to restore their bruised honor. Easton got there in April, followed by Brown several weeks later. (Tellingly, perhaps, shortly after reaching Philadelphia, James Easton was thrown into jail for debt, languishing there for three months.) Easton and Brown heaped scorn and derision on the general they so thoroughly detested, sentiments reinforced by others like Moses Hazen and echoed in letters from their friends and relatives. Illustrative of the vitriol is the statement of one such opponent, who wrote of Arnold, "I heartily wish some person would try an experiment on him, (viz,) to make the sun shine through his head with an ounce ball" to see whether the rays shone straight through or bounced around.

Against that poisonous clamor few voices could be raised. Arnold and others who knew the facts were far away tending to their military duties. The always supportive Silas Deane had departed to become an envoy to France. Some delegates who had visited the Northern Department could attest to Arnold's battlefield prowess but could not address the specific charges spewing from his angry accusers. One member, Samuel Chase, informed Arnold of the diatribes against him and warned him to beware of so-called "friends" who were in fact enemies waiting to pounce.

The Congress bowed to the uproar raised by the two bitter officers, issuing Brown a commission as a lieutenant colonel, which he had claimed Arnold had unfairly denied him. But, with far more important matters on their agenda, the delegates quickly tired of the whole unseemly mess. They threw the quarrel back into the army's lap, where it should have been all along. Washington obediently told Schuyler to convene hearings for all officers charged with malfeasance in Canada.

First up was Moses Hazen. His court-martial began on Wednesday, July 31. That was the trial dragging an exasperated Benedict Arnold away from his vital mission of establishing a fleet.

The commodore became even more agitated when he arrived at Fort Ticonderoga to discover a smug Moses Hazen basking in the comforting embrace of a packed court. The members were Hazen's peers and friends, and, for a variety of reasons, hostile to Arnold. Upon realizing the drift of the hearing, Arnold completely lost his temper. He blasted the proceedings in terms deemed by the members to be "illegal, illiberal, and ungentlemanlike." They huffily demanded an apology. Becoming apoplectic rather than apologetic, he flatly refused. Instead, he challenged them each and every one to a duel. Not one of the officers could summon the courage to face the irate general over deadly weapons. Disgusted, he stalked out, ending the hearing in chaos. Gathering some collective nerve, the cowed members met again to exonerate Hazen and to call for their challenger's arrest. General Gates accepted the ruling on Hazen, but then dissolved the board for showing "too much acrimony" towards Arnold. Besides recognizing the blatant dishonesty of the board's charade, Gates was looking at the bigger picture. In relating the action he had taken, he referred to Arnold's matchless value to the cause, saying that the nation "must not be deprived of that excellent officer's service at this important moment." Arnold returned to the shipyard at Skenesborough, his blood still hot but his eyes on the real enemy industriously constructing warships at St. Johns.

Intelligence reaching the south end of the lake described the British fleet coming together as almost certainly more powerful than the one the Americans were building at Skenesborough. General Carleton would command more ships outright and would definitely enjoy superior firepower. His expert crews would man not only more guns but bigger and longer-ranged ones as well.

Having hoped for up to thirty warships, Arnold realized he would be lucky if half that many were in the water in time to meet his foe. In addition to *Liberty* and *Enterprise*, both veterans of action on the lake in 1775, the commodore had two more schooners. Those four, each manned by about fifty men, were fast and maneuverable so long as they had wind to work with, but carried relatively light armament. Three row galleys, with crews of around eighty, provided the iron fist for battle. Large and heavily armed, the galleys were able to slug it out with hostile ships. Moreover, powered by both sails and oars, they were agile. The problem was that there just weren't enough of them. Most numerous but least effective were nine gundalows. Crewed by some forty-five men, with guns fore and aft and along both sides, the smallish vessels could sting, but were not very maneuverable. Awkward and flat-bottomed, they could sail directly with the wind but required oars for any other movement. Even if workers at Skenesborough could complete all the fighting ships in time, the patriot navy would certainly be a hodgepodge of vessels.

Worse still was the daunting problem of finding crewmen. British ships were sure to be manned by seasoned sailors and gunners, skills seriously short in the Northern Department. By and large, Americans with experience at sea preferred to ship out on privateers rather than join the army, so few experienced sailors were available. Those few, eyeing the clumsy vessels taking shape in the Skenesborough shipyard, recognized that they were unlikely to survive a clash with British warships on the lake. Only a handful responded to pleas for volunteers. So army commanders received orders to fill out the fleet's crews. They either sent misfits or forced reluctant soldiers to draw lots. Arnold fumed at the results. The untrained, unwilling, and often recalcitrant troops marching in "are a miserable set," he complained, hardly "equal to half their number of good men." But he had no recourse other than to make the best of it. He tried to place at least one qualified artillerist and one experienced seaman on each boat, and set out to train the rest in the short time remaining. The limitations of his crews, he knew, would be a major factor in the coming battle.

Taking unwieldy vessels manned by bungling soldiers into a fight with a superior fleet quite naturally raised the issue of tactics. How should the American ships be employed? Early in August

Gates issued secret written orders. "It is a defensive war we are carrying on," he said; therefore, the commodore should take "no wanton risk" by acting offensively. That meant, specifically, American warships would stay south of the Canadian border. Still, the fleet must fight, because the mission was to prevent "the enemy's invasion of our country." Arnold was to conduct a "resolute but judicious defense," making "every effort to retard" Carleton's advance. Clearly, the hostile fleet must be engaged well north of patriot defensive positions at Ticonderoga. Arnold should select a narrow point in the lake where his flanks would be protected and Carleton would be required to attack him. If the British armada proved to be of overwhelming strength, Arnold had the authority to retreat to Ticonderoga, but Gates fully expected him to act with "cool, determined valor" to give his foe full reason to pause. He knew well the fighting instincts of his combative commodore.

By this time, so did British leaders. Lord George Germain, writing from London, expressed disappointment that Arnold had not been captured or killed in Canada, as "he has shown himself the most enterprising man among the rebels." Guy Carleton himself, knowing from actual experience the belligerent character of his opponent, fully anticipated aggressive action once the American fleet set sail. He did not intend to venture south until he had an overpowering force in hand.

Aware of the Englishman's overly cautious nature, Arnold took advantage of it. Widely advertising his intention of raiding the shipyard at St. Johns, he began moving his ships beyond Ticonderoga to Crown Point in mid-August. His orders, of course, prohibited him from approaching St. Johns, but they were secret and known only to him. His bravado scared even some of his subordinate officers, who knew full well how unready they were to attack. Spies picked up the boastful talk and duly reported it to their handlers in the north, where it was taken seriously. Arnold had soldiers to turn into sailors, so he had to get his ships into open water anyway—if that worried Carleton, so much the better.

By August 24, Arnold had ten ships ready and a fair south wind. He sailed north. The small flotilla was in no shape to fight—the row galleys were not yet ready—but he needed to reconnoiter the lake, select a battle site, train his crews, and gather intelligence about British readiness. Besides, he reckoned, his bluff might actually cause Carleton to delay somewhat.

He was successful beyond even his wildest imagination. Early in September he anchored in battle array far north on the lake, well within the limits of his orders but close enough to the Canadian border to assure that his presence and posturing would become known in British headquarters. He had by then twelve ships, a pitifully small number compared to the huge force coiled in St. Johns. But Carleton blinked. Reporting that patriots were blocking the lake with "a considerable naval force," he decided to wait until his last and largest warship was ready. A giant three-masted sloop of war had been disassembled and hauled piece by piece overland past river rapids to St. Johns, where workers had just begun to reassemble it. The *Inflexible*, mounting eighteen twelve-pound guns, could sweep the lake of any other shipping. General Carleton wanted that insurance before tangling with Benedict Arnold again. *Inflexible* floated in early October, and Carleton finally gave the word to sail. Arnold's bluff had delayed the enemy advance by almost exactly one month.

That was the most crucial four weeks in the entire campaign. The hills already showed patches of snow. Nighttime temperatures were below freezing. From then on winter was a staunch American ally.

When Carleton reached open water on the lake, Arnold was nowhere to be seen. After remaining exposed in the forward position long enough to be sure of having made his foe nervous, he had sailed southward in easy stages to Valcour Island.

Arnold considered it to be the ideal place to make a stand. Roughly midway between north and south ends of the lake, Valcour stood close to the western shore. There geography offered a natural redoubt. The island and the shore formed a large bay open to maneuver only from the southern end and out of sight from ships heading south until they had passed well beyond the island itself. The little armada, formed in a crescent-shaped curve reaching half a mile across the bay from Valcour Island to the New York shore, could not be flanked or attacked from the rear. After passing Valcour Island, Carleton would have to turn his fleet around, beat back into the wind, and attack head-on into a constricted area subjected to concentrated shelling. Significantly, Arnold's poorly trained crews would not have to worry about maneuvering their vessels during the fight. Patriots had been successful on land when they could entice British commanders to attack them in carefully prepared defensive positions. It could work on water, too.

Telling Gates of his tactical scheme in mid-September, Arnold had felt confident. If hostile warships ventured forth, he wrote, "it will be impossible for them to take advantage of our situation." By the end of that month, however, he was growing increasingly worried—his strength had increased to fourteen ships, but he had none of the all-important row galleys. Without them he could not risk a battle. If Carleton arrived before they did, Arnold told Gates, he would have no choice but to abandon his plan and slip away to the south.

Most soldiers show trepidation at the thought of imminent mortal combat, but not Benedict Arnold. For him, tenseness came at the thought of missing a fight. His edginess displayed itself in several messages to Gates, badgering him with lists of shortages in the fleet.

Ammunition and swivel guns headed the items in terms of urgency. Warm clothing was vital, he said, for half the men were inadequately outfitted for cold weather. And more rum would help, as much as could be spared. Lastly, having watched the ragged performances of soldiers trying to handle warships, the commodore pleaded for a hundred more qualified seamen. But please, he wrote, "no landlubbers." Of those he had plenty. Meanwhile, aware that patriots never went into battle with all they needed anyway, he kept the men busy training, especially in gunnery. He even let them fire some of the dangerously low stocks of ammunition in hopes of improving their effectiveness. As things turned out, he had more than two weeks at the site to prepare for battle. Each extra day the British tarried was a bonus, providing added time for the row galleys to arrive and the crews to become more able.

Fortunately, a south wind slowed the British and sped the three row galleys. By October 6, *Trumbull, Washington,* and *Congress* had all taken their places in the patriot formation. Upon inspecting the powerful craft, Arnold selected *Congress* as his flagship. He then assigned his top lieutenants to command the other two, making them responsible for the right and left wings of the battle line. Arnold took his position in the center, where the fight would be thickest and he could best control the action. Then he carefully briefed his ship captains on his plans. He was none too soon, for word arrived on October 10 that Carleton's grand fleet was mere miles to the north, moving rapidly with a fresh north wind. Patriot crews went to sleep that night knowing they would be in battle the next day.

———•·•———

While Carleton and Arnold had been racing to ready their respective fleets for a lake battle, Howe and Washington were preparing to resume combat at the Hudson River's southern end.

From the beginning Americans had recognized that New York City, at the tip of Manhattan Island, was practically indefensible against a foe with complete naval superiority. Major General Charles Lee, sent from Boston early in 1776 to plan the defenses, sized up the problem right away. "What to do with the city, I own, puzzles me," he reported. "It is so encircled with deep navigable waters that whoever commands the sea must command the town." From a purely military point of view the islands around New York Harbor should simply have been evacuated and the city itself burned to deny its use to the enemy. Politically, though, that course was unacceptable. The city had to be defended. Lee's solution was to deter the British by making the cost of taking it higher in casualties than Howe would pay. Fortifying the area and defending tenaciously, he wrote, "might cost the enemy many thousands of men to get possession of it." When General Washington shifted from Boston to assume command in New York he accepted Lee's reasoning.

However, two factors forced a reevaluation after the Battle of Long Island. First, the ratio of combat power was not at all what Americans had estimated it would be. They themselves had far less strength than they had counted on in the heady days after wedging the British out of Boston, while Howe's forces were awesomely larger than anyone had predicted. Second, General Howe showed no inclination whatsoever of playing into patriot hands by launching frontal assaults. Washington convened his generals to reconsider their operational options.

At that crucial moment, when rapid decisions were called for, the Americans dithered for nearly two weeks. The Congress would not permit the destruction of the city, and only grudgingly granted Washington authority to withdraw if he thought it absolutely necessary. Finally, on September 12, the council of war voted to evacuate most of Manhattan Island. But it was too late.

Howe landed troops north of the city on September 15, catching patriots in the midst of withdrawing. Coming ashore at Kip's Bay (where today's 34th Street reaches the East River), British and Hessian units met minimal resistance. Defenders in the vicinity fled in wide-eyed fright, few so much as pausing to fire their muskets. Washington galloped toward the sound of the guns, only to encounter terrified soldiers "flying in every direction and in the greatest confusion." Mortified at the cowardly display, he rode into and through the panic-stricken soldiers, waving his sword and exhorting them to make a stand. But to no avail. All that prevented redcoats from cutting completely across Manhattan to the Hudson River, thus trapping a large portion of the Continental Army, was Howe's cautious decision to halt for the day in order to bring up reinforcements. Washington managed to get his men and artillery out, and to fall back to defensible ground at Harlem Heights. Howe had captured New York City intact, although just days later a mysterious fire destroyed much of the city. Unaccountably, the Englishman paused for a full month, handing Washington a much-needed chance to consider the new circumstances.

Watching his troop strength declining rapidly as militiamen left in droves, and mulling over the expensive lessons on maneuver that Howe was handing him, the commander in chief concluded that he would have to withdraw still farther north. Following a heated debate, however, he accepted the advice of Nathanael Greene and a majority of his other senior officers to continue occupying Forts Washington and Lee, sitting on the east and west banks of the Hudson about where today's George Washington Bridge crosses the river.

In mid-October General Howe struck again. This time he sent an amphibious force swinging deep behind the American left, landing first at Throg's Point and then at Pells' Point (on the east shore of the Bronx, where the East River joins Long Island Sound). Finding himself once more outflanked, and his avenue of retreat from Manhattan Island threatened, Washington had no choice other than to pull back to a new site at White Plains. There, on October 28, the two armies clashed once more, with Howe this time turning the patriots' right flank. Washington avoided disaster by moving at night five miles northward to stronger terrain at North Castle.

The dreary pattern repeated over and over since the Battle of Long Island was painfully apparent—Americans occupy a defensive position, British and Hessians move around one flank or the other, Americans quickly retreat to another defensive position. Washington could not stand and fight in the open against so superior an enemy, but neither could Howe catch him. It was during this period of frustration on both sides that English officers began calling the wily Virginian the "Old Fox."

Americans anticipated yet another attack against their lines at North Castle when redcoats approached, probing the position to determine its extent. This time, however, Howe surprised them. Not liking the looks of the terrain in that area, and aware that his elusive opponent could simply keep drawing him deeper and deeper into the American countryside, the Englishman suddenly broke contact on November 5 and marched back toward Manhattan.

As Washington was pondering the meaning of his opponent's abrupt operational change, couriers were carrying a stream of remarkable news from the Northern Department. Benedict Arnold's clash with Guy Carleton on Lake Champlain had produced astounding results.

——•——

Friday, October 11, 1776. Dawn came cold to the shimmering waters of Lake Champlain. Commodore Benedict Arnold's men squinted against the morning mists to catch a glimpse of hostile sails. A stiff breeze blew out of the northeast. Everyone knew it would soon drive Carleton's fleet into view. The patriots' decks were cleared for action.

Shortly after ten o'clock the first British ships appeared far out in the middle of the lake, serenely cruising straight south past Valcour Island. No swift scouting craft roamed ahead. Enemy captains did not know where the Americans were, and evidently had such confidence in their superiority that they had failed to take the most basic security measures. Arnold could hardly believe his luck.

The British formation continued for about two miles before some sentinel looked back to discover the Americans arrayed for battle. Seeing the van of the enemy fleet changing sail to come about, Arnold baited his trap. He moved out with the three row galleys and one of the schooners, charging the startled British before they could prepare fully for a fight. Quickly closing within cannon range, the four patriot vessels opened fire. The gauntlet had been thrown down; the British had been challenged to a duel. The four raiders then turned and raced back to resume their positions in the defensive formation. Thanks to their sweeps the row galleys had no trouble returning, but the schooner ran aground, becoming the first casualty of the battle. British ships also had difficulty working into the breeze, but the English leaders had committed themselves. Prudence would have called for them to drop anchor, wait for reinforcements and a shift in the wind, and then patiently use their long-range guns to methodically blow the rebels out of the water. But Arnold's goading challenge had pricked their Royal Navy pride, and overweening confidence overrode their common sense. They pressed ahead, which was precisely what the American wanted.

Except for one schooner, named *Carleton*, none of the larger British vessels managed to get into the fight until late in the day.

Along with the constricted and unfamiliar maneuver space, a spanking north wind limited them to lobbing shells at long distance. The billowing smoke of battle soon rendered even that effort inconsequential. The huge *Inflexible*, whose completion had delayed the British advance for a crucial month, was not a factor in the fight. But Carleton's gunboats, having sweeps as well as sails, could engage. By themselves, they were potentially more than a match for the entire patriot force. Twenty in number, they mounted heavier guns—with plenty of ammunition and handled by expert crews—than anything the Americans could bring to bear. By midday the opposing lines, at places almost within rifle shot of one another, were blazing away in an orgy of mutual destruction.

No one on the American side was more centrally visible or valuable than Benedict Arnold himself. Limping about the deck, aiming cannon personally, shouting orders to concentrate fire, always fully exposed, he was the consummate warrior. He was soon blackened head to toe from gunpowder and smoke, indistinguishable from any other crewman except in bottomless energy and inspirational presence.

That point-blank pounding continued until the British gunboats, having exhausted their grapeshot, backed off a few hundred yards and switched to firing solid shot. Hours passed in thunderous exchanges, with both sides dealing out and absorbing punishment. All the while other English captains struggled against the adverse weather to add their own guns to the conflict. At last, just when it appeared that Carleton's heavier ships might finally get into the melee, approaching darkness and a gathering evening fog halted the action. The two sides had fought to a bloody draw.

Human casualties, severe on both sides, were about equal. So, too, was the materiel count. Americans lost the schooner that had run aground at the outset and one gundalow (the *Philadelphia,* raised from the mud generations later and now on display in the Smith-sonian Institution in Washington, D.C.), while British losses were one gunboat and the all but destroyed schooner *Carleton.* Never-theless, in the battering, the patriots probably ended up in worse shape. Several gundalows were barely afloat, and virtually every ship had sustained damage. For instance, Arnold's flagship, *Congress,* had been hulled nearly twenty times, with seven of those hits at or near the water line. Most ammunition had been expended. And included in the dead and wounded were a good number of the sea-soned gunners and seamen. The British would be ready to fight again the next morning; the Americans would not.

Believing he had the opposing fleet trapped, Carleton gleefully anticipated totally destroying it when daylight returned. But Arnold was one step ahead of him. English captains, having no idea where rocks and shoals might lurk, could anchor safely only in deep water, leaving a gap of perhaps a quarter of a mile between their left-most ships and the New York shore. The patriots, how-ever, having reconnoitered the area well, could confidently pass through that gap. They also knew that dense fog arose most nights, offering concealment. They had an escape route.

In column, quietly, Arnold's surviving vessels slipped away in the night, with the general himself bringing up the rear in *Congress.* When the fog lifted next morning, Carleton stared in open-mouthed disbelief at the empty bay. Furious, he turned his fleet southward in pursuit of his maddening nemesis. He most assuredly no longer thought of Benedict Arnold as a "horse-jockey."

Arnold, meanwhile, was eight miles south assessing his situation. It wasn't promising. With several ships only marginally seaworthy, he would have trouble under any circumstances reaching Crown Point before Carleton caught him. Acting quickly, he scuttled two seriously battered gundalows and set a third on fire after it settled in shallow water. Then he ordered the least damaged row galley to escort the remaining ships to the American lines, hoping to save them for another fight another day. He personally remained behind with two row galleys as a rear guard to delay the enemy armada.

By early afternoon British sails could be seen on the horizon—and the wind had shifted around to blow from the south, bringing intermittent sleet and rain. Neither side could make much headway, but the patriots remained out of reach by rowing through the night. The fickle winds shifted again early on October 13, helping *Inflexible* and two schooners close rapidly on the rebel stragglers, which by then included four gundalows so filled with water that they could barely move. Ignoring the wallowing gundalows, *Inflexible* headed straight for the two row galleys. The imposing warship had finally found an opportunity to flex its muscles.

The first contest ended quickly. After "receiving a few broadsides" in his already damaged craft, Arnold's fellow row galley commander surrendered. The British then turned on the *Congress*, looking forward to a similarly easy victory. But they had misjudged. The second ship was commanded by the redoubtable Benedict Arnold.

The three warships surrounded *Congress* like wolves around a wounded animal—"two under our stern, and one on our broadside," Arnold wrote later—and closed to within musket range. For over two hours the four vessels waged a deadly, desperate, swirling action. Outgunned more than five to one, the Americans endured an "incessant fire...with round and grape shot," but kept their own guns roaring back, even after four more British craft joined the slugfest. Although "the sails, rigging, and hull of the *Congress* were shattered and torn to pieces," Arnold still would not strike his colors. The British were up against a master mariner who had one last trick to pull. At a command, his rowers planted their oars in the water, sharply jerking the mangled galley between two of the enemy ships, and headed for shore. The gundalows, rowing frantically, followed. Caught off guard and obliged to turn into the wind, the British could not stop them. Beaching their ships, patriots rapidly removed their wounded and set all five afire, flags still flying. Arnold personally put the match to *Congress* and jumped off before flames hit powder. It was a defiant thumbing of the nose at his frustrated British opponents.

After an arduous overnight trek, their third straight night without sleep, Arnold and his bedraggled troops reached the safety of American units at Crown Point. They had done all that mortal men could possibly do.

The Americans fully expected to confront Carleton yet again in a ground battle. But the British leader had no stomach for further campaigning. The season was late; ice would soon be on the lake. Further, judging from the tenacity the rebels had shown so far, an attempt to take Ticonderoga looked to be excessively costly and very uncertain of success. After dawdling near Crown Point for a few days, Carleton began withdrawing back into Canada on November 2. British forces might have taken New York City, but without Albany they did not own the Hudson River. The patriots had gained a grand strategic victory.

Acclaim for Arnold soared to new heights. General orders paid public tribute to the resolute commodore and his soldier-sailors, saying their actions on Lake Champlain would "establish the fame of American arms throughout the globe." The angels themselves, Horatio Gates added in private correspondence, must be watching over General Arnold, for there was no other way to explain "so many hairbreadth escapes in so short a time." In faraway Philadelphia, ecstatic congressmen cheered the heroic warrior who had saved "the honor of the states." Nor did the enemy spare accolades. Acknowledging that the rebel leader had increased "that renown which he had acquired on land," an English publication praised his sparkling performance on water as "that of an able naval commander." A gunboat captain who had fought against him in the lake battles summed up grudging admiration for his gallant foe, admitting that the courageous delaying action on Lake Champlain "did great honor to General Arnold." The famed American Hannibal was becoming a legendary figure in the war.

Being a legend, though, has its downside. Celebrated heroes evoke jealousy in lesser men.

Standing in his lines at North Castle, Washington watched perplexed as enemy forces marched away from him on November 5. What on earth could General Howe be up to? Why would he suddenly break contact after having pushed the Continental Army relentlessly ever since landing on Long Island in August? It could be a ruse, of course, and the Englishman might suddenly turn to attack. Or, with cold weather at hand, he could be going into winter quarters, or perhaps he intended to lay siege to Fort Washington as a step in opening the Hudson River for a possible junction with General Guy Carleton in the north. Maybe he planned to strike across New Jersey to seize Philadelphia. The possibilities seemed endless.

Whatever his foe might actually have in mind, Washington knew that he himself had to position his own units so as to permit a timely response. But how? There was no obvious or safe solution. Even so, his instinct always guided him to choose action over delay. He did so in this instance, coolly tempting fortune by splitting his already overmatched army into three parts. William Heath, with about three thousand soldiers, would occupy fortifications in the Hudson highlands to protect the ability of the Continental Army to shift either west or east of the river as circumstances dictated. Charles Lee and some seven thousand troops would remain east of the river in New York to guard against any resumption of operations there. Washington would take the remainder, maybe two thousand effectives, across the wide waterway to join Nathanael Greene on the west side to cover New Jersey. Before leaving, he told Lee to be ready to follow "with all possible dispatch" if it appeared that Howe's purpose was to threaten Philadelphia.

Elated by word of Carleton's withdrawal into Canada—the first good news since British forces had landed on Staten Island in July—Washington crossed the Hudson and deployed his elements west of Fort Lee. By the middle of November the Continental Army was as well postured as was feasible until Howe revealed his ultimate aim.

Howe had Fort Washington in his sights and intended to take the fortress by storm, not siege. Surprising the Americans by committing thousands of troops to an assault on November 16, he quickly overcame the poorly engineered defenses. The patriots lost nearly three thousand men in the shocking defeat, an indelible exclamation mark to a three-month drumbeat of reverses in New York. But Howe was not through. Three days later he sent a powerful force led by General Charles Cornwallis across the river to attack Fort Lee. Barely avoiding a repeat of the Fort Washington fiasco, Washington personally led the garrison to safety but had to abandon the bulk of the fort's supplies and equipment. When Cornwallis aggressively pursued the battered troops deeper into the state, it became evident that Howe intended to shift the scene of combat to New Jersey.

Staggered by the unexpected lightning-like blows from his previously sluggish opponent, the commander in chief sent urgent messages to his subordinates to march as quickly as possible to reinforce him. With redcoats nipping hungrily at his heels, and unable to stop his reeling army long enough to establish a coherent defensive line anywhere in New Jersey, Washington decided to concentrate his resources along the western banks of the Delaware River in Pennsylvania.

Reacting immediately to Washington's call for help, Horatio Gates and Benedict Arnold in early December embarked several under-strength units from Albany—fewer than a thousand men— and sailed south. Unloading near Newburgh, just north of the Hudson highlands, the men hastened along sleet-lashed roads to a rendezvous point in Pennsylvania.

Charles Lee was not as responsive. At first he ignored the summons, claiming that he could do more good where he was by threatening the British base in New York. When Washington insisted, he reluctantly crossed the Hudson and began moving by easy stages through northern New Jersey, evidently in no hurry to reinforce his comrades along the Delaware. The former British officer had a well-earned reputation for eccentricity, but his actions at this crucial moment verged on mutiny. Fortunately, Lee himself solved the problem. In mid-December he carelessly stayed overnight in a tavern beyond American positions, where a British patrol snared him. John Sullivan, promoted to major general, rounded up the scattered remnants of Lee's former command, reduced by sickness and desertion to just two thousand able soldiers, and hurried them toward the Delaware.

For a while it seemed that Cornwallis would chase Washington all the way to Philadelphia, right into the very lap of the Continental Congress. The Virginian reached the river town of Trenton on December 3 and completed ferrying his troops to the west side four days later, just as Cornwallis's van came into view. The patriots collected boats up and down the river and established defenses at likely crossing sites along a twenty-five-mile stretch. But the situation remained critical. Most reinforcements were still days away, and the army, such as it was, faced dissolution, with enlistments due to expire on the last day of the year. Things could hardly have been more fraught with imminent disaster. Thomas Paine published his pamphlet *The Crisis,* writing accurately and memorably, "These are the times that try men's souls." When the Congress nervously discussed moving out of the way of approaching danger, the commander in chief pointedly advised the representatives to leave. They did, packing up and heading to Baltimore on December 12. On December 13, Washington made provisional plans to retreat even beyond Philadelphia if Cornwallis managed to force a crossing of the Delaware. Just then, however, to great sighs of relief from all in the Continental Army's headquarters, word arrived of Howe's announcement of the end of that year's campaigning. The long retreat was over! European generals did not wage war in winter.

George Washington was not of their school, however. He began at once planning a counterstroke. In his own words, "Desperate diseases require desperate remedies." The very life of the Revolution was seeping away. The depressing series of setbacks simply had to be stopped. Americans needed a victory. Moreover, it had to be gained before the year ended and the army melted away. The patriots, he stated, would now "weigh every circumstance of attack."

A spate of letters to subordinate commanders flew from headquarters on December 14, all with the same message: Come quick! There will be an attack against an unsuspecting enemy. "A lucky blow in this quarter would be fatal to them," the commander in chief wrote, "and would most certainly raise the spirits of the people, which are quite sunk by our late misfortunes."

Counting heads, Washington figured that he had altogether about six thousand men under arms. In addition to the soldiers who had survived the chase across New Jersey, he now had those Lee had commanded, the contingent from the Northern Department, and militiamen mobilized in and around Philadelphia. On the other side of the Delaware, stationed invitingly in scattered packets, were some three or four thousand enemy soldiers, mostly Hessians. For a fleeting moment, until enlistments ended, Americans enjoyed a superiority in numbers.

Washington fastened his eyes on the garrison at Trenton, an estimated 1,200 Hessians commanded by Colonel Johann Rall.

———•—

One significant consideration making it so absolutely imperative to stop the long slide of defeat was a rising clamor of divisive voices. Unity was the all-important ingredient for success in the war. Internal dissension posed in many ways a greater danger to the cause than London's armies. Benedict Arnold could have testified eloquently to that point, but he was not alone in attracting criticism from fellow revolutionaries. George Washington was an even larger target. The main difference was that those undercutting the commander in chief worked behind his back. Arnold, basically bereft of political power, was more vulnerable to overt attacks.

By late 1776 General Washington had acquired a growing and increasingly vocal gaggle of detractors, inside the Congress and out. His record since ousting the British from Boston half a year earlier was one of unbroken defeat and retreat, and the muttering had started early. John Adams, chairman of the Congress's Board of War, had written after the disastrous fighting on Long Island, "In general, our generals have been outgeneralled." And things had gone downhill from there. As word got around that powerful men were contemplating replacing the commander in chief, ambitious officers began plotting to be that replacement. With the Continental Army staggering back toward the Delaware River and the Congress fleeing to Baltimore, the intrigue reached a crescendo.

Appalled at the string of defeats that autumn, Joseph Reed, Washington's former aide and confidant who had replaced Horatio Gates as adjutant general in the summer of 1776, let loose a burst of ill-considered correspondence highly demeaning of his commanding general. Charles Lee, convinced that he himself should become commander in chief, let it be known that the devastating loss of Fort Washington's garrison could have been avoided if Washington had withdrawn from that untenable position, as Lee had advised. Lee wrote to Benjamin Rush, another Washington critic, that command of the continental forces was in the wrong hands, and immodestly suggested himself as an alternative. "Had I the powers," he said, "I would do you much good."

On that point the army's adjutant general very much agreed. When Washington sent for Lee to cross the Hudson to join forces with him, Reed slipped a note into the courier's packet. "Oh! General, an indecisive mind is one of the greatest misfortunes that can befall an army; how often have I lamented it in this campaign!" Lee's immediate presence, he pleaded, was of the utmost importance for the survival of the Continental Army.

By happenstance Lee's answer came to Washington's eyes. Lee told Reed that the commander in chief was indeed inflicted by a "fatal indecision of mind which in war is a much greater disqualification than stupidity. . . ." And, yes, he would hasten to join the main army, for "I really think our chief will do better with me than without me."

Faced by inescapable evidence that his senior staff officer and his senior general were conniving against him, Benedict Arnold would have reacted with fire. George Washington reacted with ice. Forwarding the offending letter to Reed, with a frosty note about the tenor of the "correspondence," he put the adjutant general on notice that his duplicity had been discovered. That effectively ended their close relationship of trust. (Reed left Washington's service not long thereafter, but not our story. He will surface later in stormy opposition to Benedict Arnold in Philadelphia.)

By carelessly falling into the enemy's hands, Charles Lee had removed himself from the scene of intrigue. Before his capture, though, he penned a disloyal letter to Horatio Gates, who was then bringing reinforcements from the Northern Department. Between us, Lee said, "a certain great man is most damnably deficient." Perhaps his overlarge ego had blinded him to the possibility that Gates might also aspire to replace Washington as commander in chief.

Benedict Arnold strode into headquarters on a cold December day to find a particularly warm reception. It was the first time he and Washington had talked face to face since Arnold had departed for Quebec some sixteen months earlier. The then relatively unknown Connecticut colonel was now a renowned continental general. It was heartening to have in camp at that low moment someone wearing the wreath of success. Besides, the commander in chief was glad to talk with a kindred spirit whose instinct for the offensive matched his own. He had heard enough of caution, and in Arnold he found reinforcement for his conviction in the efficacy of boldness.

Their meeting was of necessity a brief one. Washington was immersed in preparations to counterattack across the Delaware River, while Arnold was preparing to ride to Rhode Island. A British force had seized Newport earlier in the month, threatening Providence and perhaps a larger part of New England. General Washington could spare no troops, so he sent Benedict Arnold, whose very name was now worth regiments.

Horatio Gates's visit to headquarters had an entirely different tone. Gates was horrified to hear that his commander intended to throw the ragtag elements remaining in the Continental Army against the victorious enemy holding New Jersey. Retreat was the only feasible course of action, he argued, even if it meant retiring still farther back into the remoteness of Pennsylvania. He was shaken when Washington rejected his advice. Feigning sickness, Gates begged off taking a role in the forthcoming battle. The whole enterprise reeked of probable failure, and he did not want his reputation tainted by the odor. Instead, he rode to Baltimore to campaign in the halls of the Congress for plum assignments.

With Charles Lee a prisoner, Gates saw himself as the next commander in chief after the inevitable disaster he was certain would overtake the patriots along the Delaware. At the very least, he believed he could replace Schuyler as commanding general of the Northern Department. He also brooded over the fact that Washington had chosen Arnold rather than him for the independent and potentially important command in Rhode Island. It seemed clear to the designing general that his former subordinate with the magnificent combat record now stood in the way of his own ambitions. From then on, Horatio Gates would be an implacable personal foe of Arnold's.

In his pocket Gates carried a document handed to him at Fort Ticonderoga by that persistently anti-Arnold zealot John Brown. It contained a listing of thirteen serious if spurious charges against Brigadier General Benedict Arnold. Gates had not told Arnold or Washington about it, but he now planned to show it to members of the Congress.

General Washington set Christmas Day as the date to launch his attack on Trenton. The Hessians stationed there, disdainful of American fighting men after previous encounters with them that fall, did not seem to be overly concerned with security. They would be even less alert, it was hoped, after celebrating a major holiday. Washington planned to lead the main effort of about 2,400 men. He would be supported by a good number of field artillery pieces, and while that group assailed the village directly, two other columns would cross downriver from Trenton to prevent the Hessians' escape and block reinforcement from other enemy posts. The crossing would be made at night for a dawn assault on December 26.

For the first time since he was a young man George Washington was about to lead an offensive action. The very thought made his adrenalin pump—a short time before he had confided to his brother that he was "wearied almost to death by the retrograde motions of things."

Boat handlers readied their large, low vessels, cargo craft designed to carry heavy loads in the swift current. Assigned to that task were the same skilled seamen who had made possible the army's escape from Long Island almost exactly four months before. Officers began loading men, horses, and cannon late on December 25 in relatively mild weather—but conditions took a sudden turn for the worst during the crossing. A fierce gale struck, driving a numbing mixture of hail, rain, sleet, and snow in blinding sheets, seriously slowing boats and thoroughly soaking men. Ice soon coated both. It was a bitterly cold winter storm certain to shatter the confidence of an ordinary leader. In fact, of the other two columns, one deemed the icy onslaught too foreboding to even attempt to cross, while one managed to ferry only a smattering of men to the far side before calling it quits. The strike force, however, driven by George Washington's personal example and indomitable force of will, continued crossing until every last man stood shivering on the far shore.

As units started moving overland toward Trenton, nine miles to the south, they were already about four hours behind schedule. The final approach would therefore have to be made after sunrise. Undeterred, the Virginian pushed on, accepting the risk, reckoning that the howling storm itself would help him gain surprise by cloaking his march. When commanders reported that their gunpowder was too wet to use, Washington stubbornly told them to fix bayonets. His immutable purpose was to take Trenton, come what may. Not a man that awful night doubted the general's steel resolve.

Rarely in war do events work out as envisioned ahead of time. Washington's assault of Trenton is one of the exceptions. His ill-clad veterans—for that's what these stalwart survivors had become—materialized like vengeful ghosts out of the snowy haze, catching the Hessians unawares and unready. Consternation reigned inside Trenton. Some defenders scrambled to rally and make a stand, but American artillery swept the streets clean. Others huddled in buildings. A few escaped. Colonel Rall paid for his complacency with his life. The fight was quickly over. In little more than an hour, the patriots had rounded up the last of hundreds of prisoners and had checked the dozens of snow-covered corpses to discover that not a single American had been killed. Barely a handful had been wounded, and they only slightly. (One was a future president of the United States, Lieutenant James Monroe.) The victory could hardly have been more resoundingly complete.

Washington's immediate problem was deciding what to do next. He knew that at least one of his two supporting columns had not made it across the river, and he had no information on the status of the second. He could very well be alone on the New Jersey side of the Delaware. Even if nearby garrisons had not already been alerted by the sounds of battle, German soldiers fleeing from Trenton would soon spread the word and enemy commanders would react. Realizing that his semi-frozen force was too weak to confront an organized counterattack, he hurried them back to the boats, taking along prisoners and numerous wagonloads of captured equipment, and recrossed the Delaware. He had lost no soldier in the attack itself, but so terrible were the conditions that some died from exposure and fatigue on the way back.

Not long after returning, he was able to piece together from reports flowing into headquarters a picture of a vastly changed situation—and of a new opportunity. Upon learning that Trenton had fallen, the other two patriot columns somewhat sheepishly crossed after all and now stood on the far shore awaiting orders. About half of Washington's army was on the New Jersey side! Moreover, the shock of Washington's attack at Trenton had spooked other nearby Hessian garrisons to decamp eastward to safety. At the moment, Washington was unopposed in the western part of New Jersey.

Washington saw a magnificent strategic opportunity. Most of his regulars were slated to leave for their homes in just a few days, so he had to act quickly. For the third time that frigid day, he transported his hardened warriors across the Delaware. He assembled at Trenton what remained of the Continental Army. By the time all units came together it was December 30, less than two full days before the enlistments of most continentals expired. There might have been as many as four or five thousand fighters in ranks (in those fluid days no one spent much time counting) but half or more were recently mobilized militiamen. These part-time soldiers were neither seasoned nor likely to remain with the army very long, because they had been mobilized to meet the threat to Philadelphia. Among the regulars only a few hundred Virginia continentals had commitments to serve beyond the start of the new year. To have any kind of a chance against British and Hessian professionals it would be absolutely necessary to convince a good percentage of the other veterans to stay on a while longer. The commander in chief became chief recruiter.

He gathered his troops on the site of their recent glorious triumph and promised there could be more such grand moments. He addressed the units one by one, pleading with the gritty veterans not to leave him in the lurch. "My brave fellows," he boomed out, "you have done more than could be expected of you. But I'm asking you to do this one more thing and re-enlist." That rousing call echoed the theme of Thomas Paine, whose recent words the men had all heard: "The summer soldier and the sunshine patriot will, in this crisis, shrink from the service of their country; but he that stands it *now*, deserves the love and thanks of man and woman." What's more, the Virginian said, anyone signing up for six additional weeks would receive a bonus of ten dollars.

Something clicked. The personal plea from a leader they had grown to admire immensely? The bounty? A tug of shame at leaving in the midst of crisis? The exuberance that sprang from tasting battlefield victory? Though no one has ever been able to say why with certainty, the historical fact is that well over a thousand Americans answered the call. Washington thereby had the reliable nucleus he needed to continue what has come to be called his Christmas Campaign. He promptly switched hats from recruiter to strategist.

General William Howe, so rudely shaken from his winter repose by what ministers in London termed "the disagreeable occurrence at Trenton," could not comprehend how "three old, established regiments of a people who make war a profession should lay down their arms to a ragged and undisciplined militia." He angrily sent General Cornwallis pounding toward the Delaware at the head of highly regarded British regiments. His mission was to sort things out, and do it quickly. Patriots were concentrated at Trenton, Cornwallis learned, so he headed straight there.

Washington was waiting. Ragged his men might be, but hardly undisciplined and most assuredly not merely militia. In his ranks stood a solid core of hardened campaigners, winter soldiers all, and they would fight. Furthermore, the "Old Fox" had in mind a scheme of maneuver that his European antagonists, schooled in European ways of war, could not have dreamed of.

Sending a strong body of soldiers to harry the hard-marching British units along the road to Trenton, the commander in chief placed the bulk of his army in a strong defensive position behind a deep creek running into the Delaware just south of the village. The delaying force did its job well, keeping Cornwallis from arriving until late afternoon on January 2, 1777. It was too late to attack that day, but, having overpowering strength, the English commander confidently planned to crush the rebels first thing next morning. He had taken the bait.

As was their custom, Americans built fires to ward off the cold. These fires also outlined their battle positions on the snow-covered heights across the stream from coiled and eager redcoat units. In the night, leaving some men to tend the fires and maintain the appearance of a strongly held defensive line, the patriots slipped away in a wide circuit and struck out toward... Princeton.

Incredibly, George Washington was marching his tiny army deeper into New Jersey, not to safety in Pennsylvania. He was placing himself between two superior forces, Cornwallis's in Trenton and Howe's in New York. It made no sense at all in terms of that era's prevailing rules for military maneuvering. And it seemed to defy common sense. Nevertheless, trusting in their commander, the patriots uncomplainingly tramped off into the darkness. Only a small number of Washington's most trusted lieutenants knew his ultimate aim. He was practicing his stated belief: "Secrecy until the moment of execution is the life of enterprise." Surprise and boldness were twin allies for his weaker army, and he planned to employ both to full advantage.

At Princeton the general intended to take the road to Brunswick, the location of a major British supply depot lying still farther into New Jersey. With almost all enemy units drawn to Trenton, Brunswick would be essentially undefended. By moving rapidly, the patriots could grab the valuable stores of equipment and supplies before Cornwallis could turn around and catch up to them. But what good would be accomplished, one might ask, in being bounteously supplied—and trapped? Washington was not saying.

As it happened, not all of Cornwallis's elements had yet joined him. When the American van reached Princeton it ran into the tail of an enemy column leaving the town on its way to Trenton. The unexpected meeting turned abruptly into a sharp fight. Redcoats formed ranks for battle, and at first took the initiative from the onrushing Americans. Washington galloped at once to the sound of guns to find confusion and hesitation at the sudden turn of events. He had not anticipated a fight here, but a battlefield setback, he knew in his gut, would spell disaster. Unhesitatingly, he took charge and rallied his men. Then, calmly, he rode out between the two lines, within easy musket range of the British. Turning his back on the hostile line of red, he raised his sword and ordered a charge. Volleys from both sides filled the winter air with thick smoke, completely obscuring the general and his horse. History held its breath. When the air cleared he was still in the saddle, untouched. Patriots surged forward, the British broke, and the fight was over.

After clearing the town of diehard resisters, Washington took stock. Brunswick and its cache of supplies were only fifteen miles away, but the clash at Princeton had cost precious time. Cornwallis could not be far behind. Moreover, his men were on their last legs. It was simply not in them to make another forced march and engage in yet one more battle. He would have to forgo capturing Brunswick's treasures. Instead, he pointed his exhausted army toward Morristown, situated in defensible hills thirty miles north.

In his dawdling march through northern New Jersey a month before, Charles Lee had seen the value of establishing an armed base at Morristown and had mentioned it to Washington. Studying that idea, the commander in chief realized its great operational potential. The site itself was practically impregnable in winter, located in terrain too rough to permit either an assault or siege operations against it. Covered valleys farther north would assure protected supply lines for the continentals, so they could not be starved out. Best of all, British routes across New Jersey would be vulnerable to interdiction by patriot patrols operating out of the hills. Howe would have to fight on very adverse terms—or evacuate the entire state of New Jersey.

The Continental Army straggled into Morristown on January 4. Soon thereafter, conceding that he had been totally outgeneraled, a most unhappy Howe ended his occupation of New Jersey except for a handful of outposts along the Hudson River.

In ten stunning days, winning two small battles and occupying a militarily decisive flanking position, Washington had completely reversed the war's six-month slide. The Revolution, at the edge of extinction just days earlier, had new life. As a later biographer wrote: "News of Trenton and Princeton traveled across America like a rainstorm across a parched land, lifting bowed heads everywhere." And the uplift lasted. Two years later, when Pennsylvania's governing body commissioned Charles Willson Peale to paint a portrait of the commander in chief for display in Philadelphia's State House, scenes from the battles of Trenton and Princeton made up the backdrop.

The amazing counterstroke restored Washington's luster in America, stilling for the moment voices seeking his removal. Across the Atlantic, too, observers of the war's progress lionized the Virginian. Frederick the Great, the most famous military luminary in Europe, stood out among the host lauding the brilliance and sheer daring of the Christmas Campaign.

George Washington in New Jersey and Benedict Arnold on Lake Champlain had assured the continuation of the Revolution.

CHAPTER ELEVEN

"LIKE APES
FOR NUTS"

————⋆◆⋆————

BECAUSE OF ITS THREE SEVENS, LOOKING TO SUPERSTITIOUS patriots like three gallows, 1777 was feared to be the "Year of the Hangman." Ominously enough, the year began with the new nation suffering its first civil-military crisis. Flaring right after Washington's Christmas Campaign had removed the threat of imminent military disaster, the crisis dimmed only when the threat itself resurfaced in mid-summer. Pitting the Continental Congress against military leaders in an unseemly clash over issues of control, the prolonged disagreement left the Continental Army markedly weakened as it took the field to face Great Britain's grand offensive that year. Among those at the vortex of the debilitating dispute were Benedict Arnold and George Washington.

————⋆◆⋆————

When the Congress fled Philadelphia for the relative safety of Baltimore, the defeat of the Revolution loomed as a very real and present possibility. In that dark moment, with events racing out of their control, members transferred to General Washington nearly full authority to act on his own, to raise forces, and to direct the war effort for the next six months. The ceding of such power, considered by many as setting up "dictatorial" control, was unprecedented. That action, taken by men viscerally fearful of a military coup, shows the depth of their despair.

But the despair didn't last long. After General Howe's retreat to the environs of New York City, and the relaxation afforded by a couple of secure weeks nestled down in Baltimore, representatives began to experience something akin to seller's remorse. The commander in chief had done nothing to abuse his new authority, but the old specter of being ruled by a "man on horseback" crept back into the collective consciousness of the Congress. Delegates began early in 1777 to take steps to reclaim their relinquished prerogatives.

Stirring the already troubled waters was none other than Horatio Gates. Having recovered with surprising rapidity from the illness that had allegedly prevented him from service in the field, he at once resumed his game of intrigue. Washington's victorious campaign in New Jersey had for the time being removed any hopes Gates might have harbored about becoming commander in chief, so he set his sights on gaining command of the Northern Department. He could count as his allies most of the New England delegates. They had long wanted to be rid of the aristocratic New Yorker, Philip Schuyler. After conferring with Gates about conditions in the northern army, Samuel Adams tipped his hand by writing, "General Gates is here. How shall we make him head of that army?"

Gates did his part by offering faint praise for Schuyler's role in stopping Carleton's 1776 invasion of upper New York. He also

released John Brown's rabidly slanderous allegations about Benedict Arnold. If New Englanders managed to succeed in ousting
Schuyler, Gates wanted no competition from America's Hannibal.
The Congress fired its first overt salvo before the new year was
much more than a week old. Probably encouraged by Gates, representatives turned their attention to the idle Northern Department. Without conferring with General Schuyler beforehand, they
fired his director of hospitals. That ignited a chain of acid messages. Schuyler complained in a tone the politicians deemed to be
disrespectful. They then reprimanded the general in an insulting
way, all but guaranteeing a sharp rejoinder. Finally, after several
weeks of bickering, the representatives took a swipe at the New
Yorker by sending Major General Horatio Gates to command at
Fort Ticonderoga. Once again, however, as had been the case in
1776, Gates traveled northward under vague orders, leaving
unclear what his relationship with General Schuyler was to be. The
Congress was reasserting itself, but not reforming itself. Old habits
die hard.

Meanwhile, relying mostly on local militia units, George Washington launched a winter-long harassment of British lodgments in
eastern New Jersey, denying them the rest and recuperation professional armies of that era normally expected to enjoy during winter. More important, he denied them the resources of the New
Jersey countryside, especially forage for horses. Arnold, discovering that British units had dug in for the winter at Newport and
posed no immediate threat to the rest of Rhode Island, promptly
made plans to attack them, also relying heavily on local militiamen. It was not in the military makeup of either general to let an
opponent take a time-out from hostilities.

In the meantime, the mumbling from Baltimore grew throatier
with each passing week. When General Washington used his new

powers to order New Jersey loyalists to choose between swearing fidelity to the United States or joining the British occupiers in New York City, several politicians were taken aback. They complained loudly that the general was usurping legislative authority. When a sizeable British foraging party pushed into New Jersey and the commander in chief elected not to confront the raiders directly, congressmen railed at his timidity. Members passed a resolution urging the Virginian to "entirely subdue" marauders rather than to be satisfied with merely limiting their incursion. John Adams, revealing his lack of knowledge of conditions in the Continental Army as well as his impatience with the patient commanding general, asked rhetorically: "Are we to go on forever this way, maintaining vast armies in idleness and losing completely the fairest opportunity that was offered [of] destroying an enemy completely in our power?" How General Washington would have loved to have had "vast armies" to wield!

For the most part, officially, Washington shrugged off the criticism. But privately he fumed. It angered him that the Congress would not or could not send money and supplies, yet offered such an abundance of gratuitous advice. He was trying desperately, "by every means in my power," to keep pressure on the enemy while at the same time striving to "keep the life and soul of this army together." Delegates far from the scene of action, he complained, did not grasp the realities he had to contend with. "In a word, when they are at a distance, they think it is but to say, 'Presto! Begone!' and everything is done."

But containing the British and contending with congressional jabs were not the worst problems facing Washington that winter. Most pressing of all was the absolute imperative of raising an army capable of standing up to British and German troops once the 1777 campaigning started. Nearly all of the men who had extended their enlistments to participate in the Christmas Campaign had gone home, leaving the commander with the task of rebuilding virtually the entire Continental Army.

Fortunately, his new powers gave him new tools. Except for money, always short, he had much of what he needed to create an effective force. The other major missing ingredient was the selection and promotion of general officers. Even in its distress, the Congress had withheld that authority from the "dictatorial powers" it had bestowed on the Virginian in late 1776. Accordingly, at the end of January the commander in chief requested that the representatives provide the Continental Army a much larger number of generals, including its first-ever lieutenant generals. He appended a private note listing the names of several officers he deemed most worthy of promotion and sent it "as a hint to Congress." That note has not survived, but it is clear from his later statements and actions that Benedict Arnold was prominent among those he recommended.

Far from passively accepting the general's "hint," however, the Congress balked. Members saw Washington's request and recommendations as an opportunity to restore their dominant control over the military establishment—and over the commander in chief. The first half of February brought a busy slate of meetings and debates on the subject. Simply put, several delegates looked at the fame accruing to George Washington with nervousness or jealousy—or both. They believed he had to be cut down to size. John Adams reflected the mood of many when he cautioned his colleagues not to be tempted "to idolize an image which their own hands have molten." The maintenance of civilian supremacy over the military argued for the Congress to do as it liked regarding military affairs, not to adhere slavishly to Washington's preferences. As good a man as the commander in chief might be, Adams proclaimed, not a little pompously, "In this house I feel myself his superior." He then added an ominous note: "It becomes us to attend early to the restraining [of] our army." Striking that combative posture, the congressmen approached the always sensitive issue of general officer promotions.

Washington's request for three lieutenant generals was dealt with almost out of hand. Creating such senior ranks was directly contrary to the Congress's intent to tighten the leash on the Continental Army. Members were not about to elevate officers who might later be in a position to challenge their authority. No one besides Washington himself would hold a rank higher than major general. Delegates did agree to entertain the request to promote several brigadiers to the next level, but even that proved to be difficult enough to do.

Representatives spent a week in "perplexed, inconclusive, and irksome" debate trying to establish "a rule of promotion." Hoping to avoid the pitfalls of regional favoritism in the selection process, they adopted three criteria to guide their choices: they would give "due regard" to seniority, merit, and a roughly proportional relationship of generals to the number of troops provided by each state. Connecticut already had two major generals—fat and ineptly active Israel Putnam, and elderly and lethargic Joseph Spencer. (Ironically, Spencer was the titular commander of forces opposing the British invasion of Rhode Island, but, knowing him to be incompetent, Washington had sent Arnold to be the de facto commander.) Among the brigadiers, Benedict Arnold was second in seniority only to his fellow townsman, the discredited David Wooster. And in terms of merit, no brigadier in the entire Continental Army had as sparkling a record of heroic exploits. His selection as major general seemed assured, especially with George Washington's endorsement.

During that "irksome" week Benedict Arnold's name came up time and again. His record was too powerful to ignore. But he had no personal champion in the halls of the Congress, where only two delegates from his home state of Connecticut were in attendance. One of those two was Roger Sherman, a fellow New Havenite but no fan of Arnold's. He had fined Arnold some eleven years earlier for publicly thrashing an informer. Moreover, in a strange twist, General Washington's support may not have been helpful in this instance. A feisty Congress wanted to demonstrate its independence. As a modern historian concludes, "Arnold's close identification with Washington worked against him in Congress's deliberations."

Furthermore, John Brown's diatribes were circulating uncontested. Horatio Gates, who could have exposed Brown's charges for the wild-eyed rantings they were, chose not to do so before leaving Baltimore for Philadelphia as the debate was under way. Controversy and Arnold were cousins. The congressmen could neither overlook his seniority nor deny his combat leadership. But there were other candidates for promotion who were not tainted by accusations of impropriety and who had loud, ardent supporters. So delegates turned away from two of their own criteria, seniority and merit, and fastened on the third, proportionality.

On February 19, the Congress approved a slate of five officers for promotion to major general. Benedict Arnold's name was not among them.

Nearly three weeks passed before Arnold learned that the Congress had chosen five brigadiers, all junior to him in rank and none anywhere near his equal in achievement, for promotion. Early March found him in Boston urging the city's leaders to send militiamen to Rhode Island so he could assail the wintering British garrison at Newport. While in the Bay City, he purchased new uniforms and accouterments befitting a major general in the Continental Army. Along with everyone else who thought about the matter, Arnold assumed he would be elevated in rank.

Washington was definitely among those who thought so. He was dumbfounded when he first saw the list. Surely there was some mistake? Or perhaps the Congress had promoted Arnold earlier in a separate action? After all, with the delegates in Baltimore communications were even less dependable than usual. In a letter to Arnold, the commander in chief admitted how perplexed he was. He felt at a loss to know "whether you have had a preceding appointment, as the newspapers announce, or whether you have been omitted by some mistake." Telling the younger officer to avoid leaping to conclusions until more information could be gathered, he counseled that time would likely "remedy any error that may have been made."

Hoping to have calmed his headstrong subordinate, at least temporarily, Washington set out to discover what had happened. He was concerned on two counts. First, the passing over of so deserving an officer might well cause him to resign. The country had all too few sterling and seasoned combat leaders as it was. Second, the stinging slight could adversely affect the morale of other officers, who might conclude that seniority and battlefield laurels meant little to their political leaders. The Continental Army did not have "a more active, a more spirited, and sensible officer," Washington told a fellow Virginian sitting then in the Congress. He asked that confidant if he knew whether "General Arnold's non-promotion was owing to accident or design." He also told General Nathanael Greene, who happened to be in Philadelphia as the Congress returned there from Baltimore, to try to get a glimpse into the promotion process. He was determined to dig to the bottom of the issue and reverse Arnold's non-selection if he possibly could.

Meanwhile, Arnold returned to Providence from Boston unaware of the hubbub swirling around the Congress's treatment of him. Washington's letter met him there.

Shocked, uncomprehending at first, Benedict read and reread his commander's words. He had not been promoted, while five lesser qualified men had been. There was no way to put a pretty face on that fact. But why? Quickly, Arnold's mind fixed on the constant chorus of malicious charges from miscreants like Brown, Easton, and Hazen. Quite obviously, he reasoned, the Congress had accepted their allegations. On March 11 he responded to Washington, saying he would remain for the time being at his post, but that he could not be expected to continue long under the circumstances. It was evident that the Congress had taken "a very civil way of requesting my resignation." Rather than resign peremptorily, however, he would first demand a court of inquiry to clear his name. After that he would decide whether he could continue serving with honor.

Arnold brooded for some two weeks before pouring out his anger in a letter to Horatio Gates, still thought to be a friend. The Congress, operating on "whim and caprice," had mortified him. Delegates had listened to voices that had "basely slandered me" without the courtesy of "giving me an opportunity to be heard in my defense." After clearing his reputation before the Congress, he would call his accusers to a duel. "By heavens, I will have justice, and I'm a villain if I seek not a brave revenge for injured honor." He then asked Gates to send him some records needed for the court of inquiry—a request Gates ignored.

By April General Washington could tell Arnold what he had learned about the Congress's approach to promoting major generals. The number of officers from each state holding that rank would be based on the number of soldiers provided by the state.

Connecticut, with two, already had its "full share." Washington thought that was "a strange mode of reasoning," but was relieved to know that Arnold had not been overlooked for lack of merit.

The commander in chief then attempted to dissuade his sorely disappointed brigadier from pursuing a court of inquiry. Public bodies cannot be held to account for their actions, he said, and, anyway, there was no specific charge against him that could be appealed.

Washington may well have been aware that the Congress was in no mood to be questioned regarding its promotion policies. The problem of dealing with disgruntled officers had been raised during the debates back in February. John Adams, speaking for a good number of the delegates, if not a majority, stated, "I have no fears from the resignation of officers if junior officers are preferred to them." If they are fully behind the cause, he went on, "they will continue with us. If not, their resignation will not hurt us." Indeed, this was not the right moment to challenge the Congress over promotions.

Although stubborn himself, Arnold could not fathom the stubbornness of the Congress. Nor did he realize how hard Washington was working behind the scenes to convince delegates to reconsider and elevate the Connecticut general to his "proper place." Always a battler, Benedict's instinct was to attack. He told the commander in chief that he could wait no more. His patience was at an end. Besides, he could now leave his post without being seen as shirking his duty. The British in Rhode Island no longer posed much of a threat, and Washington planned to use his fighting general elsewhere in the upcoming campaign. Arnold intended to travel to the seat of government and demand the privilege of defending himself before a court of inquiry. Then he would exact revenge for his "injured honor."

Feeling let down by the very country for which he had sacrificed and risked so much, the morose officer rode to New Haven in mid-April. There he spent busy days seeing his family, tending to details of his shaken business, and preparing for the trip to Philadelphia. That interlude gave him time to reflect on all that had happened since he had departed two years before as a militia captain commanding the Second Company of Foot Guards. Calendars don't lie, of course, but could it really have been only two years? Ticonderoga, Lake Champlain, the Kennebec, Quebec City, Canada, Valcour Island, Rhode Island, promotions, fame, a limp, "injured honor." Two packed years indeed.

But fate was not yet through with Benedict Arnold. Early on April 26 a frantic horseman brought startling news. British ships had landed a strong force thirty miles or so to the west of New Haven. Redcoats were at that moment marching swiftly toward Danbury, an important storage center for American supplies. That alarm transformed Benedict Arnold from aggrieved officer to irrepressible warrior. Hardly pausing to say goodbye to his boys, he raced off once more to battle.

———••———

Two thousand British raiders, crack troops led by New York's ousted royal governor, William Tryon, reached Danbury late in the afternoon of April 26. Scattering the small contingent of guards, they started straightaway burning homes and barns and destroying stocks of supplies, finishing as darkness fell. His mission accomplished, Tryon rested the soldiers and prepared to return to his ships by a different road to avoid a running fight with militia units he felt sure would be closing in on the route he had traveled to Danbury.

He was right. By the middle of that night a strong body of patriots had assembled at Bethel, on the invasion road just a few miles from the smoldering ruins of Danbury. Benedict Arnold had been joined by Brigadier General David Wooster and about a hundred militiamen from around New Haven. Wooster, given no further role in the Continental Army after his poor performance in Canada, had been relegated to homeland defense in Connecticut. Putting their former personal difficulties aside in the face of the enemy incursion, Wooster and Arnold pulled together. Also at the Bethel rendezvous were about four hundred armed men from the areas the British had marched through. Too late to save Danbury's precious stores, the Americans decided to punish the red-coated marauders as they headed back to the coast.

It became evident early on April 27 that Tryon was taking an alternative road to the coast, one running through the town of Ridgefield, not Bethel. With typical celerity Arnold led four hundred men in a cross-country dash to try to reach Ridgefield first. Wooster and the remaining soldiers marched off to overtake the raiders and slow them by harassing their rear-most units. He did his job well, precipitating a fight that held the enemy column long enough for Arnold to win the race to Ridgefield. In that skirmish, Wooster received a fatal wound.

Arnold arrived at Ridgefield with perhaps five hundred men, having gathered another hundred or so along the way. He placed them in a blocking position astride the road. Outnumbered four to one, he nevertheless planned to make a stand there. The odds seemed long, but the patriots held a naturally strong defensive position that the British could not bypass. If the citizen-soldiers could stop Tryon's march, or seriously delay it, other militiamen swarming in from nearby communities might have time to muster enough strength to overwhelm the wearied raiders.

Arnold's nervous men did not have long to wait. About three o'clock that afternoon the British van tramped into view. Well-placed patriot fire from the hastily erected defensive line repulsed an initial headlong rush intended to brush the Americans aside. Frustrated by the obstinate defenders, Tryon was obliged to deploy flanking forces. He drove into the patriot position again, this time in strength. The frightening sight of flashing bayonets and disciplined rows of advancing regulars spread panic among the militiamen. Despite Arnold's vigorous efforts to steady them, the part-time soldiers bolted as the battle opened. Arnold, as always in the fore of the fight, almost lost his life when a line of redcoats fired a volley directly at him from nearly point-blank range. Somehow he was untouched, but his horse fell, mortally wounded. Arnold freed himself from the thrashing beast, shot a threatening foe with his pistol, and vaulted over a fence to escape.

The clash at Ridgefield had been a brief affair, with Arnold unable to maintain control once his soldiers started to run. But his bravado defense led Tryon to believe that patriots were present in much greater numbers than they actually were. The Briton was still some fifteen miles from the safety of his ships, night was falling, and he had numerous wounded to care for and dead to bury. He decided to stay where he was rather than to continue in darkness against an aggressive, unpredictable enemy. Arnold had lost the battle but gained the day. He had time to rally his troops for yet another stand.

Reassembling his chastened soldiers and gathering others who had answered the call to arms, the redoubtable general occupied a second position between Tryon and the sea. With whatever splintered elements he could muster, he prepared to fight again on April 28.

Among those joining the American ranks that day was John Lamb, who had been wounded with Arnold in the futile attack on Quebec almost sixteen months earlier. After recovering from his wounds, Lamb had been paroled by the British and then exchanged. Promoted to colonel of artillery, he had spent the early part of 1777 creating an artillery regiment. Lamb was not personally wealthy. Faced with insufficient Continental funds for procuring the expensive artillery equipment, he applied to his former comrade for financial assistance in raising the regiment. Arnold responded, providing the necessary money from his own accounts. When Lamb showed up that morning with three field pieces, it was the first installment he would make on repaying Arnold's generosity. It would not be the last.

Declining to attack the entrenched Americans, Tryon swerved south and hurried toward Compo Hill, a tactically dominant piece of terrain overlooking Long Island Sound. From there he could cover his embarkation. Arnold followed, nipping at his heels and picking off stragglers. Upon reaching the security of Compo Hill, Tryon turned and launched a strong spoiling attack aimed at throwing the Americans off balance long enough for him to evacuate all of his marauders.

Once more the militia scattered before the formidable ranks of regulars. Arnold railed at the fleeing men, to no avail. Once more he was left with a mere handful of stouthearted soldiers, among them John Lamb, who was again seriously wounded. Once more the general had a horse shot out from under him. Once more he escaped without a nick, but he did have his coat collar cut by a musket ball. A participant later described how Arnold "exposed himself, almost to a fault." Under heavy fire, and leading from the front, he "exhibited the greatest marks of bravery, coolness, and fortitude" in the sharp battle.

Tryon got away, but not without paying a heavy price in casualties. It would be a long while before the British would strike into Connecticut again. (As absolutely incredible as it would have seemed to participants on both sides in that spring of 1777, a similar raid in September four years later would feature a turncoat Benedict Arnold in the role of William Tryon.)

Word of Arnold's extraordinary heroism rapidly reached the halls of the Congress, leaving delegates openly embarrassed that they had ignored Washington's recommendation to promote the best fighting general in the army. When one noted sheepishly that, all things considered, the United States could probably use another major general, a motion was quickly made. On May 2, 1777, "the ballots being taken, Brigadier General Benedict Arnold was promoted to the rank of major general."

The new major general enjoyed widespread celebrity status. John Hancock, the president of the Congress, reported to George Washington that Arnold's performance was "highly approved of" by his congressional colleagues. That was an understatement. John Adams, rarely inclined to level effusive praise at military officers, became almost rhapsodic. Arnold's most recent show of combat daring might be enshrined in a medal to inspire others, he suggested. One side would depict "a platoon firing at General Arnold, on horseback, his horse falling dead under him and he deliberately disentangling his feet from the stirrups and taking his pistols out of his holsters before his retreat." The scene on the reverse side would be of Arnold "mounted on a fresh horse, receiving another charge of musketry, with a wound in the neck of the horse." Information reached Washington that the British were speaking of Arnold as a "devilish fighting fellow," a grudging compliment. For his part, the commander in chief sent Arnold a ringing note of congratulations and alerted him to anticipate a key role in the forthcoming campaign.

Arnold himself, however, was not satisfied. The Congress had not acted to adjust his date of rank, leaving the five men promoted over him in February still senior to him. That had to be corrected. Moreover, the assaults on his character remained unanswered. Underscoring that point, a new handbill being circulated by John Brown listed old charges again and added still more claims, one of which was that Arnold was doing everything possible to avoid trial. Finally, Arnold's expense accounts from the Canadian campaign had not been entirely settled. For those three reasons he decided to resume his interrupted plans to journey to Philadelphia.

On May 12, Arnold rode into headquarters at Morristown. Washington met him with genuine enthusiasm. They had last seen each other in the dark days of December 1776, these two men who were so different yet shared the powerful bond of warriors. When Arnold explained why he felt he had no recourse other than to make his case directly to the Congress, Washington acquiesced. He would have preferred that his lieutenant just accept things as they were, but he would not stand in his way. As a matter of fact, he had already notified the Congress that promotion alone, without changing the date of rank, would very likely push Arnold to resign. Writing a supportive letter, and cautioning the sometimes fiery officer to avoid antagonizing the delegates, the Virginian wished him well.

By May 16 Arnold was in Philadelphia. Charles Carroll, one of the commissioners he had hosted in Canada a year earlier, helped him settle in. Carroll was a supporter. Like Washington, he advised the new major general to be aware of the Congress's raw nerve on the issue of promotions. Arnold was also reunited with his old mentor, Philip Schuyler, who was in town to sort out once and for all the status of command arrangements between himself and Horatio Gates. Gates, designated to command at Fort Ticonderoga, had stopped instead in Albany, where he was acting rather presumptively, as if he had more power than Schuyler believed was warranted. Being himself in the midst of a heated argument inside the Congress, Schuyler knew of the hypersensitivities prevalent in that body. He, too, counseled Arnold to tread lightly.

Early in the week of May 19 Arnold began his efforts to obtain redress. Appearing in the State House, he submitted a copy of John Brown's latest scurrilous allegations and requested to be heard by a court of inquiry to address the "catalogue of crimes" he was accused of. Next he asked to have his public accounts audited and closed out. For the time being he downplayed the date-of-rank issue.

The Congress responded with surprising speed. Referring the requests to the Board of War, the representatives resolved that a horse, "properly caparisoned," be presented to Arnold as "a token of... approbation of his gallant conduct" at Danbury. By week's end the Board of War announced itself fully satisfied "concerning the general's character and conduct, so cruelly and groundlessly aspersed" in John Brown's handbill. The findings were to be publicized, thus clearing Arnold's reputation of wrongdoing. But the delegates had dodged any discussion over changing his date of rank. That subject was off-limits.

That same week the Congress voted narrowly to endorse General Schuyler over General Gates. Schuyler left to resume command of the Northern Department, while Gates was told to choose between serving under Schuyler at Fort Ticonderoga or returning to the position of adjutant general on Washington's staff. When those orders reached him, Gates did neither. Instead he rushed back to Philadelphia to plead his case in person. John Adams grumpily confided to his wife, Abigail: "I am wearied to death with the wrangles between military officers, high and low. They quarrel like cats and dogs. They worry one another like mastiffs, scrambling for rank and pay like apes for nuts."

Adams hadn't seen the worst of it yet. At about that same time more trouble stepped off a ship from France. Philippe Charles Tronson de Coudray carried a commission as a major general in the Continental Army dating from August 1776. It had been granted by Silas Deane, the Congress's representative to France. Deane had hopes of gaining both artillery expertise in America and influence in France at the court of Louis XVI.

Coudray was one of a flood of adventurers from Europe looking for a position in the Continental Army. The Congress encouraged them, often to George Washington's chagrin. Some turned out to be genuinely helpful to the cause—many others were more a burden than a boon. Dealing with them caused yet another source of friction between the commander in chief and members of the Congress.

Because of his reputed date of rank, however, Coudray presented more of a problem than the others. Not only would he outrank Arnold and the five other recently promoted major generals, but he would be senior to officers such as Nathanael Greene, Henry Knox, and John Sullivan. Those three, in fact, soon wrote letters to the Congress threatening to resign if Coudray superceded them. The possibility of losing the services of so many of his top generals distressed Washington. On the other hand, threats of resignation hardened the Congress's determination to protect its control over the military. Observing this emerging standoff coming on the heels of the Schuyler-Gates controversy, Arnold became more convinced than ever of the Congress's inability to lead a nation at war.

———

For a brief interlude an enemy foray quieted the brouhaha. General William Howe, finally ending his winter hibernation, sent a powerful force into New Jersey in early June. It appeared that the campaign of 1777 had begun, and Philadelphia seemed to be the objective. Benedict Arnold, as the senior officer in that city after Schuyler's departure, was responsible for its protection. The Congress, preferring that the renowned field officer be in the field, turned the defenses over to another general and directed Arnold to join Washington in New Jersey.

Disgruntled at having to leave with his personal affairs still unsettled, Arnold nevertheless turned excitedly to the prospect of participating in another campaign. This time, for the first time, he would be serving in battle directly under General Washington. Stopping at Trenton, he began planning defensive positions along the Delaware River.

Washington thought (correctly as it turned out) that Howe's true purpose was to entice the Continental Army out of the hills in order to engage it in a decisive battle in the open. The American leader would not take that bait. He arrayed his troops for battle, but remained out of reach of the British army. However, in case Howe's aim really was to march on Philadelphia, the commander in chief planned a trap. Arnold and others were to confront the British east of the Delaware River while he himself would follow Howe and strike him from behind. Howe would thereby have his fight, but not on the terms he had envisioned. John Adams told his wife that Washington could be depended on to maneuver wisely and cautiously and that the ever-aggressive Arnold "will have at them, if he can." He had come to know the two leaders well.

Howe understood the folly of attempting to march overland to Pennsylvania without first removing Washington's threat to his flank and rear. But the maddening "Old Fox," unassailable in his mountain redoubt, would not come out and fight. After two weeks,

Howe gave up the effort and withdrew. By month's end he was out of New Jersey entirely.

The alarm ended with Benedict Arnold having had no opportunity to add to his combat laurels. He returned to the City of Brotherly Love, firmly resolved to try one last time to have his date of rank adjusted. Had he been more politically perceptive he would have seen that the seeking of redress was the very reason the Congress would deny him. The delegates would say no simply because he had *asked* for it. Generals had to be kept in their places.

In those early days of July, Arnold watched with growing uneasiness as the Congress sharply dismissed the complaints from Nathanael Green, Henry Knox, and John Sullivan regarding the Frenchman Coudray. Telling Washington that the impertinent letters sent by the three generals represented "an invasion of the liberties of the people," the delegates added that those three "shall be at liberty to resign their commissions and retire." About that same time, Horatio Gates rode into town, steaming. Gaining permission to address the representatives, he precipitated a row between his supporters and members backing Schuyler. John Adams may have harked back to his earlier comment: ". . . like apes for nuts."

When the Congress ordered Gates to report to the army, that angry officer left instead for his home. No reprimand ensued. Arnold, watching how generals with no political connections were treated as compared to those with influence, finally came to realize that his request would never be honored. He sat down to write a letter of resignation.

"Honor is a sacrifice no man ought to make," he stated. Because the Congress obviously felt him to be "unqualified for the post that fell to me in the common line of promotions," an assessment which amounted to "impeachment of my character," he could no longer with honor remain a member of the Continental Army. On July 11, Major General Benedict Arnold strode into the State House and submitted his resignation. He would continue serving his country, but as "a free citizen of America," not as a soldier. Could the gentlemen therefore quickly conclude the settlement of his accounts?

In upper New York, meanwhile, General John Burgoyne had attacked south on Lake Champlain, approaching Fort Ticonderoga early in July. That fortress, commanded by Major General Arthur St. Clair, one of the five brigadiers promoted ahead of Arnold back in February, was expected to stop the enemy advance. Instead, St. Clair evacuated it without a fight after British artillery appeared on a nearby hill on July 4. News of that disaster, and the implications it held for the unraveling of patriot resistance in the north, raced by courier to Washington's headquarters. Thoroughly alarmed, the commander in chief wrote to the Congress, asking that Benedict Arnold be sent north at once. His presence could rally the New England militia to help stop the British. Without Arnold, "the most disagreeable consequences may be apprehended." That letter reached the State House just as Arnold submitted his resignation.

Delegates chose to focus on Washington's letter and ignore Arnold's. At that dangerous moment the nation needed its foremost battler. The resignation was tabled. Also, at Washington's urging, his other leading generals dropped their plans to resign. The summons of the war trumpet had ended the prolonged period of civil-military bickering. Little had changed other than the development of a backlog of hard feelings on both sides.

The Congress directed Arnold to go without delay to headquarters and report to Washington. He responded that he would comply, but "as a private citizen to render my country every service in my power." He asked that his resignation still be accepted. He would fight, but not under the auspices of the Continental Congress, which he now thoroughly despised. He left Philadelphia three days later, reaching headquarters on July 17. Washington wanted him to report to Schuyler and focus on rallying militia support to the Northern Department. Arnold agreed to do so, and vowed to work harmoniously with other leaders, regardless of rank or precedence.

The Virginian then penned a circular urging all militia commanders in the region to mobilize in this emergency. He noted with special emphasis, "General Arnold, who is well known to you all, goes up at my request to take command of the militia in particular."

Arnold left immediately, heading for combat in the Lake Champlain area for the third time in as many years. Washington saw him off.

CHAPTER TWELVE

DEFENDING THE
UNITED STATES, 1777

———◆———

THE FAILURE TO STAMP OUT THE REBELLION IN 1776
shocked the king and his ministers to the core. How could
England's mightiest-ever expeditionary force have been
thwarted by mere provincials?

After the initial sense of disbelief wore off, cold reality sank in.
The Americans could not be cowed into submission. They would
have to be crushed. William Pitt rose in Parliament in February
1777 to warn his colleagues that they did not face "a wild and law-
less banditti," but rather a unified country whose leaders "have a
great stake in this great contest." No longer did policymakers in
London chuckle at the prewar boast of a British general who said
that, given a thousand grenadiers, he would "undertake to go from
one end of America to the other, and geld all the males, partly by
force and partly by a little coaxing."

Success would not come easily. On the other hand, the outlook
was far from grim. Sober reassessments of the strategic situation

showed that Great Britain's forces were much better positioned to start the campaign of 1777 than they had been the year before. Powerful land forces had already been transported across the Atlantic; the British flag flew over secure bases in New York and Rhode Island; redcoats patrolled all of Canada; and Guy Carleton possessed a dominant fleet anchored at the north end of Lake Champlain. Moreover, the American rebels had not shown much of an ability to train and sustain forces capable of standing up to British and German professionals. With reinforcements of men and materiel, and more aggressive leadership, there was every reason to expect victory in 1777.

But once again it was not to be. By year's end patriot arms were on the whole triumphant—and London soon watched the American War spiral into a worldwide conflict.

As had been the case in 1776, two of the principal actors in fashioning that astounding outcome were George Washington and Benedict Arnold.

———•———

Lord George Germain and his colleagues in London spent a disconcerting winter trying to follow the bouncing ball of William Howe's erratic strategic thinking. Before George Washington's counteroffensive brought an abrupt reversal to British fortunes in New Jersey, England's commanding general had envisioned a climactic campaign in 1777. He proposed widespread attacks directed at Boston, Albany, Philadelphia, and, later, Virginia and other southern states. To do that he reckoned he would need only fifteen thousand more troops. The Americans were so battered, he said, that merely taking Philadelphia could be done with his current strength levels. However, after the "disagreeable occurrence at Trenton," Howe began trimming his aspirations. To operate successfully in the coming year would require a major reinforcement of soldiers and the more he thought about an attack into New England the less appealing it became. Perhaps Philadelphia alone would be a suitable target. Or maybe he would send a force up the Hudson to facilitate Burgoyne's advance. In London, Germain must have thrown up his hands reading that series of indecisive letters. He concluded that Howe would receive only some three thousand more men—the rest would go to Canada.

Major General John Burgoyne had hurried back to England as soon as operations in Canada had ceased in 1776. There he convinced George III and others that a strong force (under his leadership, of course, not that of the overly cautious Guy Carleton) could quickly slice southward to Albany, seize control of the Hudson River, and thereby precipitate the collapse of the Revolution. King and cabinet sanctioned that scheme, but in a lapse incredible at the time and incomprehensible to historians ever since, no one in authority ordered Howe to cooperate with Burgoyne. Sir William (he had been knighted for his victories in New York) was allowed to operate as he saw fit.

Which he did, telling no one what his plans were. Friends and enemies alike were left guessing. Throughout the spring and early summer of 1777, George Washington admitted to being perplexed. His excellent network of spies kept him abreast of troop movements and the arrival of military shipments from Europe. But he could not fathom Howe's intentions. Would he strike northward to link up with Burgoyne? Or push on across New Jersey? Or go by sea to Philadelphia? Or attack the Continental Army itself? Washington considered each of these options. Finally, he admitted he was baffled: "We have such contradictory accounts from different quarters, that I find it impossible to form any satisfactory judgment of the real motions and intentions of the enemy." The American commander was not the only one puzzled. As late as June 24, Germain confessed, "I cannot guess by Sir William Howe's letters when he will begin operations or where he proposes carrying them out."

Washington astutely stationed American forces in a position to counter whatever Howe's plan was. He took a calculated risk that Philip Schuyler, with the bastion of Fort Ticonderoga as an anchor and vast stretches of nearly trackless forest as an ally, could handle Burgoyne, while he kept the main army—based in northern New Jersey and along the Hudson River—postured to intercept Howe's movements.

American military leaders from sergeant to general had learned much about their business, having become seasoned under the pressures of combat. Washington, using the temporary "dictatorial powers" he had been given, had made a start at enlisting a long-term force. And surreptitious support from France was easing the Continental Army's chronic shortage of arms and equipment. Seven French vessels, laden with hundreds of cannons and thousands of muskets, as well as tons of gunpowder, clothing, and field equipment, made land in March alone. More followed. Money came too, and with it the mixed blessing of advisers. The Continental Army was still far from a fully competent force, but it had come a long way, and Washington was cautiously optimistic that it would show new starch in 1777.

That June, British regiments lunged into New Jersey. But when Howe failed to goad Washington into an unequal fight, he withdrew them. In July, Washington learned that Fort Ticonderoga had surrendered without a fight. Suddenly, Albany was vulnerable; control of the Hudson River was threatened. Benedict Arnold raced north, as did several regular units Washington reluctantly detached from the central force. Finally, in late July, reports arrived indicating that Howe had embarked about fifteen thousand men aboard more than two hundred ships and was sailing south. The campaign of 1777 had begun at last.

Benedict Arnold was hard on horses. He entered Albany on July 21. But General Schuyler was at Fort Edward, the northernmost post on the Hudson River, some forty-five miles farther north. Arnold rode on, reporting for duty the next day. The commander of the Northern Department was delighted to see America's most celebrated battlefield hero arrive. He briefed his new lieutenant right away. Schuyler told him the department was in disarray. It was "weak in numbers, dispirited, naked, in a manner, destitute of provisions... with little ammunition, and not a single piece of cannon." He was trying to restore order, sort out the logistical chaos, and strengthen his units. But Burgoyne had the initiative. Patriot forces were withdrawing southward, cutting trees and destroying bridges along the way to slow the enemy's advance. The northern army at that moment consisted of fewer than five thousand men fit for duty—and just two artillery pieces. Reinforcements were arriving, both continentals and militia, but not in numbers adequate to face Burgoyne's ten thousand soldiers, who were accompanied by a host of Indians. The one bright spot was that the British main body had halted at the south end of Lake Champlain while other troops hauled the expedition's heavy baggage over the Height of Land between Fort Ticonderoga and Lake George. That delay had provided some breathing room for the reeling Americans, but lead elements of the enemy were at Fort Anne, only a few miles away, and Schuyler planned an immediate evacuation of Fort Edward.

The two generals quickly agreed on a split of responsibilities. Schuyler would coordinate successive defensive positions during the patriot retreat while Arnold commanded the rear guard, maintained contact with the enemy, and relayed information to Schuyler. That work was dangerous in the extreme, for a screen of native warriors moved ahead of the redcoats, posing a constant threat to overrun Arnold's thin outpost line.

Early on Sunday, July 27, a large force of Indians burst out of the woods near Fort Edward, chasing off Arnold's men posted there and killing and scalping six of them. The attackers also captured a young woman, Jenny McCrea, who lived in the vicinity. When some of the braves began to argue over whose prize Jenny was, they killed her. Arnold reported that the frenzied warriors "scalped, stripped, and butchered" the hapless maiden "in the most shocking manner." The gruesome story spread rapidly and far, providing further motivation for mobilizing militia units in the region.

By the last day of July Burgoyne had closed on Fort Edward. He was on the Hudson River. Not far south was Albany—and waters navigable to the Royal Navy.

Schuyler continued his harassing and delaying tactics, gradually withdrawing farther and farther south, all the while creating obstacles to impede the foe's movement and removing or destroying anything of use. In early August he crossed to the Hudson's west bank at Saratoga before shifting even farther south to a defensive position at Stillwater.

In addition to the direct approach by way of Lake Champlain, Burgoyne's overall plan included a secondary attack from the west, driving down the Mohawk River toward Albany. Lieutenant Colonel Barry St. Leger and about 750 soldiers left Montreal in June, going up the St. Lawrence River and crossing Lake Ontario to Oswego. There he rendezvoused with a warring band of perhaps a thousand Indians. The combined force struck straight into

New York, aiming first for Fort Schuyler, about halfway to Albany. St. Leger laid siege to it on August 4. An attempt by New York militiamen to relieve the defenders precipitated a fierce clash with Indians two days later, leaving both sides badly bloodied. The militiamen retreated, abandoning the fort's garrison.

General Schuyler found himself in a most difficult position. If he did nothing, St. Leger might succeed in the siege and be free to slam into Albany from the west. On the other hand, if he diverted continental units to go after St. Leger, he risked being unable to stand against a push from Burgoyne. He called a council of war.

After heated debate, Schuyler decided to send a brigadier general and nearly a thousand continentals to Fort Schuyler and concentrate the remainder of his troops nine miles north of Albany, where the Mohawk River flowed into the Hudson. When no brigadier volunteered for the dangerous mission, Benedict Arnold did. By August 18, General Schuyler's men were digging in behind the Mohawk and Arnold's detachment was approaching Fort Schuyler by forced marches.

Burgoyne, feeling the effects of Schuyler's scorched-earth strategy, had a dire need for horses, wagons, and cattle. He sent a raiding force eastward to scavenge. Near Bennington, on Saturday, August 16, it ran into a buzz saw of militiamen led by John Stark and Seth Warner, who inflicted a disastrous defeat that cost Burgoyne one-sixth of his army. Making matters worse, all but a hundred of his Indians deserted him and his supply status grew more tenuous each day.

On the way to Fort Schuyler, meanwhile, Arnold encountered a suspected loyalist named Hon Yost Schuyler. Hon Yost had been detained by local officials and feared for his life. It appeared, in fact, that he was mentally deranged. The Indians, however, understood his behavior as a sign that he was touched by the supernatural. To gain his freedom, he agreed to go into the enemy camps around Fort Schuyler proclaiming that the vaunted Benedict Arnold was approaching at the head of a massive army bent on blood. He did so on August 22, almost three weeks into the siege. The warriors, bored by the siege and unhappy about their losses against the New York militia, were receptive. They believed Hon Yost and decamped. St. Leger had no choice other than to lift the siege and retreat to Lake Ontario. Luck rode with Arnold. He had removed the threat from the west without having to fight. By August 28, he could assure himself that nothing more was "to be feared from the enemy in this quarter." He started his men back to the Hudson.

Back in Philadelphia, the Congress had sought a scapegoat for the loss of Fort Ticonderoga. Some delegates jumped at the chance to revisit the subject of command in the Northern Department. Another vote was taken, and this time Philip Schuyler lost. The Congress directed him to report to General Washington for a court of inquiry. Members then designated Horatio Gates as his successor. The new commander reached Albany shortly after Arnold had left to lift the siege of Fort Schuyler.

Gates was fortunate in his timing. Two victories that he had nothing to do with simply fell into his lap—the militia triumph at the Battle of Bennington and Arnold's vanquishing of St. Leger. True to his pattern, he wrote to the Congress praising by name the victorious commanders at Bennington, but saying nothing about Arnold's role in the west. It was left to General Washington to give due credit to America's Hannibal, which he did in general orders on the first day of September.

On August 30, Benedict Arnold returned to headquarters and reported to his one-time friend and current detractor. Gates welcomed him cordially enough and gave him command of the army's left wing, where his fighting skills could be put to good use.

As distasteful as that might have been to Gates personally, he realized that his army needed combat-tested leadership.

Any elation Arnold felt over being given a command was dampened by word that the Congress had considered—and resoundingly rejected—his request to have his date of rank adjusted. The delegates resented any suggestion that their original orders might have been wrong and were firm on not giving any impression of caving in to military pressure. Henry Laurens, a delegate from South Carolina, thought the reasoning behind the vote was nothing short of "disgusting." He also worried that the decision would cause the loss of "good old servant General Arnold" and could have "further ill effects in the army."

Major General Arnold assumed his new duties with decidedly mixed emotions. As always, his adrenaline rose with the prospect of battle, but he seethed inwardly at this latest slight from what he considered to be a most ungrateful Congress.

———

Knowing that William Howe had finally opened his campaign did not end George Washington's consternation. In fact, his foe's departure from New York began one of the most uncertain periods the commander in chief experienced in the entire war. Although Howe's apparent abandonment of Burgoyne struck Washington as "unaccountable," he nevertheless began shifting his army to protect Philadelphia. By the first of August, patriot units were astride the Delaware River, waiting for more intelligence.

A week after the British fleet sailed, reports placed it near the mouth of the Delaware. That would seem to mean that Philadelphia was indeed Howe's objective. General Washington issued orders to move the Continental Army toward Wilmington, Delaware, where it would be between the British and the city. But just a day later, word arrived informing him that the hostile fleet had turned out to sea. He canceled the orders to march. What now? Sailing south out of New York could have been a grand feint; the English armada might well be on its way up the Hudson River to join Burgoyne. Then came a report telling him that the fleet had been spotted again, this time off Maryland heading south. That made Charleston the logical objective. But there was no way American forces could march that far to counter Howe.

For eleven nail-biting days Washington waited. Then came word that the British were standing off Chesapeake Bay, poised as if to enter it. That made no sense to Washington either, but Howe had actually kept Philadelphia in his sights all along. He had calculated, correctly as it turned out, that threatening the rebels' capital city would force Washington from his strategic position in New Jersey and oblige him to stand and fight. Howe planned to take the direct water approach from the Atlantic up the Delaware River and move on Philadelphia from the general direction of Wilmington. But the position of Washington's troops and the formidable patriot defenses on the Delaware convinced him to opt instead to sail around to the Chesapeake, go as far as he could up the bay, and attack Philadelphia overland from the south. Adverse winds kept the fleet at sea for days on end, frustrating Howe and further confounding Washington.

Finally, on August 22, word reached headquarters that the British were far up into the Chesapeake. It was obvious at last where they were heading. Relieved to have the long suspense lifted, Washington wrote that Howe "must mean to reach Philadelphia by that route, though to be sure it is a very strange one." He put his men into motion once more, this time heading south beyond Philadelphia to battle.

As the army passed through the capital, congressmen and citizens would have a close look at it, many for the first time. Washington decided to cross the city on parade, in order to cheer patriots and cow loyalists. The Continental Army had never paraded like this before, but Washington sensed that he led a far readier force than he had in 1775 and 1776, and he wanted to show it off.

On August 24, ten thousand fighting men marched through the City of Brotherly Love. They were clean and proud, if ragged and far from uniformly dressed. Washington led the way, accompanied by his top officers. Then followed the various units, each regiment with fifes and drums instructed to play tunes "with such moderation that the men may step to it with ease, and without *dancing* along or totally disregarding the music as too often has been the case." Artillery pieces were much in evidence, a sign of French largesse earlier in the year. Officers kept careful watch to assure "that the men carry their arms well," and women were banned from the ranks altogether. "Not a woman belonging to the army is to be seen with the troops." There was one uniform touch. Showing confidence in victory, every soldier wore a green sprig in his hat, or, if he had no hat, in his hair. The entire column was two hours long.

Most observers were impressed. This army had the feel of toughness about it. The British and German units were in for a fight. Cheers rang in the ears of the soldiers, a new experience for most of them. Some bystanders, however, were quiet, or doubting. John Adams, somehow still under the belief that he possessed more military know-how than the seasoned leaders passing by, sniffed that the men in ranks did not "turn out their toes so exactly as they ought."

Reaching the other side of town, the army continued south. Washington rode ahead to reconnoiter—this was strange ground where he had never contemplated engaging in battle.

Howe began disembarking his army at Head of Elk, the far northeastern point of Chesapeake Bay, on August 25. The Continental

Army would have to make a stand somewhere between that land-ing site and Philadelphia. Fortunately for the patriots, British sol-diers and the surviving horses required some time to recover from the long, debilitating voyage at sea. Redcoats and Hessians did not even start northward for several days, and then advanced very slowly, foraging along the way. General Washington used that gift of time to seek the best defensive position available. He chose Brandywine Creek, about midway along the road to Philadelphia. Although the Brandywine had numerous fords, it was a major obstacle to a field army. The two armies were equivalent in troop strength, but the terrain gave the patriots an edge.

Washington thought Howe would feint a frontal assault across the Brandywine, while sending a main attack swinging around one flank or the other. It would be a maneuver similar to those the Briton had used with such success in the battles in New York a year before. Because the left of the patriot position was anchored on very rough ground, Howe would likely hook the other way. Hence, the right of the American line would have to be strong and ready to oppose the British advance. Once Howe launched his main attack, Washington planned to charge across the creek, batter the weaker units posted there, and then outflank his opponent's flankers.

The American commander, the combative side of his nature showing, was actually eager to confront the British. He expected to "give them a repulse or at most . . . a painful and dear bought vic-tory." He sensed that a patriot win could well be decisive, for Howe had essentially cut himself off from support by the Royal Navy. "One bold stroke will free the land from rapine, devastations and burnings, and female innocence from brutal lust and vio-lence," he told his soldiers. "The eyes of all America, and of Europe are turned upon us," he added.

George Washington, the soldier.

Courtesy of Mount Vernon Ladies' Association

George Washington taking command of the Continental Army.
The Granger Collection

The father of his country.
Courtesy of Mount Vernon Ladies' Association

An epic moment: George Washington crossing the Delaware.

Courtesy of Mount Vernon Ladies' Association

The house that became his monument, Mount Vernon.

Courtesy of Mount Vernon Ladies' Association

General of the Continental Army.
Courtesy of Mount Vernon Ladies' Association

Plotters: Horatio Gates and John Adams.
Courtesy of Mount Vernon Ladies' Association

Alexander Hamilton as statesman and soldier.

Left photo: Courtesy of Mount Vernon Ladies' Association
Right photo: The Granger Collection

IN CONGRESS.

The DELEGATES of the UNITED STATES of *New-Hampshire, Massachusetts-Bay, Rhode-Island, Connecticut, New-York, New-Jersey, Pennsylvania, Delaware, Maryland, Virginia, North-Carolina, South-Carolina,* and *Georgia,* TO ——

Benedict Arnold Esquire

WE, reposing especial Trust and Confidence in your Patriotism, Valour, Conduct and Fidelity, DO, by these Presents, constitute and appoint you to be ——

Major General

in the Army of the United States, raised for the Defence of American Liberty, and for repelling every hostile Invasion thereof. You are therefore carefully and diligently to discharge the Duty of *Major General* by doing and performing all manner of Things thereunto belonging. And we do strictly charge and require all Officers and Soldiers under your Command, to be obedient to your Orders as *Major General.* And you are to observe and follow such Orders and Directions from Time to Time, as you shall receive from this or a future Congress of the United States, or Committee of Congress, for that Purpose appointed, or Commander in Chief for the Time being of the Army of the United States, or any other your superior Officer, according to the Rules and Discipline of War, in Pursuance of the Trust reposed in you. This Commission to continue in Force until revoked by this or a future Congress. DATED at *Philadelphia May 2d 1777*

By *Order of the* CONGRESS,

John Hancock

PRESIDENT.

ATTEST. *Cha Thomson Secy*

Benedict Arnold's official appointment as Major General of the Continental Army.
Courtesy of Mount Vernon Ladies' Association

Conspirators: Arnold tells Major John André to conceal the plans
of West Point in his boot at their meeting on September 21, 1780.
The Granger Collection

Previously unpublished portrait of Benedict Arnold, in oil by Doug Henry.

Courtesy of Bill Stanley, president of the Norwich Historical Society

At dawn on September 11, a rattle of musketry informed the waiting Americans that the British were moving toward them. The Battle of Brandywine Creek was about to open. Washington had learned his lessons well in 1776—Howe planned to do exactly what Washington had guessed.

Far to the north loomed another clash of arms.

Tension between Benedict Arnold and Horatio Gates developed almost at once. Gates's suspicions were raised when Arnold took under his wing several young officers known to be close to General Schuyler. Those suspicions were abetted by an inveterate schemer and foe of Arnold's—James Wilkinson, his one-time aide—who now enjoyed Gates's full confidence. In just days the relationship between the two generals had chilled to the point of mutual personal disdain.

Moreover, they disagreed completely on how best to fight Burgoyne. Arnold, not surprisingly, wanted to take the offensive. Gates, having never led large formations in battle, preferred to stand behind entrenchments and oblige the British to attack. The two did agree that the army should shift farther north to more defensible terrain.

Arnold, accompanied by an engineer from Poland, Thaddeus Kosciuszko,[1] rode out to reconnoiter. The two men found a place where steep, high bluffs reached almost to the Hudson's western shore, blocking the route Burgoyne would have to take to reach

---

[1]   From the surviving documentary evidence, Americans found the Pole's name virtually impossible to spell. But they had the utmost respect for his professional ability. Kosciuszko would later be the primary engineer in the construction of Fortress West Point.

Albany. On September 12 the patriots occupied those imposing hills, known as Bemis Heights. Under the careful eye of Kosciuszko, they began digging in.

That same day Burgoyne started cautiously south, cutting himself free from his lines of support and retreat, much as Howe had done below Philadelphia. Required to repair bridges and remove obstacles as he went, his advance was slow. By September 17 he stood about four miles from the American entrenchments on Bemis Heights. The next day, Arnold led a reconnaissance-in-force to try to discern the enemy's intent. He returned to warn Gates that an attack could be expected in a day or two, and it would probably come in the form of an attempt to get around or overrun the American left, Arnold's position. Gates disagreed, saying he was sure Burgoyne would strike the opposite flank near the Hudson River.

Arnold was right. On Friday, September 19, Burgoyne moved toward him. The First Battle of Saratoga (also known as the Battle of Freeman's Farm) was about to begin.

——•——

By late morning on September 11 the confrontation along Brandywine Creek appeared to be shaping up just as General Washington had predicted. Advancing British regiments had pushed a screen of American units back across the creek. That done, they rushed artillery forward and began shelling patriot positions. But they showed no inclination to try to cross the waterway. An express rider brought Washington a report of a powerful body of infantry and artillery marching in a wide circuit, aiming at some point upstream on the Brandywine. Heavy woods throughout the area hindered observation on both sides, but it certainly appeared Howe was attempting to get around the American right. Washington gleefully prepared to launch his own counterstroke at the supposedly light forces across from him.

At that critical moment arrived a message with most disconcerting information. British forces were not marching up the far bank of the Brandywine after all, the report said. In fact, according to the new intelligence, no enemy elements opposed his right. That report was erroneous, reflecting the confusion of battle, but it jerked Washington up short. It stood to reason that if Howe was not moving to outflank the patriots, then the bulk of the British army must be drawn up across the creek—right where the Americans had been set to attack. Washington quickly canceled his plan and halted those units moving to reinforce his right flank. This turned out to be a near-fatal decision, for it permitted Howe to cross the Brandywine unimpeded and to march virtually undetected toward the American rear.

Before long, frantic reports poured into headquarters. Hostile forces had appeared suddenly on the far right of the American positions, threatening to envelop Washington's entire battle line. He reacted at once to send elements at double time to the endangered area. An account of the ensuing melee is quickly told. The Americans rushing to restore the right flank ran into the British, who were exhausted after a seventeen-mile forced march over rough tracks and poor roads in the late summer heat. The Americans checked the British advance momentarily, but were forced back. Night came before a decision could be reached, but the British were in a better position to continue the struggle the next day. Washington prudently withdrew under cover of darkness and reassembled his scattered, intermingled units near Chester, several miles from the battlefield.

Having received an unexpected bloody nose, Howe did not pursue. Instead, he paused to gather his strength before proceeding, giving George Washington time to ready his regiments for another stand.

Far from falling into despair, the continentals felt some satisfaction in the outcome. The British held the field of battle, to be sure, but their casualties had been heavy, reportedly quite heavier than those suffered by the patriots. And, tellingly, panic—that constant companion in the ranks just a year ago—was absent from the American withdrawal. The men were ready to fight again. "I am sorry to inform you," General Washington reported to the Congress, "that in this day's engagement we have been obliged to leave the field." After describing the course of the battle, he ended on an upbeat note: "Notwithstanding the misfortunes of the day, I am happy to find the troops in good spirits; and I hope another time we shall compensate for the losses now sustained." The Virginian himself had long before shown that he possessed great personal reservoirs of resilience. Now his army was demonstrating the same trait.

Howe resumed his advance northward on the September 16. For six days the two armies marched and counter-marched. Washington positioned his army to threaten the British rear if Howe should turn toward Philadelphia. But he also had to leave himself an escape route. He knew that the survival of the Continental Army was more important than saving the capital. For his part, Howe hoped to entice or trap the Americans into accepting a major battle. When he finally concluded that the Old Fox would not cooperate, he shrewdly out-maneuvered the American commander to occupy the village of Germantown on September 22, placing himself between Washington and Philadelphia. A few days later a British detachment entered the undefended capital. Washington's bedraggled men had covered altogether some 140 miles after the Battle of Brandywine, shifting first here and then there, to no avail. Philadelphia had fallen. It had been a month since the continentals had paraded bravely through it on their way to confront the invaders.

The Congress had already decamped to Lancaster and later to York. Its members were not happy with General Washington.

————

In stark contrast, good tidings flowed in from upper New York.

Having been deserted by most of his Indian allies, Burgoyne was militarily blind as he moved south. Although aware that Americans held Bemis Heights, he did not know how far to the west their defenses stretched. He decided to advance in three widely spread columns to find the extent of the rebel positions before launching an attack. One would go straight down the road alongside the Hudson River, another would sweep far to the west, and the third would approach in the center. All three stepped off in a heavy morning fog on September 19.

Burgoyne felt sure that Gates, who had been an officer in the British army, would wait passively behind his entrenchments. He was right about Gates, but had not counted on his extremely aggressive subordinate, Benedict Arnold.

General Gates's plan was merely to await developments. Although fog and forest at first obscured the patriots' view of Burgoyne's advancing right wing, it was soon detected. Arnold pleaded for permission to strike the British while they were marching through the heavy woods and defiles on the American left. He warned that if Burgoyne were allowed to get his artillery within range and maneuver against their left flank, the patriots could be forced out of Bemis Heights. Gates appeared frozen by indecision. Arnold passionately "urged, begged, and entreated" to be turned loose. Finally, Gates relented. The commander of the left wing could advance his riflemen and light infantry, and support them, but he could not expect any reinforcements. That was all Arnold needed. He leaped on his horse and galloped to the front.

Two veterans of the 1775 march to Quebec were a part of the American left. Daniel Morgan commanded his vaunted riflemen and Henry Dearborn led a special detachment of light infantry. Arnold put his old comrades in motion and followed closely with his musket regiments.

Morgan and Dearborn roared out of the woods to strike the leading British elements in the vicinity of John Freeman's farm (ironically, located on land leased from Philip Schuyler). It was not much of a site for so momentous a battle—a handful of rough buildings centered on fifteen or twenty cleared acres. But back and forth across those stump-littered fields patriots and redcoats fought for an afternoon that changed the history of America.

At first the shock of the furious patriot attack, combined with the deadly fire of the riflemen, drove the British back. More regulars came up to stop the onrushing Americans. The British center column became engaged. Arnold threw his infantry units into the fray, changing the momentum once more. Burgoyne sent an urgent call to his column on the river to march on the double to his assistance.

At that point the English leader had no more readily available units to commit. Neither did Arnold, but the rest of the American army, the entire right wing, remained fresh. Moreover, an incredible panorama came into focus right in front of the uncommitted men on Bemis Heights. They watched as a large portion of Burgoyne's left column, responding to the call for assistance, changed direction and began crossing the American front. That presented an enticing opportunity. If boldly led, the patriots could charge down from the high ground to assail the vulnerable rear of those enemy troops marching toward Freeman's farm. The British were in a bad way. Their predicament raised the unexpected possibility of an overwhelming American triumph, wanting only a bold stroke by Gates. But that officer remained inert.

No one ever used that word to describe Benedict Arnold. Men reported seeing him virtually everywhere on the battlefield. Some said the major general acted at times "like a madman." Personally leading charges, he appeared to be "inspired by the fury of a demon." It was always so with Arnold in battle. "Riding in front of the line, his eyes flashing, pointing with his sword to the advancing foe, with a voice that rung clear as a trumpet," as one witness later recounted, he was a galvanizing agent who "made heroes of all within his influence."

The incomparable warrior realized what a potentially decisive opening the enemy had presented the Americans. He spurred back to urge Gates to act.

The two argued until the commander of the Northern Army reluctantly agreed to release a single regiment. Then, as Arnold wheeled to return to the fight, Gates called him back, peremptorily ordering him to remain in the rear.

That order was the only decisive act taken by Horatio Gates all day. Ironically, it cost him any chance for a victory on the battlefield. Deprived of an overall commander, the left wing gradually lost its cohesiveness and drive, and retired from the field. Even the reinforcing regiment Gates had agreed to send got lost on the way and had no influence on the outcome of the fight. The British, though badly mauled, remained at Freeman's farm as night fell, fortunate to emerge as tactical victors. Half the American army had not been engaged in combat, sitting idle all day.

Arnold was furious—frustrated at the lost opportunity and humiliated at having been removed from the fighting. Still, he knew the

British were vulnerable to an all-out attack, if one could be launched before they reorganized. He wanted to drive the sword in to the hilt. But Gates, openly disdainful, would not hear of the idea. He simply ignored Arnold. Americans sat in their lines while Burgoyne erected entrenchments on defensible terrain around Freeman's farm.

Gates had hardly stirred from his safe headquarters, but he saw that Arnold's combat heroics had won the soldiers' admiration. More than ever, he burned to rid himself of Benedict Arnold. "General Gates despises a certain pompous little fellow," a haughty James Wilkinson wrote.

On September 22, Gates filed his official report of the engagement. He boasted about how well he had handled the battle...and chose not to mention General Arnold. That was more than the Connecticut firebrand could take. Arnold stormed into headquarters complaining about "repeated indignities" he had suffered at Gates's hands. A shouting match ensued. According to witnesses, both generals resorted to "high words and gross language."

Gates accused Arnold of being ineffective and vowed to replace him as commander of the left wing. Arnold demanded a pass to join Washington's army, and stomped out.

Word of Arnold's imminent departure shook patriot morale. Senior officers circulated a petition pleading with him to remain; nearly every general present signed it. Touched by that outpouring of support, and not wanting to ride away in the midst of a fight, Arnold announced that he would stay for the duration of the campaign. Technically, he had never been relieved, but actually he was a general without a command.

With battles near Philadelphia, along the Hudson River, and in the upper reaches of New York, the first week of October 1777 was a turning point in the Revolutionary War. Not a few historians argue that the war was won in that week.

General Howe had occupied Germantown, a village five miles from Philadelphia, with the bulk of his army. Disdainful still of the fighting prowess of the rebels, he had not bothered to throw up much in the way of entrenchments. After all, except for the desperate attempt by Benedict Arnold and Richard Montgomery to storm the citadel of Quebec in 1775, or in strikes against small outposts such as Trenton, colonials had never managed to organize an attack. They either fought defensively from behind barricades or withdrew to avoid battle. Sir William did not believe they would dare approach his sizeable garrison in Germantown. Besides, the Americans were bivouacked nearly twenty miles away; there would be time enough to react to any threat. But Howe had not reckoned with George Washington's innate sense of aggressiveness, nor had he yet fully comprehended the improving battle-worthiness of the Continental Army.

General Washington rested, refitted, and reinforced his troops. He gathered units from as far away as the Hudson highlands in New York and assembled militia formations from nearby regions, altogether enough to gain numerical superiority over enemy forces in Germantown. The enemy, meanwhile, was stretched thin. Washington surmised that Howe, his attention diverted to his supply lines; his forces divided between Germantown, Philadelphia, and supply operations; and his security lax, would be vulnerable to a surprise stroke. He decided to attack.

The Virginian inconspicuously shifted units to within fifteen miles of Germantown. Then, shortly after dark on October 3, the whole army moved out. The Americans would surprise Howe at dawn.

———•·•———

After the Battle of Freeman's Farm, Burgoyne's position was tenuous. He had either to attack or withdraw to Lake Champlain. Staying in place was not an option. As he was mulling over his situation, a courier arrived with an electrifying message from Lieutenant General Sir Henry Clinton, the British commanding general in New York City.[2] Sir Henry said he would push up the Hudson River to help Burgoyne, providing that reinforcements from England reached him as expected. He anticipated moving on September 21. Burgoyne's heart leaped. The expedition might be on its way even as he was reading Clinton's letter. He decided to remain in place after all.

For more than a dozen days, Burgoyne waited for further word from Clinton. Gates just waited. This time Gates's lack of initiative worked to his advantage, as militiamen poured into his lines, raising his overall strength to about ten thousand men by October 1. Burgoyne had only half that many, and his ranks were dwindling daily from desertion and disease. The Briton calculated that he could wait until October 12, at the latest, before his food ran out, even on short rations. If Sir Henry did not arrive soon, he would have to attack or retreat.

On October 4, Burgoyne met with his generals to determine a course of action. He thought his best chance to save his army was to attack. Other voices counseled retreat, saying the rebels had

---

[2]   Clinton had been promoted and knighted since arriving in America in 1775.

grown too strong. Torn, the commander ordered a reconnaissance-in-force to probe the American left "to discover whether there were any possible means" of getting around the Bemis Heights defenses. If forcing a passage should turn out to be infeasible, and Clinton still had not made an appearance, the army would begin withdrawing northward on October 11. An hour or so before noon on October 7, in bright sunshine, a force of about two thousand British soldiers marched against their enemy's left flank.

Unknown to General Burgoyne, British warships on that very day were engaged in breaking through patriot defenses in the Hudson highlands.

Henry Clinton's reinforcements from England had arrived late, delaying the start of his operation until October 3. But he lost no time thereafter. In a sharp maneuver, feinting one way and going another, he landed combat elements on the Hudson's west shore on October 6 and sent them circling to the rear of American fortifications there. Those works (on the west bank where Bear Mountain Bridge now spans the river), built painstakingly from the very beginning of the war, fell in mere minutes.

On October 8, Clinton wrote exuberantly to Burgoyne that he had broken through the vaunted rebel defenses. Noting that there was "nothing now between us but Gates," he sent hopes that the success would "facilitate your operations." But that glow faded quickly. Two days later, when his troops were removing the last river obstacles and nearing open water, bad news arrived: both Howe near Philadelphia and Burgoyne above Albany were in trouble. Serious trouble.

———·•·———

Howe's day of reckoning came first. At dawn on October 4, hundreds of rebel soldiers charged out of fog so thick the men could only see thirty paces ahead. When patrols had reported the American advance a short while earlier, Howe had assumed it was "a mere flying party." In fact, it was the entire patriot army under General Washington's personal command. Except for some light troops directly in the path of attack, British units were surprised, many with arms stacked. Howe himself later admitted that he had not believed "the enemy would have dared to approach after so recent a defeat as that at Brandywine."

With militia units screening both flanks, the commander in chief pointed two powerful columns of continentals at Howe's encampment in Germantown. One, commanded by John Sullivan, struck straight through the village itself. Washington, riding with the reserve, followed Sullivan. The second and stronger force hooked left to envelop the British right. Trusted Nathanael Greene commanded that wing.

The dense fog was both help and hindrance. It permitted the attackers to get very close without being observed or brought under fire, but it also mightily complicated control of the several units and severely limited coordination between the two attacking columns. At first everything fell in favor of the attackers. Despite courageous and commendatory delaying tactics by British light troops, Sullivan's column smashed its way along the road running through Germantown, nearing Howe's main body bivouacked on the other side.

Washington, forced by low visibility to judge the course of the fight from the sounds of battle, sensed momentum swinging to his side. Gathering his reserve force, he rode forward to deliver the decisive blow. Soon finding himself out front and under "the hottest fire of the enemy," he listened intently. Rolling thunder to the left might, he thought, be General Greene among the enemy's tents. At that point Washington ecstatically envisioned Howe's regiments "in the utmost confusion" and fleeing. It was time to drive forward to chase the shattered foe back into Philadelphia.

Fog plays tricks with sounds and senses. The British were indeed in some disarray, but it was the Americans who were in distress. Delayed by thick mists and unfamiliar terrain, Greene's troops were in fact not yet in position. Sullivan was basically alone. Worse, some disoriented continental units collided and began shooting into one another. In a twinkling, what had appeared to be a triumphant breakthrough turned into a panicky rout. Soldiers, hearing firing from strange quarters and imagining the worst, broke ranks and raced to the rear. Washington and other officers managed to stop the stampede, but the moment was lost.

Recognizing that regaining battlefield control was all but impossible with units so intermingled and confused, the deeply disappointed commander in chief ordered a withdrawal. As always, preserving the Continental Army was the paramount concern. Weary soldiers retraced the route they had taken into town only hours before.

As the fog slowly lifted, the shaken British were not willing to push their advantage. The attackers disappeared in as ghostly a fashion as they had arrived.

By all objective standards, Americans lost the Battle of Germantown. They had been obliged to flee to avoid disaster. But war has an all-important subjective side. Weighing the battle on psychological scales, the patriots come out on top. Washington and his senior generals had rounded out their professional training, gaining invaluable experience in conducting offensive operations. And quite significantly, the soldiers themselves were eager for a rematch. They believed they had been on the verge of victory. The men of the ragamuffin army exhibited the bravado that "all young troops gain by being in actions," Washington wrote. They were confident they could "confuse and rout even the flower of the British army with the greatest ease." Strong morale permeated the patriot ranks, and after Germantown the Continental Army was a more potent fighting force than ever before.

Spirits flared higher yet on arrival of the news that General Howe felt threatened enough to pull in his forces and consolidate them in Philadelphia. As energizing as the impact of the battle was around continental campfires, it had an even more far-reaching result in Paris. The French government, seeking signs of the effectiveness of American arms, found what it was looking for. In the words of the foreign minister himself: "To bring an army, raised within a year, to this, promised anything." Deliberations over forming an alliance with the United States accelerated.

———

Burgoyne's battering came only three days later than Howe's.

The Second Battle of Saratoga (also called the Battle of Bemis Heights) began very much like the first one. Americans arrayed in defensive positions on Bemis Heights; a portion of Burgoyne's forces advancing to feel out the extent of those positions; Horatio Gates far to the rear, out of danger but too distant from the fighting to exert much influence; Daniel Morgan and Henry Dearborn in the path of likely combat on the patriot left. The big difference was that on this day, October 7, 1777, Benedict Arnold commanded no units. He brooded in his headquarters.

After leaving their entrenchments near John Freeman's farm an hour or so before noon, Burgoyne's troops advanced nearly a mile to a slight rise offering possibilities for observation and relatively open fields of fire. There some 1,500 men formed a battle line more than half a mile long. Artillery crews muscled field pieces forward of the line while officers trained telescopes toward Bemis

Heights, hoping to penetrate the screen of trees. A smaller element eased into woods farther west to probe for the enemy's left. At first, the Americans merely watched.

Daniel Morgan always railed at inaction. A natural disciple of Benedict Arnold, he urged a counterstroke against the overextended British line. That would be the best response to Burgoyne's incursion, he argued. After all, that method had worked splendidly in the first battle back in September. This time Gates was not so slow to react—he granted Morgan permission to "begin the game."

While Morgan and Dearborn slipped through the woods to get around their enemy's right flank and fall on the rear, two regular infantry brigades were to strike straight ahead to fix the foe's attention, one aiming at the left of the hostile line and the other at its center. By mid-afternoon the battle was joined. Despite coming under galling artillery fire, the infantry brigades advanced steadily. Not wanting to be drawn into a general engagement, Burgoyne sent forward an aide-de-camp carrying an order to withdraw. But the messenger was mortally wounded and captured; the troops stayed on the field. Burgoyne would have a battle whether he wanted one or not. Meanwhile, Morgan had worked his way into position, flushing enemy soldiers out of the woods as he went. When he and Dearborn crashed into the British right, it collapsed and fell back frantically until officers rallied remnants of units to stabilize the situation temporarily. That brought a pause in the fighting as both sides regrouped, staring at each other across a corpse-littered field not much more than two hundred yards wide.

Battlefield momentum hung in the balance. It could swing either way, depending on which side first grabbed the slack reins of opportunity. At that crucial juncture the totally unexpected arrival of a fiery leader suddenly shifted the initiative to the Americans. Benedict Arnold rode into the fray.

Simmering in his headquarters as the battle opened, Arnold had been unable to contain himself as he listened to the progress of the fighting. It simply was not in his constitution to sit passively in the presence of mortal combat. Especially in this instance, with his own division in a fight without him. Leaping on his horse, he galloped to the sound of the guns.

Finding himself initially in the midst of a Connecticut regiment, he shouted, "Now come on, boys; if the day is long enough we'll see them all in hell before night." The happily surprised men cheered. Their fighting general was back!

Riding to the front of the center brigade, Arnold promptly led it in an unsuccessful assault. Undeterred by the repulse, he began to ready the men for a second try. Then, spotting Morgan off to the left, he spurred quickly over to his old comrade. Together the two warriors forced the enemy back on that side, starting a general retrograde as British units struggled desperately to withdraw into the safety of their fieldworks. They managed to do so, but the artillerymen had to abandon their guns. Soon Americans were attacking everywhere, pulled headlong by the combat charisma of Benedict Arnold. He was out ahead, visible to everyone, waving his sword high in the air, shouting to the men to give no respite to the retreating foe. An admiring New England soldier later described the inspirational impact Arnold had on the men. "He didn't care for nothing. He'd ride right in. It was 'come on boys,' not 'go boys.'... There wasn't any wasted timber in him."

With the British beaten back to their original breastworks, Arnold paused to scan the area. A push now, before darkness gave the enemy time to recover, could seal the victory. He saw, off to the left, a rare and perhaps fleeting opportunity. There the British position was weakest, and there stood a relatively fresh patriot brigade. He decided at once to seize the moment.

Unhesitatingly, he took the shortest distance straight toward that spot—dashing right down the narrow no-man's land separating the two armies. Astounded soldiers on both sides watched as the lone rider, clad in the blue and buff uniform of an American major general, steered his sturdy brown mount unscathed through that gauntlet of fire. Acts like that caused observers later to remember Arnold as a man possessed that day, a leader defying death to the reckless point of madness.

Barely stopping to make his intent known, he whirled and led a charge that broke the enemy line. That swift strike isolated a body of Germans in a key redoubt. Arnold fixed his attention on them. If they could be overrun the entire British position would come unhinged. But it was already late, and the sun was fading fast. The redoubt had to be taken before darkness ended the day's fighting. In frantic haste, Arnold found Daniel Morgan. The two quickly made their plans. Arnold would lead about two hundred men to the rear of the redoubt while Morgan would assault the front of it with the remainder of the troops available.

In the face of Morgan's rapid advance, and after a hard day's fighting, German discipline finally cracked. The scene in the redoubt was one of panic when Arnold and his men appeared to cut off retreat. In the lead as always, Arnold burst through the open rear of the redoubt. Taking a few seconds to survey the wild melee around him, silhouetted in the dim light of dusk, he was an easy target atop his panting charger. A handful of the defenders reacted to this new threat by loosing a volley of musket fire at the man on the horse.

One ball smashed into Arnold's left leg, slicing ligaments and shattering bone. Other shots struck his horse. The mortally wounded animal reared and fell heavily sideways, pinning the general to the ground, his already dangling leg twisted at a grotesque angle. Arnold and the sun fell at the same time.

When Morgan's men clambered over the redoubt's ramparts, the entire British defensive position became untenable. But night-fall and the loss of Arnold halted the American offensive. Burgoyne was able to extricate his units and withdraw in reasonably good order northward. Gates, who had never ventured out to take a hand in the battle, did not pursue. In fact, he did not even follow immediately. He did not have to. Burgoyne's expedition was doomed. Ten days after the battle, at the river village of Saratoga, the Briton surrendered what was left of his army.

News of Burgoyne's capitulation reached Paris with electrifying effect. Coming close on the heels of word about the surprising strength and resilience demonstrated by the Continental Army in the Battles of Brandywine and Germantown, it sealed the French decision to come openly to the aid of the United States.

On December 17, 1777, France announced that it would recognize American independence, the first nation in the world to do so. A few weeks later authorities notified American emissaries that France was also prepared to form an alliance with the new nation. By mid-1778 France and Great Britain were at war. Eventually Spain and the Netherlands entered the conflict against the British. The American war had become a worldwide war.

It is hard to see how London could have won in America from that point on. The island kingdom simply had too many enemies and the fighting was on too extensive a scale. King George III could not win the war against his rebellious colonies, but the United States could still lose it.

And that is almost what happened.

CHAPTER THIRTEEN

ARNOLD CRIPPLED

————✦————

A N EIGHTEENTH-CENTURY BATTLEFIELD WAS A PLACE OF awful carnage. Darkness on October 7, 1777, had ended the fighting at the Second Battle of Saratoga, but not the activity or the agony.

Officers struggled to gather their troops in preparation for a resumption of combat the next morning. Walking wounded straggled to the rear. Wagon drivers hustled food and ammunition forward. Guards herded prisoners into tight knots to prevent escape. Soldiers tried to comfort critically injured comrades in their final hours of life or to find ways to get them back to the surgeons' tents. Others searched for patriots killed in action and dragged their bodies to designated spots for later burial. Ghoulish scavengers stripped Hessian and English corpses of footwear and other useful clothing. (It was not unheard of for men wielding daggers in the dark, upon coming across a foe still living, to hasten the unfortunate victim's rendezvous with death.) Many men, wholly exhausted from the day's fighting, simply dropped where they were, fast asleep. Here and there a pistol shot signaled the killing of a wounded horse. Torches flickered everywhere. Moans punctuated the macabre scene.

Benedict Arnold became a part of that woeful tapestry. Seeing him fall, nearby soldiers rushed to free him from his horse. They cut away his trouser leg to reveal the wound and to provide strips of cloth for a tourniquet to stanch the bleeding. Veterans among them shook their heads knowingly as they inspected his mangled limb. It was beyond serious. In that day and age such wounds were fatal more often than not; amputation would be the very best of expected outcomes. Hurriedly, the soldiers fashioned a makeshift litter from materials lying about the redoubt and started carrying their general back to find a doctor.

We can only guess what a terrible ordeal that trip was. The way back was not an easy one in daytime—at night, in haste, stumbling along in the uncertain light of a torch or lantern, the stretcher bearers could hardly have been gentle. Each bounce or jolt sent paroxysms of pain surging through the helpless patient. An agonizing hour passed, maybe more, before the weary bearers eased Arnold's litter to the ground near patriot headquarters. Overburdened doctors there, involved in the grim work of casualty triage, could do little more than check and adjust the primitive first aid administered in the field, immobilize the leg as best they could, and send him in a wagon another thirty jarring miles to a military hospital set up in Albany. There, nearly four tortuous days after being shot, the famous warrior came under the care of surgeon James Thacher.

Thacher and every other doctor who looked at the wound came to the same conclusion: amputation. Otherwise one just did not recover from having a limb shattered by a musket ball. Even if the bone could somehow be coaxed into knitting together again the injured leg would end up being significantly shorter than the other and ever painful. Besides, bone splinters mingled with fragments of the musket ball itself would dangerously hinder healing. Gangrene was likely to set in, with deadly consequences. Ordinary infection was also an omnipresent threat before the discovery of antibiotics. If Arnold wanted to live, he would have to do so with much of his left leg cut off. To that everyone agreed—except Arnold.

Amputation was "damned nonsense," he shouted each time the surgeons pleaded with him for permission to operate. Taking a long-odds gamble, with the stakes being life or death, he insisted that he would rather die than be a one-legged cripple. The men of medicine shrugged their shoulders in consternation, unable to fathom such irrationality. Of course, they could not see what lurked in the warrior's heart.

Perhaps Arnold actually wanted to die. He had certainly jeered at death over and over on the day of battle. Henry Dearborn provided a personal insight when years later he recalled Arnold's first words to him after being wounded. Rushing over to the fallen officer, Dearborn had asked if he was seriously hurt. Yes, came the answer, in the same leg that had been hit under the walls of Quebec City. Then, clinching his teeth in excruciating torment, he had told his old comrade that he wished the musket ball had struck his heart instead.

Whatever his pain-drenched reasoning might have been, Benedict stubbornly stuck to his position. He would survive with two legs or not at all. That made him an almost impossible patient. Doctor Thacher, attending to him on October 11, wrote that the renowned general was "very peevish, and impatient under his misfortunes, and required all my attention during the night." Carpenters fashioned a

wooden frame to hold the limb rigid. Although absolutely necessary, total confinement to bed further soured Arnold's attitude.
When the wound was slow to heal, as the long-suffering physicians
had warned it would be, he verbally abused them as a loutish "set
of ignorant pretenders and empirics."

Then, for just a short while, it appeared that a miracle might
occur. Arnold showed signs of making an extraordinarily rapid
recovery. A visitor reported that "General Arnold is growing better very fast" only three weeks into his convalescence. But that
upbeat assessment withered in the face of harsh medical reality. By
mid-November the leg had turned grossly purulent, exuding large
quantities of bloody pus. "General Arnold is very weak, and full of
poison, his wound discharges like water," wrote one of his worried
aides. The hurting, of course, was constant. That, along with the
indignity of bedpans and the onset of bedsores, not to mention the
sheer boredom of staring at the ceiling all his waking hours, eroded
his soul. December came, with scant change in status. He remained
dangerously ill. When the hole carved by the Hessian musket ball
began to close, Dr. Thacher had to lance the swollen leg to keep it
draining ("punctured" was the word used by a witness). The recovery would be prolonged—if ever.

From the first, a stream of visitors had kept him informed of
events in the war as they tried hard to keep up his spirits: Daniel
Morgan as he passed through Albany with his riflemen on the way
south to rejoin Washington, Lieutenant Colonel Alexander Hamilton on a mission carrying instructions from the commander in chief
to Horatio Gates, and soldiers who revered the daring leader who
had shared with them the risks of combat. But to no avail. The
patient sank deep into depression. He despaired of ever recovering.

Gates himself exhibited indifference to the plight of his fellow
major general. In his after-action report of the battle, he had full

praise for Morgan and Dearborn and numerous others. But he only mentioned Arnold in passing, acknowledging merely that he had been wounded in a "gallant" assault on an enemy redoubt. News of Arnold's life-threatening injury had spread too widely for Gates to again ignore the fighting general's presence in battle.

Perhaps Arnold's physical decline could be partially attributed to his unconcealed disgust at the way fame came to rest on the head of Horatio Gates. The astounding news of General Burgoyne's surrender reverberated around the United States and across the Atlantic Ocean. The Congress honored Gates with a gold medal. His reputation soared, in many quarters approaching or eclipsing that of General Washington. Hearing all of that, Arnold fumed. He knew the truth. In a just world the laurels should have gone to others. Philip Schuyler for setting the stage. Battle leaders such as John Stark and Daniel Morgan. And, yes, to Arnold himself. Bedridden and helpless, Benedict Arnold gnashed his teeth at the distressing thought of "Granny Gates" receiving honors won by the blood and grit of better men.

Not even a gracious endorsement by General Burgoyne himself eased Arnold's depression. Stopping several days in Albany after surrendering at Saratoga, the Briton openly and clearly stated where he thought the credit for his defeat rested. It was Benedict Arnold, he pronounced, who was primarily responsible for the American success.

Nor did a resolution of the Congress, leading to the restoration of his military seniority, mollify the unhappy warrior. On November 29, members voted to let General Washington "regulate the rank of Major General Arnold," sure in their knowledge that the commander in chief would adjust his date of rank to predate the five brigadiers promoted over him some ten months earlier. When a letter from the president of the Congress arrived, informing him of this action and praising his service, Arnold interpreted the resolution as an act of sympathy, not as an apology for its previous mistreatment of him. Peeved and unreconciled, he waited three weeks before perfunctorily responding. He did not want the sympathy of a group so intent on glorifying General Gates.

As the year ended, Arnold's wound finally began to show signs of healing. With that improvement bolstering his morale, his thoughts came increasingly to center on his own personal and fiscal welfare. He stopped dwelling on death, if he had ever seriously done so, and began to look ahead to life after a sickbed. Enforced inactivity gave him time to think—perhaps too much time. He began to reassess his past willingness to sacrifice for the cause. Having been twice wounded, and very possibly fated to be an invalid for the rest of his life, he started turning his attention away from further military assignments. Poison may have stopped oozing from his leg, but his heart remained full of rancor. In those long weeks of recuperation his sense of core values shifted from selfless service to self-interest.

He had to restore not only his health but also his personal life. That included business affairs, of course, but family circumstances as well. On a trip from Rhode Island to Boston the previous spring he had met a charming teenager, Betsy DeBlois. Although the general was a widower twenty years her senior, thoughts of marriage had crowded his mind. Betsy (or her parents), not so keen on the idea, had rebuffed him. The press of war had interrupted his courtship, but now, abed and lonely, and dreaming of a new future, visions of the alluring girl returned. With the help of an aide he wrote Betsy a letter.

By mid-January he could sit up in bed and resume correspondence on his own. He told friends that he hoped to be able to leave his room with the help of a crutch before many more weeks passed. As it turned out, that estimate was quite overly optimistic. The leg, although mending, would be at least two inches shorter. He would have to wear a built-up shoe to minimize a permanent limp. Putting any weight at all on the atrophied limb was hardly bearable, and the passage of time would only diminish the pain, not eliminate it. He would need to use crutches for an extended time. It would be months, if ever, before he could mount a horse again. He would survive, it seemed, but the once superb athlete would never be physically the same again.

On January 20, 1778, from his encampment in Valley Forge, George Washington sent Arnold official notification of his restored seniority and asked about the pace of his recovery. The commander in chief was looking ahead to the coming campaign and hoped his fighting general would be able to take part in it. He had in mind "a command which I trust will be agreeable to yourself and of great advantage to the public." But Arnold had other ideas. Caring for his personal interests had overtaken his sense of duty to country. He did not respond for some six weeks.

The tormented hero decided to go home just as soon as he could manage it. When winter showed signs of ending, he decided to hazard the long trip by easy stages. He traveled on a bed in the back of a wagon, and had himself carried into and out of lodgings at each stop. Even so, he was pushing too hard too soon. Reaching Middletown on the Connecticut River, only a good day's ride from being reunited with his sister and children in New Haven, he was forced to stop for several weeks. The jolting journey had reopened his wound.

At Middletown, on March 12, Arnold finally took time to respond to Washington's inquiry about his health and possibilities for the 1778 campaign. Trouble with his injury had flared again, he wrote, "occasioned by some loose splinters of bone remaining in

the leg, which will not be serviceable until they are extracted."
That process could not be completed for at least two and possibly
up to six months. Therefore, he could not even guess when he
might be able to "take the command your Excellency has been so
good to reserve for me."

May had arrived before Benedict Arnold reached home. A
hero's welcome awaited him, and a much-delayed respite with his
family in his own house. During his enforced stay in Middletown
he had continued his pursuit by mail of the "heavenly" Betsy
DeBlois, but with no success whatsoever. There, too, he had picked
up the reins of commerce once again, beginning the tough task of
rebuilding his business interests during wartime. His mind had definitely not been focused on military matters. But that began to
change, perhaps partly in reaction to the adulation showered on
him by his neighbors in New Haven. Perhaps, also, in dawning
realization that in America's war-torn economy his rank as a major
general would be a significant asset.

The war's fourth campaigning season was obviously nearing.
Arnold had been an instrumental player in the first three. And
Washington had clearly signaled his intent to give him a major role
in 1778. He could not resist the summons of the trumpet. Despite
the shortened leg, despite the bitter disenchantment, the battler
decided to report to headquarters. His crippling wound still con-
fining him to a carriage, Benedict Arnold left for Valley Forge after
only a few days at home.

About the same time Arnold was making arrangements to
depart New Haven, Washington was preparing a packet for him.
A Frenchman had given the Virginian two sets of fancy epaulets
and sword-knots to be presented "to any friends I should choose."
The commander in chief wanted Arnold to have one set as "testimony" of his high esteem for his service. He also told his foremost

battler how hopeful he was of having him return to the Continental Army. That packet very likely intercepted Arnold along the way.

With British warships controlling the lower Hudson River, Arnold's route took him in a northwesterly direction to cross that waterway in an area where patriots had been hard at work since January erecting new defenses in the Hudson highlands. There he saw Fortress West Point for the first time.

West Point was actually an interlocking complex of many fortifications, all centered on a huge, unbroken granite ridge jutting out across the path of the mighty river, forcing it to make two sharp turns before continuing south to New York City. Arnold stayed there from May 11 to May 13, resting his leg and being briefed on the construction plan. The engineer in charge was his former colleague who had supervised the raising of patriot positions at Bemis Heights, Thaddeus Kosciuszko. West Point was slated to become the most important strategic site in the United States, one that would be called the "Gibraltar of America." It was also fated to be the rock on which Benedict Arnold would eventually crash.

The keystone fort in the entire complex was a great bastion covering much of the level plain right where the river made its sharpest bend. Honoring Arnold's visit and his combat exploits, the commander in the region named it Fort Arnold. It bore the fighting general's name from then until his treason two and a half years later.

Then, in relatively easy stages, Major General Benedict Arnold continued to Valley Forge. He could neither sit on a horse nor walk without a crutch, but there he was, resplendent, one must assume, wearing the new epaulets and sword-knot.

It had been more than seven months since he had fallen in battle. General Washington was delighted to have him back.

CHAPTER FOURTEEN

WASHINGTON
CHALLENGED

WHILE BENEDICT ARNOLD ENDURED THOSE INTER-minable winter months, George Washington also suf-fered a season of trauma, but of a much different kind. His wounds were political. At issue was nothing less than whether he would retain the helm of the Revolutionary War.

A clique of influential men, already predisposed to want to replace the commander in chief, saw an opening in the sudden rise to fame of Horatio Gates. Their shadowy hopes of undermining the Virginian blossomed in the late autumn of 1777 into a challenge to his continuation in command. That internal revolt is known to history as the Conway Cabal.

Actually, Thomas Conway himself came late to the movement that carries his name. He didn't arrive on the scene until May 1777, one of the many foreign adventurers who so complicated George Washington's life that year. Seeds of the so-called cabal had sprouted many months before, following the shock of patriot defeats in New York and New Jersey in 1776. Surfacing first was an incipient movement to replace George Washington with Major General Charles Lee, considered by many to be the most consummate military leader in the colonies. Lee himself was an active agent in the attempt, writing at one point that certain times required leaders to "commit treason against the laws of the state for the salvation of the state." He was hinting not at all subtly that the ousting of Washington would be such a "virtuous kind of treason."

All but openly abetting General Lee's conspiratorial inclinations was Joseph Reed, the adjutant general of the Continental Army. Horatio Gates joined in, albeit more circumspectly. A number of congressmen poured kerosene of criticism on the emerging flames. Acerbic New Englanders fed the fire.

Lee's capture and Washington's brilliant Christmas Campaign silenced thoughts of sacking the commander in chief, but only temporarily. Suppressed for the most part, but kept alive by civil-military clashes in the first half of 1777, the notion festered for months. It erupted with newfound vehemence after Washington's failure to defend Philadelphia. His galling reverses in Pennsylvania stood in stark contrast to Horatio Gates's glorious victory in New York.

If one man deserves to have his name linked to the anti-Washington movement in the winter of 1777–78, it would be the principal instigator, Thomas Mifflin. Curiously, however, he has generally escaped opprobrium at the bar of history. Among the reasons might be, as one modern historian suggests, that "Conway Cabal" has a catchy ring while "Mifflin Cabal" sounds rather scruffy.

Thomas Mifflin, a suave young Pennsylvania politician, rode with General Washington as an aide-de-camp when the newly appointed commander in chief departed Philadelphia for Boston in June 1775. He rose rapidly thereafter, being elevated less than two months later to quartermaster general, a job making him essentially the chief supply officer in the Continental Army. By May the next year he was a brigadier general and, in February 1777, he was one of the five brigadiers promoted to major general over Benedict Arnold. Mifflin provided valuable service early in the war, particularly in helping rally resistance in his home state during the dark days of 1776. But, like many others late in that bleak year, he began to harbor doubts about Washington's abilities. Those doubts were not lessened in the first half of 1777 as his political colleagues kept him abreast of the simmering civil-military tensions. The personal chemistry between the Virginian and the Pennsylvanian was not good. In the passage of time they simply grew to dislike each other.

Mifflin's ego suffered when Washington did not draw him into his inner circle of advisers. It was further ruffled when the commanding general chastised the quartermaster general for several failings in the performance of his duties. Nor were the bruised feelings eased when Washington restored Benedict Arnold's date of rank, in effect jumping him over the Pennsylvanian. Nathanael Greene noted later that Mifflin was upset because Washington failed to pay "such mighty deference to him as his vanity leads him to think himself entitled to."

But it was not until the latter half of 1777 that the disgruntled officer became an outright opponent of the commander in chief. When British forces entered New Jersey, ostensibly threatening Philadelphia, Mifflin thought Washington should come down out of his redoubt in the mountains and directly confront the enemy in order to save the city. When the commanding general refused to accept that advice, Mifflin became distraught. His emotions ran from disgust after the defeat at Brandywine to outrage after the British occupation of Philadelphia. The city could have been defended, he was convinced, if the patriots had been under the command of a more competent general. Mifflin set out to try to foster that change.

He did not have to look hard to find like-minded collaborators. There were many, springing from different motivations. Some were military officers, like Charles Lee, who were convinced they could do a better job than Washington. Some were political leaders who resented Washington's prestige. Some were New Englanders who had never reconciled themselves to having a Virginian in charge. Some were friends of Washington who worried that he was in over his head. Some were supporters of the commander in chief as a person but who were concerned at the growing power of any "man on horseback." Mifflin's task was to mobilize them all—and the grand victory of Horatio Gates at Saratoga seemed to be a heaven-sent opportunity to do just that.

A cacophony of complaints about Washington's performance, even before the defeats around Philadelphia, had filled the ears of anyone paying the least attention. Thomas Burke, a representative from North Carolina, encountered in the Congress "a great desire" among the delegates from New England "to insult the General." John Adams wondered aloud why Washington was holding "vast armies in idleness" rather than committing them to battle. Another impatient Massachusetts leader lamented, "I long to hear of enterprises, of battles fought and victories gained on our side." Horatio Gates, showing early signs of insubordination, sent Washington an impertinent letter regarding supplies. After the Battle of Brandywine and the subsequent occupation of Philadelphia, the noise level rose several decibels. Word of Saratoga brought it to a crescendo.

Benjamin Rush, a former congressman serving at the time as a surgeon general in the army, weighed in with words more poisonous than most, penning a cryptic assessment of "the state and disorders of the American army." Washington, he claimed, was a puppet in the hands of a few officers at headquarters. The major generals were a sorry lot. The soldiers were ragged and undisciplined. There was "bad bread, no order, universal disgust." He also told John Adams that officers referred to Gates's army as "a well-regulated family," but called the forces directly under Washington "an unformed mob." He went on to contrast Gates, at the "pinnacle of military glory," to Washington, who had been "outgeneraled and twice beaten." He was not reticent to share his views with others near and far.

James Lovell, a Massachusetts firebrand who entered the Congress early in 1777, had been an outspoken supporter of Horatio Gates in the quarrels with Philip Schuyler. He continued to be a shrill voice in favor of elevating Gates over Washington and was not reticent in pushing his beliefs. In a letter unsigned but almost certainly his, Lovell told Gates that military affairs around Philadelphia were doomed "unless you come down and collect the virtuous band who wish to fight under your banner and with their aid save the southern hemisphere." Lovell even wrote intemperate letters to Washington himself.

John Adams sang soprano in that congressional chorus. "Oh! Heaven grant us one great soul!" he cried after the Congress had been obliged to vacate Philadelphia. "One active, masterly capacity would bring order out of this confusion and save this country." He let it be known how glad he was that Burgoyne's defeat was not the work of General Washington or of southern troops. "If it had been, idolatry and adulation would have been unbounded, so excessive as to endanger our liberties," he intoned. Shortly after the Congress had found new quarters in rural Pennsylvania, Adams left to go home. He then departed on a mission to France, but his acid pen had already helped fuel mutinous fires.

By no means was the gathering movement limited to sniping from congressmen. Horatio Gates, basking in the afterglow of his triumph in northern New York, saw his star rising and Washington's falling. Emboldened, he sent his report of victory at Saratoga straight to the Congress, pointedly bypassing the commander in chief. Grown haughty beyond any measure of propriety, he left it to others to inform the overall commander.

When Washington heard rumors of Burgoyne's surrender at Saratoga, he was thrilled and hoped that troops from the Northern Department could be released to reinforce those in Pennsylvania. But he needed some sort of official word. Finally, after waiting two weeks without receiving "authentic advice of the victory," he sent his aide, Alexander Hamilton, hurrying northward to find out what had happened. Hamilton carried a sharp letter from Washington to Gates, and had authority to direct that general to send continental regiments south at once.

The young officer was not prepared for what he found. Horatio Gates did not want to provide the required reinforcements. He claimed to need them in his own theater of war, where he felt shorthanded. Militiamen were already on their way home, Daniel Morgan and others earlier ordered north by Washington had been released to return, and some forces had been sent down the Hudson to help patriots in the highlands. A few good regiments were being held around Albany in case of a British attack, although there was no real reason to anticipate any such threat. Benedict Arnold suspected Gates of holding back in hopes that the Congress would dismiss Washington and summon the victor of Saratoga to save the sputtering Revolution. Arnold shared that thought with his own aides, and most probably with Alexander Hamilton as well. In hindsight, it appears he was right.

Not only was General Gates loath to release combat troops, but, as Hamilton quickly discovered, he had powerful friends who had led him to believe he could disobey Washington with impunity. Hamilton became thoroughly alarmed at the extent of the internal insurrection he was uncovering. When Gates finally agreed to send a token force south, Hamilton accepted. It would be "dangerous," Hamilton told Washington, to insist on more from a man "whose successes have raised him into the highest importance" and had earned him extraordinary influence, especially with the New England states. Among those warning Hamilton of the brewing movement against Washington was New York's governor, George Clinton. If the Virginian had not previously been aware of the gathering threat to his position, he surely was after hearing from Hamilton.

Another young officer close to the commander in chief also alerted him to signs of political maneuvering. The Marquis de Lafayette, receiving reports from the dozens of French volunteers embedded throughout the Continental Army, got wind of behind-the-scenes machinations. The commander in chief was under siege from "secret enemies," he warned, some in the Congress and some inside the army itself. Much to Lafayette's later chagrin, one of those turned out to be a fellow Frenchman, Thomas Conway.

Washington had initially been impressed with Conway; he spoke English when so many foreigners did not. The Congress had given the Irish Frenchman an appointment to brigadier general in May 1777. Later that year he had performed in combat to the satisfaction of his immediate commanders, and appeared headed for larger responsibilities until overweening ambition tripped him up.

Although he was the most junior brigadier in the army, Conway had become convinced that he deserved to be a major general. He began campaigning openly for that promotion. Hearing the chatter against Washington, and learning that some of it emanated from the halls of government, he sought to take advantage of the situation. In a message intended for the congressmen, he shared his low opinion of the commander in chief. While General Washington was a good man, "his talents for the command of an Army...were miserable indeed." The adventurer also penned a fawning letter to Horatio Gates, hoping to climb aboard that general's accelerating bandwagon. Referring to George Washington, Conway wrote: "Heaven has been determined to save your country; or a weak General and bad Councellors would have ruined it."

For his part, Washington had over time changed his earlier favorable opinion of Conway's abilities. Upon learning that the Congress was considering elevating the brigadier, the commander in chief reacted in unusually strident terms. Writing to congressman Richard Henry Lee on October 17, he stated unequivocally that Conway did not merit promotion. The Frenchman, he said, was not nearly the leader he claimed to be. Adding emphatically that "his importance in this Army, exists more in his own imagination than in reality," Washington could hardly have been more scathingly negative. He also argued vehemently that such a promotion, leapfrogging the foreign officer over nearly two dozen other brigadiers, would create havoc by starting "a train of evils unforeseen and irremediable." Then, his frustration getting the better of him, he hinted that he himself might resign "if such insuperable difficulties are thrown in my way."

What the commanding general did not know was that Lee was in cahoots with Mifflin and others in the effort to replace him. When his letter arrived, a surge of excitement swept the ranks of the junta.

For weeks the conspirators had been constrained in what they could do—Washington was too widely popular a figure to attack openly. Beyond holding meetings of small numbers of like-minded men, prudence would not permit much more than composing letters casting doubts on the commanding general's abilities and the circulation of anonymous tracts defaming his character. None of the plotters had been able up to that moment to see a way clear to oust the Virginian, but his letter to Lee raised a tantalizing thought. What if Washington could be provoked into resigning on his own? Might not Conway be just the instrument to effect that?

In another encouraging event, the cabal gained a large boost when the Congress established an external Board of War to superintend military matters. The new board, replacing a long-standing internal congressional committee of the same name, would have oversight of Washington's conduct of the war. Delegates soon appointed Horatio Gates to the presidency of the board, although his responsibilities in the north would prevent him from assuming his duties at once. A Connecticut member wrote him a congratulatory letter, saying there was "universal applause at this appointment." The Continental Army needed "a total reform and regulation, both internal and external," he said, and Gates was just the man to do that.

The Congress also assigned Thomas Mifflin to serve on the board. That position gave the malcontent an ideal vantage point from which to orchestrate the previously uncoordinated barrage of anti-Washington sentiment

Meanwhile, fate was intervening in the form of a supercilious young man to whom Horatio Gates had entrusted the responsibility of delivering to the Congress the details of Burgoyne's surrender. James Wilkinson, a thoroughgoing rascal if ever there was one, and quite full of himself, felt no urgency to speed the news to the delegates waiting at York. He loitered along the way, calling on friends and visiting his fiancée, burning up the better part of two weeks on a journey that could have been completed in a few days. Spending a rainy evening in Reading, Wilkinson sat up late drinking and talking with officers on the staff of Major General William Alexander. With rum loosening his tongue, he told one of them about Thomas Conway's disparaging remarks to Gates about General Washington. That officer dutifully reported the conversation to General Alexander. Sensing that the information exposed "such wicked duplicity of conduct" that it could not be ignored, Alexander relayed it to Washington.

When the commander in chief read Alexander's message, early in November, he realized that at least two of his generals were involved in disloyal correspondence—or worse. That corroborated what he had been hearing from several sources. Shrewdly, without mentioning any name other than Gates, he prepared a short note to Conway. "A letter which I received last night, contained the following paragraph," he stated simply, and then quoted Conway's own words to Gates: "Heaven has been determined to save your country; or a weak General and bad Councellors would have ruined it." Conway, missing the significance of the brief message, responded limply that he doubted having used the term "weak general," but he did not disavow having written the letter in the first place. Providing grist for future historians to debate whether he was a mere dupe in the cabal or was an unbelievably inept plotter, he did not tell Mifflin about Washington's discovery of the correspondence for some three weeks. When he did, Mifflin grasped instantly the magnitude of the problem. Washington had put the conspirators on notice that he was aware of something going on, but he had carefully concealed how much he actually knew. They would have to move faster, and with less caution.

Mifflin at once alerted Gates, warning him to be more careful with his correspondence. Gates puffed up, responding angrily that his papers were in fact secure. Someone with access must have "played me this treacherous trick." Hamilton! When Washington's aide was in Albany he must have seen and copied the letter from Conway. Indignant, Gates wrote to Washington complaining of the theft and urging the commander in chief to help identify the culprit who placed "extracts from General Conway's letters to me into your hands." Claiming that "crimes of that magnitude" could damage "the safety of the states," he added that he was providing a copy of his letter to the Congress. He privately sent one to Mifflin as well so the two could act in concert as circumstances evolved.

In the meantime, back in mid-November, Conway had stirred the bubbling cauldron again. Angered at the promotion of another foreign officer while his own case lingered, the volatile Frenchman abruptly contacted the Congress and threatened to resign. The delegates turned the matter over to the Board of War. It was still sitting there when Mifflin and Richard Henry Lee learned that George Washington knew of the Gates-Conway correspondence.

They saw their chance. Now was the time to promote Conway. Elevating him in spite of Washington's express wishes, and in light of his disparaging remarks about the Continental Army's commanding general, might trigger the very resignation they sought.

Mifflin wasted no time. He convinced the board to propose advancing Conway to the grade of major general, with assignment as the Continental Army's inspector general. In that capacity he would have independent authority to oversee Washington's work and report directly to the Board of War, facts sure to add further insult to the promotion itself. Then, at Lee's urging, the Congress approved the board's recommendation in mid-December. But, incredibly, on purpose or unintentionally, no one informed General Washington. Conway left for headquarters to deliver the news himself.

——•—•——

In the midst of that swirling intrigue, the commander in chief had been fully engaged in waging the war. Coping with a conspiracy was a secondary concern.

Washington and Sir William Howe were focused on the Delaware River, where stubborn American defenses blocked the British fleet from reaching Philadelphia. Opening that waterway to navigation was vital for the British—otherwise, they would remain isolated deep inside a hostile countryside without reliable supply lines. Washington recognized the military noose into which Howe had stuck his head, but he sorely needed reinforcements from the Northern Department to sustain what amounted to a blockade of Philadelphia. In the end, though, Howe's combined fleet and army were too much for the Americans. They overpowered the string of defensive posts along the river, removed water obstacles, and reached Philadelphia's wharves with resupply vessels in late November.

With winter nearing, Sir William tried once more to bring Washington to battle. When that failed, he withdrew his men into winter quarters behind Philadelphia's defenses. Washington, for his part, chose Valley Forge, a defensible site west of Philadelphia, as winter quarters for his men. It was far enough away from the enemy to be secure but close enough to oblige the British to keep up their guard. Continentals began arriving there on December 19 and started building huts, for the open ground provided no other shelter.

The Americans' own supply situation was desperate. Rations were extremely short and winter clothing was practically nonexistent. The quartermaster general, Thomas Mifflin, had never been very effective, and for months had done nothing at all, other than conspire against Washington. Moreover, the Congress, after appointing Mifflin to the Board of War, had not named a replacement.

Washington was thus obliged to be his own supply officer. The Congress authorized him to seize what he needed from citizens in the area. When he resisted taking that draconian course, congressmen chastised him for being too squeamish. That chiding resolution, gloated James Lovell to fellow Massachusetts schemer Samuel Adams, "was meant to rap a demi-God over the knuckles." It was clearly going to be a terrible winter for the men and a galling one for their commander.

Not all Americans understood the trying circumstances. Pennsylvania's legislature complained publicly about the fact that Washington was closing down the year's campaigning while the enemy occupied part of their state. That criticism elicited one of the strongest responses the commanding general ever penned. "I can assure those gentlemen that it is a much easier and less distressing thing to draw remonstrances in a comfortable room by a good fireside than to occupy a cold bleak hill and sleep under frost and snow without clothes or blankets. However, although they seem to have little feeling for the naked, distressed soldiers, I feel superabundantly for them, and from my soul pity those miseries which it is neither in my power to relieve or prevent."

It was in that combative mindset that Washington met Thomas Conway when he rode into camp. One can imagine his irritation when the arrogant Frenchman announced his promotion and new role as inspector general. The commanding general deemed that appointment "extraordinary," and dealt with Conway by simply ignoring him. Confounded, Conway withdrew from headquarters to sulk and contemplate his next steps.

Gates's letter blaming someone (Hamilton?) for stealing his private correspondence reached Washington's desk at about that time. Reading it, the harried commander in chief might have permitted himself a wee smirk of satisfaction. He responded with exquisite calmness, informing the commander of the Northern Department that the person who had leaked the contents of his mail had been none other than his own aide-de-camp, James Wilkinson. (The fury unleashed by that disclosure led to bitter words between Gates and Wilkinson, and almost to a duel.) Then, observing that Gates had provided the Congress a copy of his message, Washington said he would be obliged to do the same in order to keep the delegates fully informed.

With Conway sidelined, Gates on notice, and the Congress made officially aware of the situation, Washington had deftly begun to let the air out of the cabal. Alexander Hamilton later wrote that the plot failed because "it unmasked its batteries too soon." That is, the intrigue was exposed in its formative stage before it was ready to withstand public scrutiny.

At the turn of the year, unbeknownst to Mifflin or anyone else who might have clamped down on his impetuosity, Conway wrote the commanding general a couple of near-ranting letters. At one point he sarcastically rated Washington as being on par with Frederick the Great; at another he compared him to an admiral who had never been to sea; at yet another he admitted to making insulting comments in his letter to Gates, but berated the commander in chief for launching an "odious and tyrannical inquisition" after intercepting private mail. Washington did not react strongly to the wild missives, other than to send at least one of them along to the

Congress, stating flatly that Conway was "a man I deem my enemy." That was an unmistakable way of informing the representatives that they could anticipate scant value from the work of the army's new inspector general.

At that moment the cabal had passed its zenith. It could only subside thereafter. The work of the plotters was all but certain to become too widely known—the Congress was demonstrably unable to keep anything secret and Washington's admirers (including a vast majority of army officers, as events were to show) would spread the word rapidly among themselves. And in fact the gist of the scheme did come quickly to light, along with the names of several of the leading schemers, in particular Thomas Mifflin.

The plan to prod Washington into resigning and boost Gates as his successor collapsed of its own weight once it was exposed. Support for General Washington came from the military, from outside government, and, not least, from inside the Congress itself. For one, Henry Laurens, the president at the time, came down strongly on the side of Washington and worked to terminate the intrigue. Patrick Henry was typical of most when he wrote to assure Washington "of that estimation in which the public hold you," and to label Mifflin and others of his ilk "enemies to America." Almost all of those involved in the movement rapidly scurried to distance themselves from it and any repercussions.

The unmasked plot caused thinking men everywhere to ask, "If not Washington, who?" Certainly not Horatio Gates, whose conniving personality was fast becoming evident. Indeed, there was no answer. George Washington was the indispensable man. The failed attempt to unseat the Virginian had left him more firmly in control than ever.

Thomas Conway paid the steepest price for the failed conspiracy. While Mifflin and others disavowed involvement and got away mostly untarnished, Conway was tarred indelibly. Nathanael Greene stated succinctly what most observers thought: "General Conway is a man of much intrigue and little judgment." Later that spring Conway again threatened to resign. The Congress, to his utter astonishment, promptly accepted the resignation. After losing part of his jaw in a duel with a Washington supporter, he returned to France.

When General Gates arrived in Pennsylvania to assume his duties as president of the Board of War, on January 19, he found the movement to replace Washington was in tatters and the players in retreat or denial. He quickly distanced himself from the aborted effort and immersed himself in the work of the board. However, his once close relationship with Washington was damaged beyond repair.

The board, controlled by men not inclined to be supportive of the commander in chief, was a remnant of the cabal. Desirous of avoiding further conflict with the commanding general, Gates turned the members' attention to a pet project of his: an "irruption into Canada." Reasoning that the defeat of Burgoyne had left the potential fourteenth state vulnerable to attack, the board forged a plan to strike northward from Albany. The Congress granted approval. The Marquis de Lafayette would command the invasion (it was thought he could win over the French inhabitants), with Conway second in command. Lafayette accepted the mission, but refused to take Conway as his deputy. Washington, who had not been consulted, frowned on the project as infeasible in the midst of winter, but otherwise merely stepped aside to let events take their course.

When Lafayette reached Albany, he found to his great consternation that the board's planning had been egregiously deficient. Virtually nothing had been done to enable the offensive to proceed. Units were not available, nor were supplies. Philip Schuyler and Benedict Arnold, both experienced veterans of campaigning in that region, told him that attempting an invasion at that time of year was ludicrous, even if resources had been ready. Those two almost surely told Lafayette their low opinion of Gates, an opinion he already held in the aftermath of the cabal. Embarrassed for having accepted command of a non-invasion, the young Frenchman returned to join Washington. He loudly blamed the board for "recommending a measure of such consequence without certain assurance of the means."

The Congress agreed. More than a few members had grown disenchanted with the victor of Saratoga. In April, Gates was relieved of his board responsibilities and was sent back to the now-idle Northern Department. The Board of War ceased to be an alternative to the command of General Washington.

By May, when Benedict Arnold arrived in Valley Forge, the Revolutionary War stood on the verge of entering a new phase. France had formed an alliance with the United States, altering the strategic equation dramatically in favor of the Americans. The operational arena, too, saw vast improvements. The long-suffering soldiers of the Continental Army had emerged from the rigors of that terrible winter healthier and more professional than ever. Washington had filled the vacant post of quartermaster general with his most able subordinate, Nathanael Greene—and positive effects were immediately evident. Under the tutelage of Baron von Steuben, who had replaced Conway as inspector general, patriot units were trained and ready. At long last Americans would be more than competent to stand up to Germans and Englishmen on the field of battle. It was the dawn of a new day

It was a new day in another important way. The internal troubles of the past winter were history. Washington later wrote of the cabal: "It appeared in general, that General Gates was to be exalted, on the ruin of my reputation and influence. This I am authorised to say, from undeniable facts in my possession. . . . General Mifflin, it is commonly supposed, bore the second part in the Cabal; and General Conway, I know was a very Active and malignant Partisan; but I have good reasons to believe that their machinations have recoiled most sensibly upon themselves."

Conway was returning to France, Gates was banished to a distant post, Mifflin was no longer on the Board of War, detractors of Washington were few and mostly quiet. The Congress, while drawn by force of habit to interject itself occasionally into operational affairs, was henceforth generally inclined to leave those matters to the commander in chief. The Virginian would remain in unchallenged command of the Continental Army for the remainder of the war.

CHAPTER FIFTEEN

DIFFERENT ROADS

———◆———

MAJOR GENERAL ARNOLD'S RETURN TO ACTIVE DUTY cheered the soldiers in Valley Forge. Many of the veterans there had personally witnessed his valor under fire, and the rest knew him well by reputation. The fighting general's arrival brought "great joy to the army," recorded Henry Dearborn, who had fought beside him at Quebec and in the battles of Saratoga. No one was more pleased than the commander in chief himself.

Washington could not have been happy, though, to find that the redoubtable warrior remained too incapacitated to take to the field. It was clear that any fighting in 1778 would be done without Arnold's participation. That was particularly unfortunate for the army—a clash of arms was imminent, and proven combat leadership would be a crucial commodity.

By the time Arnold reached headquarters, on May 21, it was evident to all that the enemy would soon evacuate Philadelphia.

Lieutenant General Sir Henry Clinton, who had replaced Sir William Howe, had the galling mission of withdrawing from that hard-won city. The French alliance with the United States had abruptly altered the strategic equation, forcing the British to consolidate their forces. Sir Henry was planning to move as much equipment as possible by sea to New York City, and to send invalids and non-combatants the same way. He had insufficient shipping to transport the bulk of his fighting forces, so they would march overland across New Jersey. General Washington, buoyed by the new circumstances, and boasting a much improved army after the period of intensive training at Valley Forge, was eager to engage.

Washington appointed Arnold to be the military commander of the Philadelphia region. One would be hard-pressed to find a worse personnel decision made by Washington in the entire war. While it was true that the position called for an officer of high rank and prestige, and would not force the hobbled veteran onto the battlefield, it also required exquisite patience, supreme tact, and unusual political sensitivity, all traits conspicuously missing in Arnold's personality. Moreover, Arnold, the once supreme patriot, was a changed man.

Day after interminable day during his long convalescence, Benedict Arnold had time to ponder his years of service to the Revolution. Old slights and troubles flooded his memory: acrimony at Fort Ticonderoga; the contemptible way Massachusetts had treated him after he had seized control of Lake Champlain; political indecisiveness that had lost Canada; the promotion of lesser men over him; being belittled by members of Congress; the two-facedness of Horatio Gates; a constant stream of slander from jealous men; risking his life over and over. And what had all of it earned him?

Crippled for life while others received accolades he deserved. Well, no more. From that point on he would place his own interests before those of the cause. The disillusioned major general arriving in a wagon at Valley Forge had little in common with the captain who had marched in full patriotic fervor from New Haven to Boston three years earlier.

Philadelphia was changed as well. Seven months of British occupation had left scars both social and physical on America's largest city. The physical damage was most readily apparent. A wartime army is not the most careful of tenants. Areas at the edge of town had suffered in particular, where barricades had been raised and soldiers had been quartered. Campfires and cook stoves consumed fence rails, furniture, and other burnable items. Broken windows gaped open, doors hung from one hinge. Debris left by hastily departing regiments littered streets and gardens. But that could be easily fixed. The social wounds were not so easy to see or to heal.

Many Philadelphians had supported the occupiers. The presence of the king's troops had emboldened closet loyalists to emerge. Pacifist Quakers, opposed to the rebellion as a matter of principle, had cooperated with the British. Opportunists, seeking profit from whatever source, dealt with royal purchasing agents. Many saw nothing amiss in social fraternization with the enemy— from matrons who had English officers in for dinner to young ladies who happily accepted invitations to balls.

Outside the occupied city paced angry men, outraged by such activities and eager to return to punish the offenders. General Clinton, knowing that loyalists would pay a terrible price, planned to take away some three thousand of them aboard his ships. But plenty would remain to face retribution. Fear permeated the City of Brotherly Love.

So did politics. The Continental Congress planned to return to its old site in the State House, which it would share with the government of Pennsylvania. Those two bodies, with their different perspectives on the war, were bound to clash. In addition, the collapse of the Conway Cabal had left bruised egos and resentment. Representatives Samuel Adams, Richard Henry Lee, Joseph Reed, and James Lovell, for instance, had been among the ringleaders of the cabal. Outside the Congress itself but active in the area were others who had been agitators in the anti-Washington movement, men like Benjamin Rush and Thomas Mifflin. Washington was now beyond the reach of their spite, but General Arnold had no such immunity. A protégé of George Washington and a certifiable enemy of Horatio Gates, he could serve as a surrogate target.

Arnold, however, was oblivious to the political quicksand he was wading into. He had his mind on money. There was profit to be made in his new position. Lots of it. That became his focus even as he waited at Valley Forge for the British to leave.

By mid-June, General Clinton had sent his shipping down the Delaware. He had also crossed the river with his land force of 10,000 soldiers, field artillery, and a supply train of 1,500 wagons. Having to clear roads and repair bridges that had been obstructed or destroyed by the patriots, the heavily laden force could not march rapidly.

Washington, however, moved at once. He had with him 13,500 troops, not counting hundreds of militiamen roaming New Jersey. Less weighted down by wagons, the patriots could move faster than their foe. They were also solidly trained, well equipped, and highly spirited. Washington wanted a fight; Clinton wanted to escape.

Washington convened a council of war on June 24. The results were not what he had anticipated.

Major General Charles Lee, released from captivity in a prisoner exchange, had rejoined the army just weeks before. He argued that intercepting and attacking Clinton's forces was too risky. Besides, he said, a battle was unnecessary. The entry of France meant that the war was as good as won. Many of the generals, who still thought of Lee as having a brilliant military mind, went along with his argument. Anthony Wayne, Lafayette, and Nathanael Greene disagreed, but the consensus was against attacking. Alexander Hamilton, taking notes at the meeting, fumed afterward that only a "body of midwives" could have taken refuge in such a cowardly recommendation. Washington decided to commit a strong detachment to nibble at Clinton's left flank. Charles Lee demanded, by virtue of rank, to command the detachment. Washington reluctantly concurred.

By June 27, the advance guard of five thousand patriots supported by twelve cannons had closed on the British, who were halted near Monmouth, New Jersey. The British were exhausted from hard marching with heavy packs in sweltering heat and humidity. But Lee issued no plan of attack. On the morning of June 28, after receiving reports the British were marching, Lee ordered his troops forward.

Clinton, however, took part of his army, wheeled around, and struck the approaching Americans. With no plan and no leadership from Lee, the patriots fell back in a three-mile long retreat. George Washington, galloping forward toward the sound of the guns, quickly sized up the situation, confronted Lee, chewed him out in thunderous anger, relieved him of command, and took charge himself.

The commander in chief threw in units to hold the British while he formed a defensive line on strong terrain farther back. Charging redcoats were stopped short. Numerous attempts to break the newly established American line failed. Clinton then wisely pulled back, only to find his foe coming after him. Finally, nightfall and sheer exhaustion in the ranks on both sides stalled the action. In the dark the British commander was able to move his forces off the battlefield.

In the battle he had not wanted, Clinton suffered more than a thousand casualties, with up to 250 dead from battle wounds and sunstroke. Scores more deserted, especially Germans. About a hundred patriots died from bullets and heat. Although seriously frightened, the British made good their escape. Americans, well led after Washington took over from Lee, had fought them to a draw. Monmouth was a landmark in the war—it was the first battle in which Americans stood toe-to-toe with Europeans in the open, giving as good as they got.

By June 30, Sir Henry was at Sandy Hook and safety. A few days later the Royal Navy had transported all survivors to New York City. Washington marched his army to the Hudson River and took positions in an arc north of the city. The opposing armies then occupied basically the same ground they had held in late 1776, before Howe had crossed into New Jersey. Their circumstances were reversed, however. In 1776 the Americans had been struggling to survive; now the redcoats huddled worriedly behind their barricades.

George Washington, taking stock of the changed situation, could not forebear a touch of gloating. "It is not a little pleasing, nor less wonderful to contemplate, that after two years of maneuvering and undergoing the strangest vicissitudes that perhaps ever attended any one contest since creation, both armies are brought back to the very point they set out from."

He must also have been pleased to be finally rid of Charles Lee. Convicted by a court-martial for failures at Monmouth, Lee was eventually cashiered from the army. There remained no contenders for the top leadership in the Continental Army— Washington would be the unchallenged commanding general for the rest of the war.

—•—

While Washington chased Clinton across New Jersey, Arnold settled into Philadelphia, where he intended to live on a grand scale. He moved into the elegant Penn mansion, which only days before had been the headquarters of the British commander. That showy choice gave an unfortunate first impression that the new military commander intended to adopt the regal lifestyle of the British occupiers.

Arnold, however, was blind to such impressions, or maybe he just did not care. He fully intended to take advantage of his new post to restore some portion of his personal wealth, so severely depleted by the war. To that end, in fact, he had not even waited until he moved into the Penn mansion.

While still at Valley Forge, he had met with one Robert Shewell, a shady Philadelphia merchant suspected of having loyalist leanings. That alone raised eyebrows. Shewell had access to wares certain to bring a handsome profit if his ship, *Charming Nancy*, could safely evade American privateers waiting to pounce on any trading vessel leaving Philadelphia. Arnold could help. He signed a pass—a paper of safe conduct—for the ship.[1]

Prior to the Revolutionary War, smuggling was considered practically legal in New England. Avoiding onerous fiscal laws promulgated by a despised government was essentially normal practice. Benedict Arnold, merchant and trader, had been a leading practitioner of that sly art. So evading such regulations established by another government he had come to despise—that of the United States of America, the Continental Congress—was but a small step for him in the spring of 1778.

Only days after assuming his duties in Philadelphia, Arnold entered into a secret arrangement to obtain and sell surplus items confiscated largely from stocks abandoned by the British or left by departing loyalists. That was certainly unethical, if not outright illegal, and set the pattern for Arnold's avaricious and nefarious activities.

Openly exploiting his position and adopting an in-your-face attitude, Arnold quickly became a controversial figure. He irritated the Congress, clashed with Pennsylvania radicals who wanted to punish or hang collaborators, and thumbed his nose at the radicals by living lavishly and entertaining often, including among his guests those who had fraternized with British officers.

Foremost among his radical critics was Joseph Reed, who transferred his animosity from Washington to Arnold. Arnold struck him more and more as a budding military dictator, the dreaded "man on horseback." Never mind that the general rode in a carriage, not on a horse—it was an especially ostentatious carriage.

Summer passed rapidly. Silas Deane, Arnold's old mentor, returned from France under a cloud of suspicion for alleged impro-

---

[1]   Raiders grabbed *Charming Nancy* anyway and took her to a port in New Jersey, pending judicial resolution of the validity of Arnold's pass. Later, in an attempt to retrieve a share of the cargo, Arnold sent a train of military wagons to fetch goods back to Philadelphia where they could be sold. Issuing a pass for *Charming Nancy* and using the wagons in that way would be only two among many blatantly self-serving acts marking his troubled tenure in Philadelphia, but those two would return to haunt him.

prieties there, which did not help the military commander's standing in the Congress. A French ambassador arrived, reminding the patriots how Arnold's gallantry had fostered the alliance. Arnold considered becoming an admiral, which would permit him to enrich himself as a privateer. Then he worked through General Philip Schuyler and others to convince state officials to offer him a vast parcel of land in northern New York, so that he could join the landed gentry. Schemes to profit from his position as military governor continued. Autumn came and went.

Meanwhile, acrimony flourished. In addition to problems of his own creation, Arnold found himself often caught in the crossfire between federal and state officials. An informant told Nathanael Greene that, although complaints leveled at General Arnold were "too absurd to deserve a serious answer," he was nevertheless growing "unpopular among the men in power in Congress, and among those of this state in general."

When Joseph Reed became the president of the Supreme Executive Council of the State of Pennsylvania in December 1778, Benedict Arnold's days as military commander were numbered. Personal attacks against the general mushroomed. Tired of the thankless job of military governor, Arnold talked with Washington about stepping down.

He also continued to press sympathetic leading citizens of New York to make him a land baron. In early 1779, just as Arnold was about to leave for a visit to New York, Joseph Reed published a list of eight charges against him, some valid, some ludicrous, but all in one way or the other accusing him of malfeasance in command. Arnold canceled the trip. He would have to stay to defend himself.

That near-miss victory at Monmouth had sharpened General Washington's desire to smite his foe. Hardly had he placed his army astride the Hudson before joyous news arrived, informing him that a chance to attack was at hand. Paris and London had broken off diplomatic relations in March and had gone to war in June—and a French fleet commanded by the Comte d'Estaing stood offshore in New York waters. French warships overwhelmingly outnumbered and outgunned English vessels bottled up in the confines of the city's harbor. Moreover, Admiral d'Estaing had several thousand marines aboard transports. A crushing victory seemed to be within grasp.

The admiral, though, was timorous. A general assigned duties as an admiral, d'Estaing did not like the looks of the sandbar his deep-draft warships would have to cross to get into the harbor, and he was uneasy about a naval slugfest inside such a constricted area. Anxious lest he lose the opportunity to work with a friendly fleet, Washington turned to an alternative objective, overwhelming an isolated garrison in Newport, Rhode Island, manned mostly by Hessians. Agreeing to that plan, Admiral d'Estaing set sail for Newport while Washington sent reinforcements to Major General John Sullivan, who commanded there.

The battle opened with great expectations of a smashing allied success, but British daring and unfriendly weather conspired to bring defeat instead. In a desperate effort to relieve his forces at Newport, General Clinton boldly sent his smaller fleet to engage the French. Admiral d'Estaing quickly re-boarded his marines and sailed out to meet the threat, confident of warding off the weaker British flotilla. At that crucial moment, however, a ferocious storm struck, scattering and battering both fleets, thereby ending all thoughts of a battle at sea. British vessels limped back to New York while d'Estaing headed for Boston to refit. General Sullivan, left suddenly uncovered in an awkwardly extended position, had to retreat precipitously to avoid disaster. Despite American entreaties, the French sailed south to the Caribbean as soon as repairs were made, ending hopes for further combined attacks that year. The setback was especially galling for thoughts of what might have been.

Still, in all, 1778 was a busy and on the whole an upbeat year for patriots. In addition to instigating battles at Monmouth and Newport, Americans had aggressively lashed out elsewhere. The state of Virginia sent George Rogers Clark west that year in an effort to combat Indian forays against frontier settlements. John Paul Jones carried the war to England, cruising the island kingdom's waters and raiding coastal areas. A band of frontiersmen sailed down the Mississippi River in an armed riverboat, raising havoc as they went. Major General Robert Howe led a bold but ultimately unsuccessful attempt to conquer East Florida. The Congress proposed yet again an invasion of Canada. A busy year indeed.

Late that fall spies brought into headquarters indications that Henry Clinton was preparing to launch a campaign. But where? Although evidence pointed toward some southern clime, Washington could not fathom why. Only three objectives, he reasoned, could be decisive: destroy the Continental Army, defeat the French navy, or capture Fortress West Point. But whatever Sir Henry had in mind appeared to be to the south, away from West Point and the Continental Army. That would be folly, the commander in chief opined, for the "possession of our towns, while we have an army in the field, will avail them of little." To be victorious, "it is our arms, not defenseless towns, they have to subdue." If the enemy does head south, he said, moving away from patriot land forces but closer to the reach of French warships, they will encounter "inevitable ruin." The accuracy of the Virginian's assessment was borne out three years later at a southern place called Yorktown.

But Henry Clinton did not see things the same way—he did in fact go south to seize Savannah, Georgia, on December 29, 1778.

At year's end, Washington rode to Philadelphia to confer with the Congress on campaign plans for 1779. What he saw there astounded him, leading him to exclaim that he would never "be again surprised at anything." Coming from the army in the field, which was saddled with shortages of all kinds and where men had to scrounge for food, he found the wealth of the capital city shocking. Soldiers needed shoes; lackeys in the city were well shod. Soldiers went hungry many a day; pantries in the city had full shelves. Soldiers remained unpaid; affluence marked life in the city. Thinking of his brave, loyal, suffering men, the commanding general railed at the unfairness of it all: "Speculation, peculation, and an insatiable thirst for riches seem to have got the better of every other consideration and almost of every order of men."

Washington did not enjoy his stay in Philadelphia—society was too fast and the Congress was too slow. With his winter headquarters located not far away in New Jersey, he could keep in touch, but he grew increasingly impatient at the torpid pace of planning in Philadelphia. Believing the army needed his "constant attention and presence" lest it crumble under the weight of its impoverished circumstances, he chafed at the manifest inefficiency of the central government. Important matters were "postponed from day to day, from week to week," while members focused on petty disputes and "personal quarrels." It was evident to the general, who had himself first been a congressman, that the "ablest and best men" had departed, leaving the Continental Congress a faint shadow of its former self. Finally, by mid-February the commanding general and the lawmakers had hammered out a broad concept of operations for 1779. Washington had endured an uneasy period of nearly two months. Nathanael Greene noted that the luxury of Philadelphia had given the commander in chief "infinitely more pain than pleasure."

Quite surprisingly, Washington apparently took little notice of Benedict Arnold's expansive lifestyle. While he often fumed about "speculators, various tribes of money-makers, and stockjobbers of all denominations," he never aimed those barbs at Arnold. Maybe he assumed that the Connecticut general was living on his private fortune, for his prewar wealth had been no secret. Perhaps in the social whirl so obvious in Philadelphia, Arnold did not stick out all that much. Surely no credible word of the major general's shady business deals reached the commander in chief. Even if he heard complaints, the Virginian's previous negative experiences with Joseph Reed would have predisposed him to discount any of his rabid charges, some of which were in fact laughable on their very face. Maybe he simply cut the disabled hero a bit of slack. For whatever reason, the commanding general left the city either unaware of or unconcerned with the looming clash between local radicals and his military commandant.

In addition to his distaste for the unseemly pace of Philadelphia society, General Washington rode back to headquarters filled with disappointment over the military outlook for the months ahead.

Despite all the visible evidence of pockets of plenty in various places, the long war (entering its fifth campaigning season) had upset the normal financial equilibrium. Inflation ravaged the economy. Hard money was scarce, and printing still more paper money hurt rather than helped. The marching and counter-marching of armies hindered the free movement of goods. States had less and less ability to raise funds to support the Continental Army, never mind their declining will to do so. The Congress, able only to ask the states for money, not to tax them, could not afford to strengthen the army. As a matter of fact, merely maintaining it was problematic. On top of all that, the outlook for outside help had turned grim. The alliance with France, after having generated an initial period of soaring optimism, had failed so far to provide the anticipated victories. General Washington would be obliged to await developments. Perhaps the arrival of a French army, perhaps the entry of Spain in the war, perhaps the return of Admiral d'Estaing with his marines, perhaps a decision in London to withdraw. . . . The initiative did not belong to Americans.

Acting passively ran counter to Washington's aggressive nature. Nevertheless, he lamented, "when I consider the necessity of economy in our present circumstances," there was no other way. "It is to be regretted that our prospect of any capital offensive operation is so slender that we seem in a manner to be driven to the necessity of . . . remaining entirely on the defensive." For him, the spring of 1779 would be one of waiting.

That was definitely not the case with Benedict Arnold. He found himself fighting on two fronts. There was, of course, the ongoing struggle of wills with local politicians headed by Joseph Reed. But predating even that longstanding problem was an affair of the heart. The indefatigable warrior had fallen in love.

Beneath the outward aplomb and pride of his arrival in Philadelphia in June 1778, the new military commandant's ego was hurting. He was suffering the pangs of rejection. Betsy DeBlois, the alluring teenager from Boston, had turned him down. Those pangs would not last long, however. Within two weeks he encountered vivacious Margaret (Peggy) Shippen. Visions of Betsy evaporated like spring snow in Georgia.

During his short stay in Philadelphia when the First Continental Congress had met there in 1774, Benedict had been a married man and Peggy Shippen had been a precocious fourteen-year-old. Now he was a lovelorn widower and she was a dazzling young woman of eighteen. She was everything he wanted in a wife. Besides being enchanting and sensuous, the desirable young woman was from a well-known and well-to-do family. Smitten at once, he lost no time in paying court.

The general approached courtship as he approached battle: attack, attack, attack. Soon his aggressive pursuit of the charming maiden became the talk of the town, giving wags a grand opportunity to overlay martial expressions on matters amorous. "I must tell you that Cupid has given our little general a more mortal wound than all the host of Britons could," said one matron. Word was out that Peggy "intends to surrender soon," wrote a Shippen family friend. "I thought the fort would not hold out long." His "close siege" would be victorious if "perseverance and a regular attack" could carry the day.

It appears that Peggy put up a most feeble defense. She rather liked the attention of America's Hannibal, and found herself more reciprocating his advances than resisting. By September, Arnold, a lovesick swain of the first order, was penning gushy sentiments alluding to a "union of hearts" and speaking of his "tender and ardent passion." Never one to leave forces uncommitted in a close encounter, he borrowed extensively from a letter he had composed in a less hurried time. Over half of one love letter to Peggy Shippen was copied word for word from one he had sent to Betsy DeBlois five months before. The words worked better this time; it was not long before Peggy was ready for matrimony. The last obstacle Arnold had to overcome was convincing her father to sanction the marriage.

Judge Edward Shippen had undertaken to weather the war by following a neutral course, neither fully supporting nor fully abandoning either side. An eminent position in prewar Pennsylvania and a substantial family fortune enabled him to tread such a narrow course, but not without consequences. Radical patriots, holding that anyone not for the cause was against it, deemed the judge to be a borderline loyalist, if not an outright supporter of King George III. It did not help that his daughter was often seen on the arms of young British officers during the occupation. In contemplating those circumstances the judge may have seen a certain amount of security in a marriage between Peggy and the famous general. No one could accuse the twice-wounded warrior hero of loyalist sentiments. For his part, Benedict Arnold did not care one whit what Joseph Reed and his ilk thought about the Shippen family.

Still, Judge Shippen had qualms. Was the handicapped officer healthy enough? The extent of damage to his slowly healing leg was widely discussed, a tantalizing topic of gossip. Would a May-December union work for Peggy? She was a passionate young woman not yet beyond her teen years, while he was more than twice her age and the father of three. Was the Connecticut merchant a financially sound suitor? To marry into the Shippen family one had to be a man of proven substance.

Arnold finessed the first point by relying less and less on crutches, providing evidence of the continued strengthening of his left leg. Peggy herself settled the second issue with her obviously strong attraction to the charismatic and vibrant suitor. Always the consummate businessman, Benedict knew instinctively how to handle the third matter. The likelihood of becoming one of the landed gentry in the upper reaches of New York was part of the solution, showing his potential for long-term success. It remained only to demonstrate the reach of his current wealth. He did that in dramatic fashion by purchasing the most imposing mansion available on the outskirts of Philadelphia, Mount Pleasant. John Adams had called the estate "the most elegant seat in Pennsylvania," and so it was. When Arnold gave Mount Pleasant to Peggy in a pre-nuptial arrangement, the last barrier to their marriage was removed. The couple set their wedding date for April 8, 1779.

Judge Shippen may have been won over, but Joseph Reed was not. Watching the patriot hero's courtship of the girl with loyalist ties who had been a fixture in British society during the occupation had hardened Reed's animosity.

———•·•———

Meanwhile, on the battlefront, not much happened in North America in the spring of 1779. Fighting was essentially at a stand-still. Neither Washington nor Henry Clinton had the wherewithal to act offensively in the absence of reinforcements. The American waited astride the Hudson River, hoping against hope for the arrival of French forces; the Briton waited in New York City, antic-ipating new regiments due in from England. They simply sat star-ing at one another as the somnolent weeks passed.

George Washington could not abide inactivity. The fire of rebel-lion fades unless it is continually stoked by combat. He felt to his core that momentum was either maintained or lost. Accordingly, he assembled a striking force powerful enough to attack several hostile tribes in the west, planning to commit it as soon as he was certain that Admiral d'Estaing would not be sailing north that spring or summer. In May, after concluding that the French fleet would remain in the south, he launched the western expedition. Patriots would at least be attacking *somewhere*.

That same month Sir Henry attempted a bold stroke aimed at grabbing West Point and precipitating a battle with the Old Fox. On one point he and Washington both agreed: Fortress West Point, where the Hudson River sliced a crooked path through the high-lands, was the strategic key to the war, the center of gravity around which everything else revolved. Retaining that bastion was an absolute imperative for the Americans. Seizing it was a prime goal for the British. The problem was, if well defended, the fortress was all but impregnable. Aware that several thousand fresh reserves were aboard ships crossing the Atlantic, Clinton hatched a complex scheme to snatch the grand prize.

First, he sent a large portion of his troops on transports to operate along the Virginia coast. That was a feint to lull patriots into complacency. The Americans would surely let down their guard once they realized that the British garrison in New York City had been so weakened that any kind of offensive operation from that base was clearly out of the question. The movement southward would also divert Washington's attention from the highlands. Then, at sea and unseen, those forces would dash back to New York to link up with the transatlantic reinforcements. With that combined armada appearing suddenly on the scene, Clinton would rush up the river on the wings of surprise to overpower the unready defenses before the Americans could react. The Englishman believed that Washington, forced to fight to try to save West Point, could be drawn into battle "in an angle between the mountains and the river, on terms replete with risk on his part and little or none on mine."

The scheme did not work. The ocean crossing was much delayed, and the soldiers, fever-ridden, were in no condition to conduct combat operations when they eventually arrived. Nevertheless, in the preparatory phase, redcoats did seize two small forts guarding King's Ferry, the primary patriot crossing site over the Hudson just south of the Hudson highlands. By controlling that site, Clinton obliged the American commander to shift his logistical activities to a more roundabout route farther north, a bother but hardly a decisive stroke.

However, by leaving troops out of close supporting range from elements in New York City, Clinton handed Washington an opening to take offensive action. It also set the stage for one of the long war's most splendid little battles.

———•••———

While Benedict Arnold was waging his winning campaign for the hand of Peggy Shippen, he was fighting a losing rear-guard action against Joseph Reed. Postponement of his quest to secure the proprietorship of immense tracts of land in upper New York was only the first setback.

February 1779 opened with the two men locked in a vitriolic war of words. Even before announcing any allegations, Reed had petitioned the Congress to remove Arnold from command "until the charges against him are examined." Congressmen cautiously asked to see just what charges he was referring to. When Reed did present a document listing eight complaints, readers might have wondered what all the fuss was about. Most hardly sounded all that bad, much less criminal. They ranged from granting passes he was not authorized to issue to showing disrespect toward state officials. Arnold promptly asked the Congress to order a court-martial to address all eight. That court, he stated, would reveal the Pennsylvania council's claims for what they were: "as gross a prostitution of power as ever disgraced a weak and wicked administration."

Reed rejected the idea of giving the military jurisdiction to rule on state matters. He thus raised the sensitive issue of state versus federal rights. The Congress, unsure of its ground and wanting to avoid a struggle with its host state government, did what political bodies do when faced with tough choices: it appointed a committee to investigate the matter. A hearing was set for March 5.

Finding it harder to produce evidence than to levy charges, Reed continued to attack Arnold in print, piling up still more allegations, to include those made some two years earlier by John Brown. Exasperated that his old nemesis had surfaced yet again, Arnold acidly noted that the Congress had long ago discredited those claims. The squabbling grew nastier and more public.

At the hearing, General Arnold served as his own attorney. Aggressively refuting all charges, he was aided immensely by the paucity of evidence mustered against him. (Ironically, he was in fact not only guilty of all eight allegations but had committed even more unethical or illegal acts than Reed had uncovered.) The committee cleared Arnold of six charges its members believed they had jurisdiction over. Claiming that the other two—using army wagons for private business and sending a soldier to summon a barber—were military matters, they referred them to be heard by a court-martial. Arnold was ecstatic. The results seemed to exonerate him. Excitedly, he began to make plans to move on.

"A committee of Congress having ruled in my favor," he informed Washington, he could now step down from the Philadelphia post. The still-weak leg needed more rehabilitation. "As soon as my wounds will permit, I shall be happy to take a command in the line of the army," he added.

But Pennsylvania authorities were not about to concede. The findings merely made Joseph Reed more determined than ever. The debate between state and nation escalated. Reed accused the Congress, led by Arnold's New York supporters, of attempting a whitewash. The sovereign state of Pennsylvania would not accept the outcome. What is more, Reed had the power to withhold support from the central government, such as refusing to call out the militia when asked. His radical threats raised the stakes.

Shaken by the intensely negative reaction, the Congress met to chart a course out of the brouhaha. In a lengthy session, marked by arguments deemed by one member to be "peevish and childish," that body voted to override its own committee's report in order to appease Pennsylvania. Political considerations trumped the reputation or rights of any one person. With Joseph Reed's concurrence—or connivance—representatives ruled that General Arnold was to be tried by court-martial on a total of four charges from the original list of eight. The two additional counts were providing a pass for *Charming Nancy* and making personal purchases from closed shops. The Congress forwarded the accusations to Washington on April 3. The commander in chief set May 1 as the trial date.

Although the change aggravated him, Arnold accepted it stoically enough. He had originally asked for a military panel to examine all eight accusations; now a court would be looking into only four of them. Confident that he would prevail before a board of senior army officers, he turned his attention to a more pleasant event: his marriage.

In the parlor of Judge Edward Shippen's Philadelphia mansion, with only family and close friends in attendance, Benedict Arnold and Margaret Shippen exchanged vows on April 8, 1779. One of Peggy's sisters joked that the bride had been "Burgoyned" by the famous general. While Arnold took some time off for a brief honeymoon, Joseph Reed remained busy. He still did not have sufficient evidence to assure a conviction, and he distrusted the military anyway. Warning both the Congress and the commander in chief of his ability to withhold support if events did not unfold in a manner agreeable to him, he requested an indefinite postponement of the trial to permit him to gather more evidence. Arnold argued vehemently against waiting, saying that Reed would "use every artifice to delay the proceedings" because he lacked proof. (He also knew that he was guilty, and any delay increased the chances that some new information might surface.) The process had already dragged on for two months, he complained, and it was high time to end it.

Washington, trapped in the unhappy triangle of the Congress, Pennsylvania, and the maligned general, felt he had no choice but to agree to Reed's application for delay. Three days before the hearing would have started, Arnold received a brief note from the commanding general. "I find myself under a necessity of postponing your trial," he wrote, adding that he would explain later. Arnold was crushed. A feckless Congress he expected—but Washington too?

When days passed with no further word, Arnold grew increasingly nervous. Then his worst fear crashed in on him. A witness materialized, an officer who apparently had some specific evidence corroborating Reed's claims of fraudulent behavior. Shocked and distraught, the battler could contain himself no longer. "Delay in the present case is worse than death," he wrote in a shrill letter to Washington on May 5. "If your Excellency thinks me criminal, for heaven's sake let me be immediately tried and, if found guilty, executed."

Reminding the commander in chief that his own reputation had been slandered not so very long ago by "a set of artful, unprincipled men in office," he did not need to state the obvious fact that many of those who had participated in the Conway Cabal were now playing roles in the anti-Arnold plot. It was a shrewd statement designed to elicit support by showing that he and Washington had common enemies. Furthermore, he contended, such malicious treatment was unjust action against a true patriot.

"Having made every sacrifice of fortune and blood, and become a cripple in the service of my country, I little expected to meet the ungrateful returns I have received from my countrymen; but as Congress have stamped ingratitude as a current coin, I must take it."

At about the same time that he penned those self-pitying and hypocritical words, Benedict Arnold was crossing a decisive threshold. Having been driven by avarice ever since rejoining the army a year earlier, he now switched to an even more potent motivator. His long, futile search for vindication had finally turned into a quest for vengeance.

----·----

On May 10, 1779, a secret agent slipped into British headquarters in New York City. He had startling news for General Henry Clinton's newly appointed spymaster, Captain John André. A celebrated rebel leader was ready to defect.

Major General Benedict Arnold, America's Hannibal, was offering his services to the British.

CHAPTER SIXTEEN

STILLNESS
BEFORE THE STORM

———◆———

IN HIS WINSOME PEGGY, BENEDICT ARNOLD HAD NOT ONLY AN adoring young wife but also a surprisingly competent co-conspirator. She had been aware of the persistent drumfire of criticism against the general during the months of their courtship, and had sided with her man every step of the way. Her support deepened and hardened as the tirade escalated. What manner of men were these to so wickedly malign such a genuine American hero? From her faintly loyalist leaning it was but a slight shift to accept Arnold's utter contempt of the Congress and the Pennsylvania Supreme Executive Council. And just another small step to begin to think that their future might well be brighter under the British flag. Before they had been married a month, Benedict and Peggy had together crossed the line of loyalty. They would switch sides in the war.

Moreover, Peggy had an avenue for surreptitious contact with Sir Henry Clinton. Joseph Stansbury and John André were the vehicles. On the surface, Stansbury was a society merchant in Philadelphia whose business occasionally took him into New York City. In point of fact, though, he operated as an agent (a double agent?) in the shadowy back alleys of espionage. While Peggy probably did not know for certain that he was a spy, she did have faith that he could be trusted to convey a message behind enemy lines. How she came to believe that is not altogether clear, but a factor might well have been her close relationship with Captain John André, an officer on General Clinton's staff. He had recently been charged with overseeing clandestine affairs. During the British stay in Philadelphia, Peggy had become well acquainted with the young Englishman; at one point he had done a pen-and-ink sketch of her that exists today. She knew that Stansbury could reach André. He did so often for the young ladies of town who sent notes to their gallants from the occupation. Arnold, too, from knowledge gleaned in the performance of his duties as military commander, may have been able to ascertain that Stansbury could be counted on to be discreet. In the first week of May, he quietly summoned the merchant to his home.

Behind closed doors, the general gave the agent an extraordinary message he was to deliver orally to Captain André. Beyond his willingness to become a turncoat, Arnold would contrive to help Clinton gain a major victory over the Continental Army. He expected the British to arrange secure channels of communication, to let him know what they wanted him to do, and—not least importantly—to compensate him handsomely for the deadly risk he would be undertaking. It was an electric meeting that Stansbury would recall with clarity years later. He left at once on the long trip, reaching André's office on May 10.

The captain could hardly credit the words springing from the spy's mouth. Benedict Arnold, the best battlefield commander in rebel ranks, was offering to turn against his fellow revolutionaries. After a hurried conference with General Clinton, André sat down to write out a response. Stansbury was to memorize the instructions, make undecipherable notes to bolster his recall, and hasten back to Arnold.

"On our part we meet Monk's overtures with full reliance on his honorable intentions," André wrote. "Monk" had an inescapable meaning for educated Englishmen of that era. General George Monk, in the turmoil following the English Civil War and the death of Oliver Cromwell, had switched sides to help restore the monarchy, thereby earning renown and honors. It was a role Benedict Arnold relished for himself.

Continued André: Arnold could count on liberal compensation, including indemnity for losses of personal property. Furthermore, if he could arrange for the capture of "an obnoxious band of men" the British would prove generous beyond "his most sanguine hopes." In the meantime, General Clinton would anticipate receiving a steady stream of insider intelligence from his high-level mole in the rebel camp.

Messages back and forth were to be encoded using identical copies of a specified book, with words expressed in a set of three numbers. The first would designate a page, the second a line, and the third the position of the word on that line. It would also be wise, André thought, to send the coded messages written in invisible ink between the lines of apparently innocent letters from or to Peggy Arnold and some of her friends.

Burdened with the weight of his mission, Stansbury set out that very night to retrace his route to Philadelphia. In due time and caution, the agent sat down with the anxious general to deliver the British instructions. The course of treason was under way.

Arnold sent his first encoded message on May 21. Thus began a cumbersome dialogue lasting more than a year. The dangerous exchanges were fraught with delays, lost or destroyed messages, misunderstandings, and not a little distrust on both sides. Throughout, however, and rather surprisingly, the secret discussions were never compromised.

Arnold's earliest messages provided military intelligence, information on America's relationship with the French, analyses of patriot morale, and so forth. He also pressed the British to be specific regarding the amount of money they would pay him, a request they were at that time quite unwilling to meet.

Meanwhile, the war went on. Arnold left for headquarters in New Jersey, where his court-martial was to be held on June 1, 1779. This time it convened as scheduled. Once again Arnold conducted his own defense. A good part of the first day was spent in arguments over the composition of the panel itself, with Arnold complaining about the number of Pennsylvania officers sitting on it. He won that opening skirmish—but to no effect. That very night a military emergency forced another postponement. British forces had attacked up the Hudson River, threatening Fortress West Point. General Washington hastily threw his army in motion to concentrate it near that critical point. A court-martial, even of a senior officer, was a far lesser priority.

Glumly, Arnold waited. Weeks passed. Unfolding events continued to preclude a timely resumption of the trial. Benedict Arnold was angrier than ever. He was also consumed with disappointment in General Washington for what he deemed to be inconsiderate treatment from the one person who had always before supported him. He resumed his clandestine correspondence with the British.

———•———

Henry Clinton's abortive attempt to seize West Point had drawn George Washington to the Hudson highlands. Establishing his headquarters there and tucking his army in close, the American commander in chief prepared to defend the essential fortress.

It became obvious by the latter part of June that the British intended for the time being to do little more than remain in control of the major crossing site they had taken. They had strengthened the defenses at the terminals on both banks and had manned them with some of their best troops. Establishing that enclave right under the gaze of rebels holding the nearby mountains was an arrogant affront to patriot pride, a gesture of disdain all but daring George Washington to do anything about it. He took the dare.

Stony Point, the west bank terminus, was a rocky near-island jutting out into the river. With its steep granite sides soaring 150 feet above the water, it had the feel of a medieval castle. Approachable only from the land by a narrow causeway and marshy tidal shallows, it exuded an aura of invincibility. The British garrison felt secure, protected as they were by natural and man-made works and confident in their superior fighting capabilities. Washington thought otherwise—Henry Clinton had handed him an opportunity to strike back. "The works are formidable," he acknowledged, but not impregnable.

He assembled a hand-picked body of some 1,300 of his best troops, assigned Brigadier General "Mad Anthony" Wayne to lead them, and started preparing them for the specialized operation. The Continental Army's professional drillmaster, Baron von

Steuben, trained the men at West Point, many of them on the plain behind Fort Arnold. (That flat area would become a parade ground for future generations of cadets.) By mid-July the assaulting force was ready.

Approaching late at night on July 15, in what some have called the war's "boldest venture," Wayne assailed Stony Point head-on. Using only bayonets, the elite light infantrymen waded the marsh, breached the barricades, and roared into the fortification shortly after midnight, bayoneting anyone who resisted and shrieking, "The fort's our own!" It was all over in half an hour.

Americans had suffered a hundred casualties, and the British far more in killed and wounded. Almost five hundred prisoners were taken. Wayne sent a message to Washington, laconic in the extreme considering the smashing victory he had just gained: "The fort and garrison and Colonel Johnson are ours. Our officers and men behaved like men who are determined to be free."

Washington was elated. He knew full well that word of the triumph, racing across the land, would be a sorely needed tonic for the nation's sagging revolutionary spirits. After hauling away captured artillery and supplies and ordering the destruction of the fort, he withdrew back into the fastness of the Hudson highlands before Clinton could launch a counterstroke.

The English general, fuming at the embarrassing loss, reoccupied Stony Point with a garrison twice the size of the former one. Guessing that Clinton, with reserves arriving from across the Atlantic, might attempt to attack West Point, Washington shifted his personal lodgings there in late July. If there were to be a struggle for the fortress, he wanted to be right in the middle of it. He moved into a large home at the river's edge near the ridge holding Fort Arnold.

Both Henry Clinton and George Washington had West Point very much on their minds through the summer of 1779. Always a key strategic factor in the planning of both sides, it had become the focal point of their operations.

———·•·———

Again, as so often in the tale of Washington and Arnold, one can imagine the inventive hand of a fiction writer at work. West Point, fated to be the magnet of Arnold's future treason, was the proximate reason for the temporary derailment of the sensitive negotiations between Henry Clinton and Benedict Arnold.

By July both sides had grown frustrated over delays and misunderstandings. Some gaps were inevitable, given the indirect and tenuous method of communicating, but military events added to the difficulties. Clinton's attempt to open the Hudson highlands, Washington's riposte at Stony Point, and the subsequent fixation of both generals on West Point left Sir Henry less attentive to the conversation with Arnold than the would-be turncoat thought proper. Clinton was a very busy commander, while Arnold had little to divert him while he waited in Philadelphia for his long-delayed court-martial.

Arnold submitted strength reports on continental forces from Rhode Island to Georgia, presented updates on patriot planning, and sent other information he deemed to be of interest to the British commander. But above all he pushed for agreement on a guaranteed amount of money to be paid him for his services. Assurances of generosity were not enough. The merchant thought he had a good product to sell, and he wanted a contract up front. He set his price: ten thousand British pounds, no matter how the war ended.

On top of the irritating delays, the American officer thought he detected an evasive tone in responses from enemy headquarters. He in turn adopted a less enthusiastic attitude. Joseph Stansbury, noticing the cooling on Arnold's part, reported that Mrs. Arnold herself was striving to hold the channels of exchange open, hoping to keep the two sides talking.

Clinton would not accede to Arnold's demands until he was surer of the rebel general's commitment. The Briton was indeed busy, but he was also a bit suspicious. He wanted Arnold to do more to prove himself, to show "a little exertion" in his effort to defect.

For one thing, the British commander required more than general information from Arnold. Specifically, with the bad taste of Stony Point still in his mouth, he needed detailed information on Washington's defenses in the Hudson highlands. Thus West Point first entered the negotiations. Furthermore, the American should try to obtain a field command, where he could be more valuable in providing timely intelligence. Finally, Arnold should attempt to arrange the exchange of a senior British prisoner with whom he could meet face to face, thereby verifying his intentions.

Seeing no progress after desultory exchanges all summer, Arnold drew back. A curtain of silence fell on the discussions, a lull broken only by a social note from Peggy to André in October, indicating that the whole idea was not dead.

Meanwhile, back at West Point, General Washington was enjoying a quieter and more fruitful season than he would have dared forecast earlier in the year.

After the dazzling victory at Stony Point, he had pulled off a similar stroke in New Jersey, across the Hudson River from New York City. Major "Light-Horse Harry" Lee surprised and stormed a British outpost at Paulus Hook, adding still another uplifting moment to cheer Americans. John Paul Jones sailed the *Bonhomme Richard* to fame in British home waters. Word arrived from the west of the thorough triumph of the expedition against hostile Indians. Finally, although Admiral d'Estaing had refused to bring his fleet all the way north, he did sail as far as Savannah in October to assist in attacking the British garrison there. The battle itself failed to dislodge the enemy, but the very presence of the French fleet on the Atlantic Coast gave Henry Clinton enormous concern for the safety of New York City. He hurriedly evacuated Rhode Island and withdrew forces from the crossing site at Stony Point to strengthen his base at the mouth of the Hudson.

So, in a year when he possessed insufficient resources to launch a major offensive anywhere, Washington could nevertheless tally up a string of successes. Not one of them was grand in size or scope, the way Saratoga had been. The storming of Stony Point had been more akin to the triumph at Trenton. Still, the collective sum of all the small wins produced a level of accomplishment beyond anything anticipated when he had concluded his planning sessions with the Congress back in February. It was bargain-basement war, to be sure, but it had been effective.

The final few months of the campaigning season passed calmly, with Washington and his soldiers basking in a warm, sunny, almost lazy autumn around West Point. Relaxed as he seldom was, the Virginian referred to the home he had lived in ever since July as "this happy spot." Leaving for winter quarters at the end of November, he was satisfied with the way things had worked out.

———

Benedict Arnold's autumn had not been so agreeable. He still waited impatiently in Philadelphia for Washington to set a date for his court-martial. He fretted over the sidelined negotiations with Henry Clinton. The leg wound, two years old, continued to give him trouble. Congressional committees dallied inconclusively with his tangled fiscal accounts tracing back to operations some three years before. A serious run-in with a mob in October left him more convinced than ever, if that were possible, of the ineffectiveness— even the duplicity—of the Congress. Peggy was pregnant.

Finally, with the Continental Army settled into winter quarters, enough general officers were available for his trial. It opened in Morristown, New Jersey, on December 23, 1779. Arnold strode in, fully expecting that he would be acquitted.

He was doomed to disappointment yet again. The hearing began well enough, but, incredibly, a key witness failed to appear. The president of the court was forced to adjourn the proceedings until the man could be found and brought to Morristown. That took weeks. By the time the court reconvened, almost a full year had passed since Joseph Reed had first released the charges being addressed. Arnold could only gnash his teeth at what he saw as the absurdity of it all.

The calendar had turned over to 1780—the "Black Year" of the Revolution.

CHAPTER SEVENTEEN

THE BLACK YEAR

———◆·◆·◆———

THE SOFT INDIAN SUMMER OF LATE 1779 GAVE WAY TO THE worst winter of the war. Old-timers said it was in fact the worst ever. The weather turned bad in December, very bad, and hit bottom in January. A blizzard slammed the northeastern states on the second day of the year, bringing suffocating snows, ferocious winds, and temperatures in the double digits below zero. The Hudson River froze solid nearly to the ocean—men and horses crossed from Staten Island to Manhattan on the ice. The great blizzard lasted three days, but a remorseless deep freeze lay over the land until late February. Military units, relegated to makeshift shelter for the most part, were brought to their knees. Soldiers struggled desperately merely to survive; many did not.

As omens go, that terrible storm ushering in 1780 could not have been more accurate. For patriots, the year would skid from start to finish along the crumbling edge of doom. Mutinies hammered the Continental Army, battlefield disasters rattled confidence, starvation stalked military camps, a dreadful economic situation wracked the nation, and patience with the long war waned. The undisputed low point of the Revolutionary War, 1780 came close to being the last year of a losing cause.

The commanding general of the West Point region sat down at his desk in a house commandeered from a loyalist to pen a New Year's message to his soldiers. "The Major General wishes the year may be productive of success, honor, and happiness in the army," he wrote. Unfortunately, it would be productive of defeat, dishonor, and unhappiness. With ultimate victory or defeat for the Revolution teetering in the balance, fate would hold her breath when another major general, one bent on treason, moved into that same house seven months later.

To gain a sense of how tenuous matters became that year, listen to the woeful litany of events from January through August:

Desertions. On the very first day of the year, about a hundred men of the Massachusetts Line, fed up with atrocious conditions in army encampments, headed home in a body. Loyal troops rounded them up and returned them to camp to face punishment, but the stage had been set. Desertions would become commonplace, outnumbering enlistments throughout the year

Severe shortages. Surviving the blasts of that particularly bone-chilling winter would have been a daunting challenge under any circumstances, but doing so without adequate food or clothing or shelter beggars description. The commander in the Hudson highlands reported, "The garrison of West Point have during the winter been at a scanty allowance of bread, and often without any at all. This has been the case these four or five days past." His men sarcastically called the distribution of winter rations "a system of starving." One soldier at a camp in New Jersey remembered his own ordeal in stark terms. "I do solemnly declare that I did not put a single morsel of victuals into my mouth for four days and as many nights, except a little birch bark which I gnawed off a stick of wood, if that can be called victuals." Even the generals grew caustic about the shortages. "Mad Anthony" Wayne wrote that the Congress appeared ready to leave the army "uniformly bare-headed—as well as bare-footed—and if they find that we can *bare* it tolerably well in the two extremes, perhaps they may try it in the *center*." The weather finally improved; the supply situation did not. "Our poor soldiers are reduced to the very edge of famine," wrote one doctor, "their patience is exhausted by complicated sufferings, and their spirits are almost broken."

Rampant inflation. Continental dollars became virtually worthless. They exchanged at the preposterous rate of thousands of paper dollars to one of gold or silver, giving rise to the expression, "not worth a continental." The long-suffering soldiers had not been paid even in that ludicrous currency in months. They sank ever deeper in debt and despair. "I assure you," General Washington informed the Congress, "every idea you can form of our distresses will fall short of reality."

Mutiny. Two Connecticut regiments banded together on May 25 and started for home. One of their colonels, trying to talk them out of leaving, was bayoneted for his efforts. When other officers blocked their route with Pennsylvania troops, the rebellious men "returned with grumbling" to camp rather than fight their comrades. Outright insurrection had been averted, but the probability of further attempts remained. Washington reported that he could sense "in every line of the army the most serious features of mutiny and sedition."

The largest single loss of the war. General Henry Clinton left New York City in the midst of the terrible winter, leading an expedition to Charleston, South Carolina. He eventually laid siege to the city when the patriot commander let himself be bottled up. After a lackluster defense, unable to shake the Englishman's vise-like grip, the Americans capitulated on May 12, surrendering nearly five thousand men. Irreplaceable continentals made up more than half that total. Patriots everywhere were thunderstruck—such a staggering loss of men was incomprehensible.

The worst disaster of the war. Trying to recoup the defeat at Charleston, the Congress sent Horatio Gates hurrying south to rally forces there. The representatives did not consult with Washington beforehand, correctly figuring that he would have resisted their choice. Gates quickly settled once and for all the debate over his capacity for field command. Leading about four thousand men, he blundered into battle at Camden, South Carolina, on August 16. There a force not much more than half his size practically annihilated his army. The defeat was so overwhelming that casualty figures were never accurately recorded. Only a few hundred continentals later straggled back to recovery points.

Gates himself, swept up in a panicky rush of retreating militiamen, escaped by galloping from the field of battle, not stopping until he reached safety in North Carolina. (Alexander Hamilton, who had despised Gates ever since their 1777 encounter, wrote the most damning appraisal of that general's inglorious retreat: "Was there ever an instance of a general running away as Gates has done from his whole army? And was there ever so precipitous a flight? One hundred and eighty miles in three days and a half! It does admirable credit to the activity of a man at his time of life. But it disgraces the general and the soldier.) Benedict Arnold, deep into his treasonous scheme, had to experience unbridled glee at Gates's undoing. To Nathanael Greene he wrote, "It is an unfortunate piece of business to that hero," and may mark his reputation with "indelible infamy." Hanging on by the slimmest of margins anyway, the Continental Army could not afford so thorough a beating. Those who had thought that the black year could not be blacker were wrong.

Disappointment with allies. By the third year of the alliance with France, great expectations had turned to immense disappointment. In fact, the alliance had brought a seriously negative component. Americans, thinking victory was at hand, had shown a lessening of the focus necessary to see the Revolution through. Their will to persevere and sacrifice weakened. Paris, having some second thoughts about partnering with the patriots, had warned early in 1780 that Americans would have to do more on their own. Nevertheless, one bright streak of sunshine peeked through the year's otherwise uniformly bleak cloud cover. Washington learned in the spring that France was sending an expeditionary force comprised of both a powerful naval squadron and a land contingent of seven thousand or more men. For a moment the Virginian turned optimistic; he had visions of a joint attack to retake New York City. But that gap in the clouds closed suddenly, causing the disappointment to cut all the deeper. In July part of the French army, under the Comte de Rochambeau, landed unopposed in Newport, Rhode Island, but British warships bottled up his partnering fleet and a second division of soldiers in the port of Brest—on the wrong side of the Atlantic. Without those forces on hand, the French general would not even consider a campaign. The summer ended with scant hope for a battle.

Militia spirit nosedives. In previous years, militiamen could generally be counted upon to answer calls to mobilize when threats arose or when urged to join the regulars for a campaign. By this sixth year of the war, however, local units appeared to be running out of enthusiasm. They had answered the battle tocsin too many times. To General Washington's utmost chagrin, very few responded to his calls in 1780. "We may expect soon to be reduced to the humiliating condition of seeing the cause of America, in America, upheld by foreign arms," he concluded sadly.

All of that and much more left the American Revolution gasping like a beached whale. It could not live much longer under existing circumstances, yet no one could see how to get it back into the water. That spring, King George III, noting the abysmal state of morale among the rebels, predicted that the United States would sue for peace before the summer was out. For once the monarch was not so far off in sensing the mood of his former subjects. The war had been long, times were tough, and reservoirs of resistance were drained.

Alexander Hamilton, watching from the vantage point of aide to the commander in chief, neatly summed up the appalling apathy sweeping the country, saying that "our countrymen have all the folly of the ass and all the passiveness of the sheep in their compositions. They are determined not to be free and they can neither be frightened, discouraged nor persuaded to change their resolution."

Americans were not alone in their concern. General Rochambeau, ensconced in Newport and looking inquisitively out over the landscape of rebellion, was immensely discouraged by what he saw. The American Revolution was succumbing to sheer exhaustion. "Do not depend upon these people, nor upon their means," he frankly told his superiors in Paris.

———————

Set against that foreboding background, Benedict Arnold continued his march to infamy. His trial resumed that frigid January.

When all witnesses had been heard and Arnold's heated oratory had been delivered, the panel withdrew to decide upon guilt or innocence. The case had sifted down to a strong-willed clash between a continental general and a state governing body. That was uncharted ground, making deliberations less than easy for the members of the court. Arnold, however, remained confident of acquittal.

The court delivered its verdict on January 26. It exonerated the general on two of the charges, but held him at fault on the other two. Members found no illegal intent regarding his use of army wagons for personal business, but stated that it was "imprudent and improper" for an officer in his position to have done that. They also ruled that he had overstepped in granting a pass to *Charming*

Nancy. The court sentenced him to be reprimanded by General Washington, which sounded like a slap on the wrist.

While complete absolution would have been preferable, Arnold was nevertheless relieved. For one thing, it was good just to have the trial finally concluded. And, importantly, he considered the outcome to have vindicated him in the bitter feud with Joseph Reed. He circulated the results widely, taking a less than subtle swipe at his Pennsylvania adversaries.

He then turned his mind to other matters. Henry Clinton, as was well known, was away campaigning in Georgia and South Carolina. So, whether or not Arnold wanted to resume his treasonous correspondence, it was of necessity on hold. A large part of February was consumed in the laborious attempt to untangle his official financial records, which the Congress had been struggling with unsuccessfully for an inordinate length of time. The drawn-out process was particularly galling, for Arnold's personal cash reserves were disturbingly low. Telling Washington in March that surgeons examining his wounded leg thought it would be imprudent for him "to take a command in the army for some time to come," he raised again the idea of a command at sea. One could profit hugely from capturing enemy ships. That proposal went nowhere, for the nation had no means in that bleak year to form a navy. On March 19, Peggy gave birth to a boy. George Washington congratulated the new parents on March 28, and granted Arnold's request for a leave of absence from the army.

After holding the court-martial report for weeks, the Congress finally sent it to General Washington in late March for execution of the sentence. Arnold, having considered the findings to be more favorable than not, may well have thought the long passage of time without action meant that the report had simply been filed away, a dead matter. If so, he was set up for a shock when the commander in chief acted on it forcefully.

General orders on April 6 carried the public reprimand. In them, Washington stated that, while he would have been happier bestowing praise on so illustrious a patriot, duty required him to do otherwise. He termed Arnold's conduct in granting a pass to the *Charming Nancy* as "peculiarly reprehensible" and in misusing the wagons as misguided and improper. That same day, in a private letter, the commander in chief pointedly let the famous general know how disappointed he was in him. "Even the shadow of a fault tarnishes the luster of our finest achievements," he wrote. "I reprimand you for having forgotten that, in proportion as you have rendered yourself formidable to our enemies, you should have been guarded and temperate in your deportment towards your fellow citizens."

Still, Washington had the utmost respect for Arnold's battlefield leadership, and very much wanted to keep him in the Continental Army. Mistakes might be made, but they could be redeemed. He tried to move beyond the reprimand, saying, "I will myself furnish you, as far as it may be in my power, with opportunities of regaining the esteem of your country."

But it was too late. Harsh words from the commander who had always been so supportive and understanding floored Arnold. The one powerful man he had thought would never turn against him had. Washington clearly believed that he, Benedict Arnold, had lost the respect of his countrymen. That was a devastating revelation.

On the heels of that low moment, a decision on his finances came from the Congress. Not only would he receive no money at that time, but it turned out that he might actually owe some! There would at best be more delays, no cash. It was too much. If he had not already made an irretrievable decision in his own mind to defect, he did so now. He took down the codebook to compose a letter to the British commander.

Once again the confidential courier, Joseph Stansbury, journeyed to New York City bearing a message from Benedict Arnold. General Clinton himself was still in South Carolina, as was recently promoted Major John André, so the spy met with Wilhelm von Knyphausen, a German general acting as commander in Sir Henry's absence.

Arnold was ready to do Clinton's bidding if he could be assured that his compensation requests would be honored. He would be returning to duty with the American army, and would take a central part in case "a capital stroke can be struck." To arrange that, he wanted to meet with a trusted agent to discuss details, and he asked for some secret sign by which he could be assured that the agent was genuine. Finally, he wanted command of a military unit under the flag of Great Britain after he changed sides, and requested the advance of a small amount of cash. The German officer may have been surprised by the information being presented to him, but he reacted calmly and forthrightly. He provided money "for cultivating the connection" with the rebel general, and he sent one of a pair of identical rings, saying the agent who would meet with Arnold would carry the other one for identification. For everything else, he would have to await the return of General Clinton.

Arnold did not wait. His decision made, he wanted to close the deal as soon as possible. He sent intelligence of various patriot activities and plans and provided information about the French expeditionary force heading for Rhode Island. He carefully described his own movements—to headquarters in the field and then on to Connecticut for private business—so a messenger would know where to find him.

Then, in a coded message sent in mid-June, Arnold announced that he expected soon to be appointed commander of West Point. That was his big bait—he knew that the fortress in the Hudson highlands was what Sir Henry most wanted.

In poker terms, Arnold was betting on the draw to complete his hand, for Washington had made no command arrangements. The commander in chief was playing his own cards close to his vest.

To win the West Point assignment, Arnold had been reaching out to his network of New York friends. Within days of being reprimanded, he met with Philip Schuyler, now a member of the Congress from New York. Would Schuyler speak to Washington about assigning him to the West Point command? His old friend did, in early May. Afterward, he informed the anxious traitor that Washington spoke warmly of him, "in terms such as the friends who love you could wish." The Virginian deferred a decision, however, still hoping Arnold might be able to operate in the field in event a campaign could be mounted. Schuyler summarized, "If the command at West Point is offered, it will be honorable; if a division in the field, you must judge whether you can support the fatigues, circumstanced as you are."

Benedict and Peggy both enlisted the assistance of another congressman from New York, their good friend Robert R. Livingston, who was particularly susceptible to Peggy's flirtatious overtures. Eager to help, Livingston wrote a strong endorsement in June. The current commanding general of the highlands fortress did not have the confidence of New York, he said. He urged Washington to replace him with General Arnold, "whose courage is undoubted, who is the favorite of the militia, and who will agree perfectly with our Governor." Having such powerful backing from prominent New Yorkers gave Arnold confidence that he would no doubt receive the West Point assignment he coveted.

On his way to New Haven, he stopped to look around that key bastion, where the central fort bore his name. Afterward, as soon as he could open his codebook in privacy, he sent an assessment of the works to the British. His report was cleverly aimed at elevating Clinton's interest in trying to seize the fortress. "It is surprising a post of so much importance should be so totally neglected," he said. Furthermore, "The works appear to me (though well executed) most wretchedly planned to answer the purpose designed, viz to maintain the Post and stop the passage of the river." He described how the huge chain across the Hudson could be broken, and he indicated avenues of attack that could succeed despite the fort's reputation for impregnability. The shrewd implication throughout was that English forces would have an easy time of it if their assaults were aided by an insider. And not just any insider, but the commander himself, Benedict Arnold. The former merchant had not lost his marketing skills.

Completing his affairs in Connecticut—consisting mainly of efforts to raise money by selling his home and other possessions at a steep discount—Arnold returned to Philadelphia. July had arrived, Henry Clinton was back in New York City, but, disappointingly, no responses to Arnold's spate of messages awaited. Right off, he sent more intelligence, updated from his previous input. He reiterated earlier demands for assurances of indemnity, and told Sir Henry that he would take command of West Point "in the course of a month." He was bluffing, for Washington had still made no arrangements.

The delicate business of consummating a treason was wearing on all concerned. Messages crossed one another in their tortuous passage, while their necessarily indirect wording imparted a frustrating sense of vagueness. Both sides saw a need to arrange a face-to-face meeting. "I expect to command W. Pt and most seriously wish an interview with some intelligent officer in whom a mutual confidence could be placed," wrote Arnold in mid-July. As that letter was on its way, Arnold heard from André. Sir Henry did in fact want West Point, the major reported, and he suggested that Arnold himself come close to a British position for a clandestine conference where details could be worked out.

Arnold, sensing that he now held a stronger hand in the negotiations, raised his price for success. "If I point out a plan of cooperation by which Sir Henry shall possess himself of West Point," he wrote, "twenty thousand pounds Sterling I think will be a cheap purchase for an object of so much importance." He also requested an immediate advance of a thousand pounds. He would be leaving for West Point in late July, he informed André, thus requiring that any correspondence would have to be forwarded to him by Peggy until more direct channels could be established between New York City and his new post in the Hudson highlands.

André responded on July 24, confirming that Clinton had agreed to Arnold's fee for delivering West Point. That letter, however, would not reach the American until late August. He left to join the patriot army along the Hudson, unsure of the actual status of his treasonous negotiations. After a year of little or no progress, things were suddenly sprinting ahead at breakneck speed.

Nor did Arnold know definitely what his new assignment would be, but he felt sure it would be the command of West Point. On the last day of July he found General Washington near Stony Point, watching units crossing the Hudson. The commanding general had hopes of combining his own army with the newly arrived French expeditionary force for a joint attack on New York City.

Washington, delighted to see his most renowned warrior back in the saddle and looking fit, welcomed him warmly. After exchanging pleasantries, Arnold inquired if the commander in chief "had thought of anything" for him. Happily, the Virginian responded that indeed he had—Arnold would have "a post of honor" with the main army, serving directly under him in the coming campaign.

Arnold's reaction astounded Washington. Recalling the encounter later, he said, "His countenance changed and he appeared to be quite fallen, and, instead of thanking me or expressing any pleasure at the appointment, never opened his mouth." Arnold was in fact dumbstruck. He could not speak. His face reddened. With some concern, Washington sent the shocked general to his own quarters to get out of the heat and rest, saying he would talk with him there.

Later, as Washington rode toward the quarters for that conversation, an aide intercepted him to report that Arnold's disposition was one of "great uneasiness." He was limping back and forth, muttering that his wounded leg would not allow him to stay on horseback the length of time duties in the field would require. When the commander in chief arrived, Arnold insisted that he was too crippled to fight, that he could only serve at the stationary post of West Point. Such an unanticipated stance by America's Hannibal struck Washington as exceedingly "strange and unaccountable."

Thinking the hero may have momentarily lost his confidence, Washington tried to calm him, telling the once irrepressible warrior that he was surely more capable than he imagined himself to be. After all, nearly three years had passed since the Hessian musket ball had smashed his leg. No, for the good of the cause, the best place for Benedict Arnold was command in combat. Washington did not suspect that the good of the cause was not what Arnold had in mind.

General orders for the next day announced that Major General Benedict Arnold would command the left wing of the army. Arnold could not believe what was happening to his grand scheme. (Neither could Peggy. Back in Philadelphia, upon hearing the great honor paid to Benedict, the co-conspirator lapsed into hysterics. Surprised friends assumed it was the overwrought reaction of a young wife and new mother to the fact that her husband might soon be in battle.) Arnold's wound suddenly if not mysteriously took a turn for the worse. He pleaded with Washington that he was so handicapped that only the West Point assignment would fit.

As it happened, hard reality came to Washington at about that time. There would be no attack. The French were not going to cooperate, recruits were not joining the colors, and Henry Clinton had reinforced the New York City lines. The concentrated Continental Army would have to disperse again. Arnold would not be needed in the field after all—but he could be of value at West Point.

Besides, did not the Revolution itself owe the crippled general some special consideration for his heroics in 1775, 1776, and 1777? More than anyone else, Washington knew that the war would have taken a different course without Arnold's bravery and leadership in those years. Although it hurt the commanding general to see the once proud warrior essentially begging for a soft assignment, he relented.

General orders on August 3, 1780, announced, "Major General Arnold will take command of the garrison at West Point." The stage was set for treason. The Black Year had not yet reached its lowest point.

CHAPTER EIGHTEEN

ON THE EDGE

———◆•◆•◆———

AFTER SEEING THE COMMAND OF WEST POINT ALMOST jerked from his grasp, Arnold recovered quickly as soon as Washington changed his mind and sent him there. In rainy, dreary weather, the renowned warrior dismounted in front of his new home, a large house two miles south of West Point and set back about the distance of a cannon shot from the east bank of the Hudson River. It belonged to Colonel Beverley Robinson, a loyalist who commanded a regiment of Americans serving with the British army in New York City. Garrison orders for August 5, 1780, announced the password for the day: "Arnold." The countersign was "West Point." The traitor had arrived.

His very first act—selecting where he would live—reflected his treacherous intent. The outgoing commander had recommended that he take up residence near Fort Arnold, in the house Washington had occupied the year before. Security would be tighter. Arnold, however, opted to move into the Robinson House, on the opposite side of the river and much closer to British lines. It would be far easier to make an escape from there if the need arose.

He had much to do. Foremost was to establish direct communications from his new headquarters to Sir Henry Clinton, now only fifty miles away. The roundabout path through Philadelphia was simply unworkable. Second was arranging for Peggy and their baby to join him. He sorely needed someone he could confide in. Moreover, they could take flight together if their scheme unraveled. Third, he had to present himself as a fully involved commander of the vital fortress complex. That final goal had a twofold purpose: to shield his nefarious dealings and to enable him to cooperate more effectively with the British when time came to betray his men.

Arnold made his presence felt at once. Directions tumbled one after the other from his desk. The number of guards was to be increased. A field-grade officer would inspect every sentry in the middle of the night. Repairs were to be hastened. Controls on watercraft were tightened. Units were told to submit fresh returns regarding the status of soldiers. He changed how patients were to be treated and even revised rules for baking bread. He issued orders to a new chief engineer to survey all the works right away, which that officer did, reporting back on August 8 that there was "a vast deal to do to complete them." Before the new commander had been a week on the job, hundreds of men were toiling to strengthen the defensive complex. There could be no doubting that a dynamic leader was in charge of West Point.

The traitor did not neglect his own special needs. He requested from Washington a map of the region between West Point and New York City, "particularly on the east side of the river, which would be very useful to me." Useful to him as commander of the area, of course, but also highly useful to a turncoat who might have to flee that way to safety.

Nor did he lose sight of the need to prepare West Point to succumb easily to a British attack. While the engineer's construction teams were much in evidence, levies for work parties cut into their numbers, eroding their effectiveness. Woodcutting and a myriad of other tasks consumed large labor gangs, slowing or stalling progress on the defenses. By the end of the month the number of workers actually employed on the fortifications stood in the dozens, not the hundreds.

Colonel John Lamb, who had fought beside Arnold at Quebec and Danbury and carried disfiguring scars from wounds suffered in both battles, commanded the central position of West Point itself. Recognizing right away that the semblance of activity was misleading, giving only an illusion of progress, he complained bluntly to the commanding general: "If such drafts as are called for are made from the garrison we shall neither be able to finish the works that are incomplete nor be in a situation to defend those that are finished." Exactly.

Making matters worse in the eyes of many officers, militia units had been called in to help make up the shortage of regulars. One major wrote acidly that the defenses were "under the care of ingovernable and undisciplined militia," which gave the post an appearance quite different from "that shining fortification all America thinks." A doctor confided to his diary that the militia soldiers were "very uncleanly," making West Point smell "more disagreeably than ever I before knew it." The militia troops chopped up logs set aside to float the great chain, used fence rails for firewood, and let pigs run loose. Unwittingly, they were helping General Arnold weaken the place.

Colonel Lamb warned Arnold that if the British ever learned "what kind of troops" defended West Point they might be tempted to try to seize it. He could never have dreamed that his own commander was at that very time sending the enemy, via Peggy in Philadelphia, intelligence reports making precisely that point.

As more and more time passed with no word from Henry Clinton, Arnold grew increasingly apprehensive. Isolated in the Hudson highlands and unable to share his fears with anyone, he could not avoid the tug of helplessness. The double game he had been playing for over a year was having an effect on his nerves. Secretive, distracted, edgy, compulsive about running household affairs, he raised worries among close subordinates, especially his two aides, Lieutenant Colonel Richard Varick and Major David Franks. The overwrought man they now saw was a very different person from the open, almost transparent commander they had known in the battles of Saratoga nearly three years before. Arnold's obsessive concern over rations and other small matters startled Varick, who had taken the position as aide only that August. Franks, who had been with the general in Philadelphia, was not so surprised at the streak of greed, but both officers bore the burden of their commander's prickly attitude. They surmised that his irritability might be caused by the separation from Peggy. In a way, they were right: she was his only co-conspirator.

After nearly three weeks in command, Arnold sent Major Franks to Philadelphia to escort Peggy and her infant to the Robinson House. He still had received no response from his final offer to Sir Henry, but he decided to relocate Peggy anyway. Her departure would close off the Philadelphia link to New York City, making it even more imperative to find a secure way to communicate with British headquarters from West Point.

He had been working at that from the outset. On his very first day in command he had begun seeking spies who could slip messages into and out of British headquarters. That sensitive search required extreme care. Moreover, it took time, which he could hardly spare. Although aware that double agents worked the area, he was at first unable to find out who they were. He later learned that Joshua Hett Smith, a resident of Haverstraw across the river, could help him find men for clandestine missions.

Arnold knew Smith slightly, having met him briefly in Philadelphia and having more recently stopped at his Haverstraw house. He began cautiously feeling out the New Yorker to determine how dependable he might be. That immediately sparked tension in headquarters, for suspicions of double-dealing swirled around Joshua Smith. Arnold and his aides argued over the seemliness of letting a possibly disloyal man dine with the commanding general. Whether or not Arnold appreciated the irony of their concerns, he knew he had to tread very lightly. Days turned into weeks, with no notable progress. Despite the urgency of re-establishing contact with André, the would-be defector forced himself to control his impatience. One slip could ruin everything. Besides, he had not heard from the English major since arriving in the Hudson highlands. Not knowing whether General Clinton had bought into the plot to take West Point, he had nothing to send into New York even if a trusted agent had been available. Still, the frustration was excruciating.

Then, on August 24, only a day after his aide had left to retrieve Peggy, a long-delayed message arrived, abruptly changing the pace of perfidy.

Nature staged a panoramic sound and light show dramatizing the letter's arrival, a show quite equal to anything a modern Hollywood producer might have conjured up. On that oppressively hot and humid day, powerful thunderstorms lashed the Hudson highlands. Dark clouds unleashed "hail as big as musket balls." Lightning danced among the hills, illuminating the way for a drenched courier bearing a coded message forwarded from Philadelphia by Peggy. The response from André!

Arnold surely trembled in suspense as he decoded the letter. It had been written, he noted ruefully, a full month earlier. As the content emerged, he became ecstatic. André's words were nearly everything he had hoped for: if he succeeded, the British would pay the twenty thousand pounds he had demanded. Success was defined as the seizing of West Point, along with three thousand prisoners and all the artillery and equipment in the fortress. While Clinton would not guarantee a specific amount in case of failure, he promised that the rebel defector could depend upon just and fair compensation. Benedict Arnold had a contract.

There was just one catch—a most serious one. The American commander would need to coordinate beforehand with a representative of Clinton. How could that be arranged when no line of communication existed? And a long month had passed since the offer itself had been extended. Circumstances could already have changed. Arnold accelerated his search for a messenger.

Fortuitously, an opportunity soon surfaced. It came in the form of a request for a pass for one William Heron to go into the city on business. Nervously, Arnold decided to take a chance. Couching his words in mercantile language, he wrote a letter, signing it "Gustavus" and addressing it to "John Anderson," André's code name. He asked Heron to deliver it. In addition to signaling acceptance of the month-old offer, the letter included a call for a meeting. "Mr. Moore flatters himself that in the course of ten days he will have the pleasure of seeing you." André would know that "Mr. Moore" was Arnold himself. The two men needed to meet face to face to coordinate the British attack.

Something in Arnold's furtive manner aroused Heron's suspicions, perhaps his secretiveness or maybe the obviously feigned handwriting. The courier carried the letter to the city, but kept it in his pocket instead of delivering it. He brought it back and gave it to another senior American officer. (That officer, glancing at the content, thought it merely dealt with business matters and absently filed it away.) Heron's action was strange, for he was actually a British spy. Perhaps he did not want to risk compromising his position. For whatever reason, though, Arnold's first attempt to restore contact with André had misfired. He was unaware of the failure, of course, but he had planned to send multiple messages anyway. The information was too vital to trust to a single courier. Trouble was, he had no one else at hand.

———·•·———

George Washington fared no better in that bitter month. It started for him with the deeply disappointing realization that General Rochambeau would not budge from Rhode Island until the remainder of his expeditionary force arrived. From then on it worsened.

Troubles surrounded his two best generals. Benedict Arnold seemed to be psychologically scarred by his war wounds, while Nathanael Greene was embroiled in an acrimonious dispute with the Congress. It could be hoped that Arnold would recover his warrior spirit as he went about his duties at West Point, but losing Greene loomed suddenly as a very real possibility.

Unable any longer to endure congressional criticism and inter-ference, Greene had huffily submitted his resignation as quartermaster general. On August 3, the Congress accepted it, with some delegates angrily pushing to expel him from the army altogether. A very concerned Washington intervened quietly to calm frayed tempers and to save his most trusted lieutenant, but the effort to do so was yet one more burden piled on top of so many others. He could be forgiven if he had wondered why a formerly benevolent Providence had seemingly turned so squarely against the cause.

Ministers in London were cheered by the bleak outlook for the Americans' rebellion. Lord Germain expressed their ebullient mood in a letter written early in the month lauding General Clinton for his resounding success in South Carolina. That, he said, "together with the reduced state of Mr. Washington's force, the decay of the power of Congress, and the total failure of their paper money, open a flattering prospect of a speedy and happy termination of the American war." This concise appraisal of the situation would have sounded uncomfortably realistic to George Washington.

Rochambeau, too, had been alarmed to discover how weak the patriots actually were. One prominent twentieth-century historian has said that Rochambeau might well "have concluded that he had been assigned to encourage a riot, rather than to support a revolution." The French commander would not move until he had assembled adequate strength of his own—he dared not rely on the Americans.

As much as he hated to admit it, Washington knew that Rochambeau was right. He told Lafayette that he would not push his ally to undertake operations before his remaining forces arrived from France. The Americans were at that low moment in no shape to be of much help. "Our prospects are not so flattering," Washington said, "as to justify our being very pressing to engage them in our views." He could only "hope circumstances will ultimately favour us." But hope, as he understood all too well, was a weak substitute for an operational plan.

Nevertheless, even the faintest chance of a combined French and American campaign evaporated totally with unfortunate news from Rochambeau on August 25. His reinforcing echelons would not be coming. They had been bottled up in the port of Brest by British warships. For the time being, French forces in America would remain on the defensive in Newport. "The flattering prospect which seemed to be opening to our view in the month of May," Washington lamented, "is vanishing like the morning dew."

That disheartening information came at a time when Washington found himself forced to beg states to send food to his starving men. "I am under the disagreeable necessity of informing you that the Army is again reduced to an extremity of distress," he wrote nearby governors. Units were obliged to scour the countryside merely to survive, slaughtering even milk cows and calves. But such drastic steps could not continue. "Military coercion is no longer of any avail, as nothing further can be collected" in the areas surrounding military camps. Without support from the states, the army itself could dissolve, or worse. Although the troops so far had borne their privations "with unparalleled patience," he warned that it would "be dangerous to trust too often to a repetition of causes of dissent."

As the unhappy month ended, Washington poured out his anguish in a private letter to his brother. Instead of sending promised men and supplies, the states "have not furnished one half of them yet," while those soldiers who were in camp "are only fed from hand to mouth and for the last four or five days have been without meat." The dejected commander moaned that "the wretched manner in which our business is conducted" was beyond his power to describe.

As the calendar turned from August to September, the Black Year was growing ever blacker. The American Revolution balanced on the brink of disaster.

CHAPTER NINETEEN

SETTING THE STAGE

BY THE START OF SEPTEMBER, GENERAL WASHINGTON'S superb intelligence network had detected signs of British preparations for an expedition. But his agents had not discovered its target. Attacking Rochambeau's forces in Rhode Island was one plausible possibility, as was reinforcing British operations in the south. But persistent indicators pointed toward something closer to the New York base. Was the English commander considering a move against Washington himself? Or was he perhaps aiming a blow at Fortress West Point?

The commander in chief immediately alerted General Arnold. Clinton's objective, he warned, "will be an attack on the main army or an attempt on the post in the Highlands. I wish you therefore to put the latter in the most defensible state which is possible." The traitor must have smirked as he read that message. He knew better than Washington what the enemy objective was. And he was indeed putting West Point in a "defensible state"—designed to facilitate his own nefarious purposes.

Ironically, about that same time spies picked up wisps of rumors that a senior American general was on the verge of defecting to the British. No one in authority seems to have given that information much credence. Even if it had been taken seriously, the renowned warrior Benedict Arnold would have been beyond suspicion. Moreover, no patriot would have linked mere defection to an insidious attempt to bring down the Revolution itself.

Meanwhile, weeks of efforts to find couriers had finally paid off for Arnold. He learned that Colonel Elisha Sheldon, commanding troops in the northern reaches of Westchester County, employed a double agent who could convey messages. That agent, as well as another still mysterious "very honest fellow," and perhaps others lost in the shadows of time, were put into service in September.

On September 3, a refugee from Quebec, Mary McCarthy, appeared bearing a pass signed by New York's governor permitting her to go into New York City. Arnold seized that opportunity, entrusting her with a letter for John Anderson (André). Again couched in mercantile language, the message informed André that he could contact Arnold through Colonel Sheldon. Mrs. McCarthy must have been surprised and most appreciative when an escort of a lieutenant, a sergeant, and seven privates took her in an army boat all the way to Manhattan Island under a flag provided by Major General Arnold himself.

Arnold's anxious desire to arrange a conference was matched by that of Henry Clinton. Before the Briton would commit himself to an attack against West Point, he wanted conclusive proof that the rebel with whom he had been dealing was in fact who he claimed to be. That could only be done in a face-to-face meeting. Major André had to expedite matters.

When the letter delivered by Mrs. McCarthy arrived, the British spymaster leapt at the opening. Wasting no time, he wrote to Colonel Sheldon, signing himself John Anderson, saying he would travel under a flag to the eastern terminus of Dobb's Ferry, under British control at that time. He would be there at noon on Monday, September 11, when he "should be happy to see Mr. G___," that is, Gustavus, one of Arnold's cover names. However, André was rightfully reluctant to enter or come near American lines in civilian clothing, an act certain to define him as a spy, which meant death by hanging if he were found out. "Should I not be able to go," he added, "the officer who is to command the escort, between whom and myself no distinction need be made, can speak on the affair." To Arnold it would be clear that André himself would show up for the conference, in the role of escort officer. But that was not at all clear to Sheldon. How could a British officer enter openly into such a discussion? Puzzled, he nevertheless sent the message along to his commanding general, who received it on Saturday, September 9.

Arnold was shaken. Feeling pushed to arrange a meeting as soon as possible, André had been irresponsible in using names and in saying a uniformed British officer would be involved. Arnold had damage control to perform before suspicions arose. "You must be sensible my situation will not permit" a private meeting with a British officer, he wrote right back, prudently sending his note through Colonel Sheldon. But if Anderson would come to Sheldon's headquarters his safety would be guaranteed.

However, even as he penned those words Arnold realized that they would probably not reach André before the Briton departed for the Monday rendezvous. As dangerous as it might be, he saw no recourse other than to attend the meeting André had scheduled. Monday morning, September 11, he pushed off in his barge, rowed by a crew of eight sturdy soldiers.

That very weekend the stress on André had intensified. British naval reinforcements, a dozen or more heavy warships and numerous smaller vessels, had begun anchoring in New York's harbor. Sir Henry now had his striking force in hand. All that remained to be done was to hold a meeting with Benedict Arnold.

As the American general's barge approached Dobb's Ferry shortly before noon, a British gunboat suddenly sped out to attack it. Pulling frantically on their oars, with cannon balls splashing around them, Arnold's boatmen reversed course and rowed away, barely escaping to safety on the western shore. Incredibly, André had neglected to alert his own forces of the planned meeting, nearly causing the death of the very man the British were relying on to throw West Point to them.

For the remainder of the day Arnold waited on one bank of the river and André on the other, a mile away. Neither dared make the first move. Gnashing his teeth, the general pointed his barge back upriver at dusk. Obviously, he had to devise an alternative plan to meet André.

In the meantime, he had a reputation to uphold. The pugnacious battler could not simply accept the near-fatal ambush without some response. "The enemy's boats come up almost every day and insult the post," he wrote angrily to Colonel John Lamb at West Point, directing him to send two heavy artillery pieces to the patriot side of Dobb's Ferry. That would take some time for Lamb to accomplish, given British command of the water, but the seeds of an idea were planted. If Arnold later thought about the order, as events in the treason unfolded, he surely regretted issuing it.

Still, the main challenge remained: how to meet André in secrecy and safety? If the British officer would not enter American lines, maybe a meeting could take place in an area controlled by neither side. Joshua Hett Smith's house overlooked Haverstraw Bay and stood a comfortable distance from patriot camps. Arnold intercepted Peggy and her traveling entourage there on September 14, where the reunited plotters spent the night. Arnold had visited the house on several occasions, but this time he looked at it from a different perspective. Near a secluded beach, hidden in trees, away from major military activities, it was ideally suited for a clandestine encounter. It could serve as a secure rendezvous site if the owner would remove his family for several days and arrange for a nighttime boat and crew. The two men talked. Smith, believing Arnold was engaged in intelligence gathering, agreed to participate. As Arnold's barge made its way north the next morning, carrying Benedict and Peggy to the Robinson House, the new plan had taken shape.

A coded message was already on its way to André, telling him he could stick with the land approach if he wanted, but proposing a safer way. "I will send a person in whom you may confide, by water, to meet you at Dobb's Ferry on Wednesday the 20th instant between 11 and 12 o'clock at night, who will conduct you to a place of safety where I will meet you." He urged the Englishman to accept the revised plan. "You may rest assured that if there is no danger in passing your lines, you will be perfectly safe where I propose the meeting."

One readily apparent flaw in the plan, a strange one considering Arnold's knowledge of watercraft, was the water distance between the midnight meeting site and Dobb's Ferry, a dozen miles or more. It would be a difficult trip, at night, on a river affected by tides as well as current. As it turned out, events would cut the distance by perhaps two-thirds, but it would still prove to be a most fatiguing pull. One is left only to wonder what might have happened if the original scheme had been attempted.

Upon returning to the Robinson House, Arnold found waiting on his desk a message from the commander in chief. Although Rochambeau had been in the United States more than two months, Washington had not yet met personally with him. The two leaders had agreed to a conference in Connecticut, about halfway between their respective headquarters, on September 20. Washington, who would be traveling with a very small party, needed some security and logistical assistance from Arnold as he crossed the Hudson River. "I shall be at Peekskill on Sunday evening, on my way to Hartford to meet the French Admiral and General. You will be pleased to send down a guard of a captain and fifty at that time, and direct the quartermaster to endeavor to have a night's forage for about forty horses. You will keep this to yourself, as I want to make my journey a secret." The traitor promptly encoded that information and sent it to Henry Clinton.

If Benedict Arnold's aides had hoped Peggy's arrival would calm their irascible commander, they were disappointed. On the cusp of conclusive action after nearly a year and a half of suspense, he was not in the least inclined to relax. Moreover, he found himself squeezed between Washington's arrival two days hence and André's in five. With much to do in a short span of time, he was more on edge than ever.

That Saturday Joshua Smith, with his wife and two nephews, stopped over at the Robinson House on the way to visit relatives farther north. As per the plan, Smith was clearing his house for Arnold's use on September 20. His overnight stay also gave the two collaborators another chance to confirm details of their project.

The next day Arnold hosted a dinner in honor of Peggy's arrival. Guests included the Smiths and several officers from West Point. The meal was served earlier than normal to give Arnold time to be with Washington as he crossed the Hudson on his way to Hartford. In the midst of dinner a courier arrived bearing a letter from Colonel Beverley Robinson. That officer, writing from a British ship on the Hudson River not far from Washington's planned crossing point, was requesting an audience with General Arnold.

Before receiving Arnold's message proposing a new method for their rendezvous, an anxious André had launched his own revised scheme. Colonel Robinson, who could plausibly be concerned about his home and belongings, would try to set up a meeting to discuss such matters with the current occupant, which would in turn provide André a chance to talk with Arnold. The idea may have been somewhat far-fetched, but André was feeling more and more pressed to bring the much-delayed affair to fruition. General Clinton's forces were ready to be put in motion toward West Point, awaiting only the required preliminary meeting with Benedict Arnold.

Robinson was aboard a fourteen-gun sloop of war, named, of all things, *Vulture*. As soon as the *Vulture* dropped anchor off Teller's Point at the southern end of Haverstraw Bay, Robinson had sent his request for a discussion, ostensibly about his property. But his casual mention in the message of a person central to the prolonged negotiations between Arnold and André signaled his real purpose.

Seeing that name, Arnold realized at once the burden of the letter. André would be on the *Vulture*. Calmly folding the note and putting it in his pocket, he mentioned that it was a request from Robinson for an interview. Colonel John Lamb, whose mangled face became frightening when it reddened, snorted angrily upon hearing Robinson's name that Arnold should have nothing to do with the loyalist leader. Rather, he should tell General Washington of the "improper correspondence." Arnold appeared to agree, thereby ending conversation about the letter. A short while later he excused himself and left for King's Ferry.

After joining Washington at Stony Point, the storied site of a patriot victory the previous year, Arnold accompanied him across the Hudson. From their boat they could see the *Vulture*, riding serenely at anchor in the distance, sails furled. Arnold told the Virginian about the request from Beverley Robinson, who was aboard the vessel. The commander in chief studied the ship through his telescope for a long while, saying nothing. That likely made Arnold nervous; he felt sure that André was on board. Washington, no novice at the intelligence gathering business, may have been wondering about the unusual use of a warship to conduct private affairs. But then again he may have been merely recalling memories of former times, for Beverley Robinson had been a good prewar friend of his. Turning back to Arnold, he reaffirmed Colonel Lamb's guidance to have nothing to do with the loyalist colonel.

As the entire party reassembled on the eastern shore for the short ride to Peekskill, Arnold had time to brief Washington on the status of the defenses in the Hudson highlands. Something bothered the commander in chief, setting off small alarm bells deep in his mind. Maybe it was just his sixth sense, triggered by so many things blowing in the wind: the weakness of the garrisons at West Point and its outlying forts; the near impotence of the Continental Army itself; the strange voyage of the *Vulture*; the recent arrival of British naval reinforcements, including a large number of troop transports; Clinton's continuing preparations for some sort of military action. All in all, it was enough to make him uneasy. He told Arnold that he would visit the fortress complex on his way back from Hartford, and would probably remain overnight at the Robinson House on Saturday, September 23. But he would not wait until then to bolster patriot strength in the area. Fearing that West Point was "so weak that it seems essential to reinforce it," he would send orders the very next day directing a shift of forces toward the highlands.

Then they parted. Washington to continue his trip to Hartford, Arnold to return to his post. Now, as the traitor made his way back to the Robinson House, the stage was set. His climactic moment had arrived.

CHAPTER TWENTY

"ARNOLD HAS BETRAYED US!"

T HE WEEK FROM SEPTEMBER 18 TO SEPTEMBER 25, 1780, WAS a momentous period in the American Revolution. It would not be overreaching to claim that events during those few days had a consequential impact on the very founding of the United States. Beyond doubt, they affected the course of the war itself, and they most assuredly shaped the lives thereafter of Benedict Arnold and George Washington.

MONDAY, SEPTEMBER 18, 1780

This day saw both Washington and Arnold penning messages regarding West Point, with one seeking to strengthen it and the other striving to sell it.

Washington wrote to Nathanael Greene, who was commanding the main army in his absence. The enemy had recently been reinforced, he warned, and appeared to be on the verge of some major effort. Sir Henry Clinton had concentrated mobile forces in New York City, where "70 transports were ready to receive them." Greene was to shift patriot units nearer to the Hudson River and "send a good Continental regiment" to the highlands. West Point, Washington feared, might not be strong enough to resist an assault unaided. Having done all he could before leaving for Hartford, the Virginian then led his party of forty horsemen on toward the rendezvous with General Rochambeau, a two-day ride eastward.

Arnold promptly disobeyed General Washington's admonition to ignore Beverley Robinson. In a letter intended to be seen by others at headquarters, he informed the loyalist leader that he could not discuss non-military matters with him, but he would be willing to listen to any proposals "of a public nature of which I can officially take notice." He also assured him that "the greatest secrecy shall be observed, if required." The bearer of his message, a Captain Archibald, could be trusted to "take particular care of your letters and deliver them to me with his own hand." The traitor had finally found an open but secure and rapid channel of communications with the enemy.

Then, when his aides were not looking, Arnold slipped a private letter into Captain Archibald's packet. His meeting with Major André would have to be done clandestinely. It seemed to Arnold that his earlier proposal for the British spymaster to come ashore near Joshua Smith's house made even more sense in light of the changed circumstances. "I shall send a person to Dobb's Ferry, or on board the *Vulture*, Wednesday night the 20th," he wrote. "You may depend on his secrecy and honour, and that your business, of whatever nature, shall be kept a profound secret." To facilitate the contact, it would "be advisable for the *Vulture* to remain where she is until the time mentioned." In Haverstraw Bay, the ship was many miles closer to Smith's house than it would be at Dobb's Ferry. To make sure there was no confusion over which British officer should actually be involved in the meeting, Arnold also included information specifically for André, who, he averred, would "no doubt" be present.

With Captain Archibald on the road to Teller's Point, near where *Vulture* swayed at anchor, Arnold could only wait in suspense to learn whether André would agree to come ashore for a secret conference. In the meantime, he sought to lessen chances of accidental discovery by reducing patriot river traffic. In general orders he specified that "no person whatever" could cross the river without a pass.

TUESDAY, SEPTEMBER 19, 1780

Tuesday of that fateful week was uneventful for George Washington. He and his retinue clattered without interruption toward Hartford, eager to take the measure of their new French allies.

As the miles passed, the commander in chief surely experienced emotions his compatriots could not. He had begun his military career fighting French forces. Now he rode in somewhat nervous anticipation to meet the commander of the French army in America, an officer seven years his senior, quite more experienced at war, and undoubtedly aware that the outcome of the Revolution itself hinged on the assistance of French land and naval forces. He probably felt more anxiety than eagerness as he traveled through the rugged Connecticut hills.

For Benedict Arnold, the day was one of suspenseful preparation and anticipation. His projected meeting with André was only two days away, but he had yet to receive positive concurrence from the other side. Then came word from Colonel Robinson, aboard the *Vulture*. Yes, the sloop would remain on station until the next day, and the Briton would be prepared to meet the American general "at any place you please." The meaning was clear—the rendezvous would be held as Arnold wanted, ashore at Smith's house and in secrecy.

By the time Joshua Smith arrived at the Robinson House—in the middle of the day, after having deposited his family in Fishkill—Arnold was set to conclude the necessary details. As previously discussed, Smith would go to the *Vulture* in the middle of the night on Wednesday, September 20. He would row out to the ship, using as oarsmen two local tenant farmers, pick up a passenger, row back, and deliver that person to his house, where Arnold would confer with him. If Smith ever wondered why an agent would be aboard a British warship, he kept his thoughts to himself. Believing the whole affair was an attempt to gather intelligence, he apparently was not disposed to ask questions.

Arnold wrote a note of safe conduct authorizing Smith, two servants, and a man named John Anderson "to pass and repass the guards near King's Ferry at all times." He also ordered a boat to be made ready. With all that finished, he had essentially placed the success or failure of the entire effort in the hands of Joshua Hett Smith. They happened to be very inept hands.

Smith enjoyed the intrigue of espionage, but as a go-between, not as a man of resolution himself. A dreamer who yearned to participate in big things but who lacked the personal force to achieve them, a sycophant rather than a doer, he was the wrong person to rely on in so sensitive a situation.

Wednesday, September 20, 1780

Hartford was hardly a place "worth lingering over," wrote a contemporary traveler. "It consists of a long, very long street parallel to the river." But it was not the town on the Connecticut River that Rochambeau and his officers were coming to see, it was George Washington.

What they saw "enchanted" the worldly Frenchmen. The renowned rebel leader "surpassed our expectations and won every heart," said one. Another, commenting on the Virginian's "handsome and majestic" countenance, stated simply, "He looks the hero." Yet another lamented his own inability to "find strong enough words to describe" the persuasive power with which the American spoke.

Washington found the French general amiable enough and eager to establish cordial relations. Although obliged to work through an interpreter, the two men forged a mutually respectful if somewhat wary affinity.

It was good that they got along personally, because their official positions were bound to diverge.

On the Hudson, Arnold's painstakingly constructed scheme began to come apart.

Somehow he had failed to convey his own sense of urgency to Joshua Smith, who made his way leisurely south toward his home, failing for some unexplained reason to take possession of the boat Arnold requisitioned for him. By the time he had rounded up the two men who were to serve as rowers—brothers Samuel and Joseph Cahoon—it was late in the day, there was no boat at hand,

and the brothers balked at going. They knew it would be a tiring and dangerous trip. Smith went limp. He sent Samuel Cahoon on a nighttime ride to inform Arnold that the rendezvous with the British agent had not taken place. Then he went to bed.

Arnold, too, slept that night. André did not. The Englishman paced the deck all night waiting for a boat that never came.

THURSDAY, SEPTEMBER 21, 1780

Well before discussions in Hartford ended on the first full day of the conference, Washington and Rochambeau had reached an understanding on the improbability of any combined actions of their armies that year.

Although the American general had arrived hoping to entice the Frenchman into participating in at least a minor campaign before the onset of winter, his practical mind told him that Rochambeau would not be so inclined. The patriots were too weak to be of much help in any undertaking, and the French army had yet to complete its buildup in Rhode Island. He was right. Rochambeau had already concluded that, militarily, 1780 was over. He had come to Hartford primarily to coordinate plans for the next year.

Even though the French general was nominally under Washington's command, it was clear that he would not risk his army by relying on hopes without substance.

It is quite evident, Washington sadly confided to Lafayette, " that my command of the French troops stands upon a very limited scale."

Arnold's day opened with the startling word that André was still on the *Vulture*. Furious, he rushed to King's Ferry to see what had gone wrong.

There, on the eastern terminus, he found awaiting him a letter from the ship's captain. Ostensibly sent to complain about the behavior of some American troops the day before, the words were in the unmistakable handwriting of Major André. Lest the point be missed, the message was countersigned "John Anderson." André remained ready to hold the meeting in spite of the missed connection and would expect to see the American contact person that night.

Arnold decided to stay in the vicinity himself to assure that this second chance was not lost by further bumbling. Had he not been so agitated, Lieutenant Colonel James Livingston, the patriot commander, might have told him about the surprise he had in store for the *Vulture*.

Crossing quickly to Stony Point, Arnold began picking up the pieces of his plan. He located the boat and had it drawn up a nearby creek, then rushed on horseback to Smith's house. He had the Cahoon brothers hauled before him to explain their reluctance to participate in the venture. Despite their continued resistance—in addition to the danger, they were now fatigued from a largely sleepless night—Arnold was not to be denied. He browbeat them into going.

Smith and the Cahoons pushed off long after nightfall. Oars muffled, gliding with the tide, they made their way to the British sloop without incident. Smith climbed aboard and was taken straight to the captain's cabin, where André and Robinson waited. In addition to private business letters carried as cover, he had a pass for John Anderson to return in the small boat with him, and a scrap of paper on which Arnold had written merely "Gustavus to John Anderson." Smith informed the two men that Arnold would be waiting alone near a landing place on the western shore, with a spare horse for Mr. Anderson.

Conferring hastily, the British major and the loyalist colonel realized the obvious: Arnold meant for André to come alone. With some reluctance, Robinson agreed to remain behind. André, concealing his regimental uniform under a dark overcoat, indicated to Smith that he would go back with him. It was midnight or shortly after.

FRIDAY, SEPTEMBER 22, 1780

The two weary oarsmen struggled against the tide on the return trip, making slower headway than had been anticipated. It was around two o'clock when they edged the boat onto the rocky shore near the rendezvous point. Smith led André to a nearby clump of fir trees where Arnold was waiting. There, at last, in darkness broken only by a shielded lantern, the traitor and the spymaster met.

Originally, the intent had been for André to go to Smith's house, where he and Arnold would plot the attack on and surrender of West Point. Then, after waiting for dark, André would return to the *Vulture*. But the botched first attempt had scrambled that plan. Arnold had horses for the ride to Smith's house, but André apparently believed they could conduct their business quickly enough on the spot, permitting him to return to the safety of his ship that same night. They huddled in the fir trees.

What actually transpired in the next couple of hours has disappeared into the mists of time. If either man ever spoke of it, his words have been lost. Surely they talked of coordinating the arrangements for assaulting West Point. Arnold would have told André of vulnerabilities in the fortress complex and would have gone over the timing of his capitulation. In all probability the Connecticut merchant insisted on confirming details of the arrangements for his compensation. Papers were passed—fateful papers, as it would turn out.

Those topics and perhaps others consumed more time than the two plotters had counted on. The minutes raced by. Around four o'clock, Joshua Smith approached to warn Arnold of the time. André should leave right away if he hoped to reach the British warship before daylight. The major was ready. He and the turncoat general had completed their necessary coordination. He would return by boat and Arnold would ride to Smith's house alone.

But the conspirators had not reckoned on the stubbornness of the Cahoon brothers. The hour was late, the two farmers were dead tired, and the tide had turned. Rowing back to the *Vulture* against it would be twice as hard as the first trip had been. And in all likelihood the passage could not be made before morning sun illuminated Haverstraw Bay. The Cahoons said no.

Arnold did not argue. He recognized the logic in their position. Besides, his thinking all along had envisioned André spending the day on land. He and André mounted the two waiting horses and rode to Smith's house—crossing patriot lines on the way.

Upon arriving, Arnold led the British major to a large second-floor room with a sweeping view of the bay. The first rays of light silhouetted *Vulture*, still at anchor near Teller's Point.

Then, to the surprise of both men, a distant booming carried across the river, and white puffs of smoke rose from Teller's Point. The Americans were shelling the British sloop. The warship's guns soon returned fire, and a cannon duel unfolded before the unbelieving eyes of the two observers in Smith's house. Arnold's face reflected consternation—as far as he knew, there had been no artillery at that forward post. But he was wrong.

Lieutenant Colonel Livingston had watched the *Vulture* with increasing irritation ever since the vessel had anchored near Teller's Point. The offending ship had been sitting there for days—arrogantly, it seemed to him—almost daring the Americans to do anything about it. Livingston decided on his own to take that dare. He asked Colonel John Lamb at West Point for ammunition for two small field pieces. Lamb was not enthusiastic about the idea, but he recalled that Arnold himself had recently urged him to take steps to bring British watercraft under fire. He sent the ammunition but was dismissive. "Firing at a ship with a four-pounder is, in my opinion, a waste of powder as the damage she will sustain is not equal to the expense." Never would he be more wrong about anything.

Livingston dragged the guns to an earthwork on Teller's Point, shrewdly waiting for a time of slack tide and low wind. Becalmed, the enemy sloop was an easy target. In the short exchange, *Vulture* had quite the worst of it. "Six shots hulled us," wrote Beverley Robinson, "one between wind and water, many others struck the sails, rigging, and boats on deck." Unable to get under way and unwilling to continue the slugfest, the ship's captain lowered longboats and began pulling downstream.

Arnold and André watched in dismay as the damaged vessel dropped slowly from sight behind a land mass at the south end of Haverstraw Bay. They had no way of knowing how far the captain would take his ship. Would he remain nearby or continue to Dobb's Ferry? The Englishman's method of return was now drastically uncertain.

Needing to hurry back to his headquarters to prepare for the arrival of General Washington, Arnold wrote passes to cover a return to British lines by either water or land. Telling Smith and

André that they could decide on their own which course seemed the better, he departed. The pair sat down to ponder the odds.

After the morning duel between Livingston's shore battery and the hostile warship, the patriots were likely to be more vigilant in checking river traffic, or so Smith reasoned. Maybe more to the point, he had no stomach for another argument with the Cahoon brothers, especially for a long haul to Dobb's Ferry. He convinced André that escaping by land would be much surer and safer. However, he insisted that "Mr. Anderson" could no longer wear a British officer's uniform.

Late in the day, when traffic at King's Ferry thinned, the two men crossed to the east side of the Hudson using Major General Arnold's paper of safe conduct. André wore civilian clothing Smith had given him. They continued until darkness forced them to take shelter in a house along the way. They shared a single bed, all the family had to offer. Although he had endured a sleepless night and a nerve-wracking day, André slept only fitfully.

———•·•———

Meanwhile, that Friday was much quieter for George Washington. Concluding the conference with Rochambeau and preparing to return to the Continental Army had none of the high drama under way seventy-five miles to the west on the Hudson. But it certainly had its downside.

Washington was embarrassed by the evident weakness of the United States. The Continental Army was staggering from a long-standing shortage of supplies and funds. Morale had sunk to serious depths of uncertainty. Militiamen were staying home. The Congress had been unable to settle on either the size of its military establishment for 1781 or for its support. Worse yet, the American commander had to admit that he did not even know how he would keep his current forces in being after the heavy losses sure to occur as enlistments ended in just three months. He endorsed Rochambeau's plan to build the French strength to 15,000 soldiers over the winter and spring, but he could only offer unsupported hopes that the United States, "by a new effort," could match those numbers. In the dim light of such vagueness, the conference ended on an inconclusive note.

SATURDAY, SEPTEMBER 23, 1780

Washington was leaving Hartford later than he had planned. As a result he now expected to reach the Robinson House on Sunday, not on Saturday as he had told Arnold when they last met.

For security reasons, the commander in chief chose not to retrace his steps back to the Hudson. To follow the same path so close to enemy lines risked running into an ambush, for spies might have informed Sir Henry of his route going to the Hartford meeting. Benedict Arnold had in fact done just that.

The new course passed north of the Hudson highlands, rather than through Peekskill to the south of that mountainous barrier. Washington and his entourage spent the night in Litchfield, Connecticut, planning a long Sunday ride in order to reach General Arnold's headquarters late that day.

Dawn came to the Hudson promising a fair, pleasant day ahead. Smith and André were already on the road. André, perhaps moved by memories of the daybreak cannonade the day before, had awakened Smith early, and the two men had started in darkness. Several miles along the way Smith reined in. British lines were some fifteen miles farther on, he informed the agent, a stretch he could cover on his own. Competing bands of patriots and loyalists patrolled that area, but he was sure the Englishman would be safe alone. If stopped by patriots, Arnold's pass would get him by; if stopped by loyalists, he would be escorted to a nearby British unit.

André rode on, acutely aware of the bulge in his boots caused by the papers Arnold had given him. All went well at first. Then, shortly before ten o'clock, at a bridge near Tarrytown and safety, three men stepped out of hiding. With leveled muskets they ordered the horseman to halt and dismount. Rattled, André aroused suspicions by first claiming to be British and only later showing Arnold's pass. Searching him, the men found the concealed documents and realized they had a big catch. They took him to Lieutenant Colonel John Jameson at North Castle, who had very recently replaced Colonel Elisha Sheldon.

Jameson had standing instructions to be on the watch for a John Anderson coming from New York City to see General Arnold. Here was Anderson—but he had been riding *toward* the city. Moreover, the papers found on him were "of a very dangerous tendency," containing sensitive details regarding the West Point defenses. Still, the pass from Arnold was valid and was in that general's handwriting. Jameson was puzzled. He had to do something, but what? He may have been a good soldier, but in this case he was out of his depth. Sheldon's departure had taken from the scene the most experienced hand in such matters.

Choosing a course of action defying all logic, Jameson decided to split the evidence. He directed a lieutenant with a guard detail to escort "Anderson" to General Arnold at the Robinson House, along with a letter describing the circumstances of his capture. Then he sent André's documents to General Washington. "Inclos'd you'll receive a parcel of papers taken from a certain John Anderson who has a pass signed by General Arnold," he wrote. Anderson had been "very desirous of the papers and everything being sent with him," Jameson went on, adding, "I thought it more proper your Excellency should see them." Not knowing of Washington's revised return route, he sent the packet by courier to intercept the commanding general in Danbury, Connecticut.

About that time an American officer who did know something of the shadowy world of espionage arrived at Jameson's headquarters. Major Benjamin Tallmadge had worked for years as one of Washington's intelligence officers. On hearing the strange tale, he suspected straightaway that Arnold was a traitor. He implored Jameson to return "Anderson" to North Castle and to recall the message to Arnold.

The hapless colonel, now more confused than ever, equivocated once again. He sent a fast rider to overtake the guard detail with orders for the lieutenant to take Anderson to a secure site at South Salem, where he would be farther from the reach of any British rescue attempt than he would have been at North Castle. But he remained conflicted. Perhaps he simply could not imagine that the celebrated Benedict Arnold was a traitor. For whatever reason, he continued to see his duty as notifying Arnold, who was, after all, his commander. Accordingly, he gave the lieutenant a second note to carry to Arnold, informing him that he had detained Anderson. By then, however, it was very late in the day. The lieutenant decided to wait until the next morning to start.

Unaware of the turmoil at Jameson's headquarters, Benedict Arnold was spending a most unpleasant afternoon at his own headquarters. Joshua Smith rode in to report what he supposed had been Anderson's safe return to New York City. Arnold's aides, deeply distrusting the man they detested as a probable loyalist, ignited a heated argument at dinner, causing Peggy to plead that they drop the matter. Tempers boiled over until Arnold quieted his aides, after Smith departed, by promising never to see him again. Thinking André safely back at British headquarters, he no longer needed Joshua Smith.

SUNDAY, SEPTEMBER 24, 1780

Benedict and Peggy, anticipating the arrival of General Washington that evening and assuming that André would already have delivered his report to Sir Henry, had a final few quiet hours alone to discuss the coming explosion.

For others it was a day of activity as various players converged on Beverley Robinson's house in the Hudson highlands. Appropriately enough, the day also brought drenching rainstorms.

Major André, hearing the incriminating papers found on him were on their way to General Washington, realized his neck was measured for a noose. Hanging was the only punishment for spies. He admitted his identity to his captors and wrote a letter to Washington explaining his predicament. Through no fault of his own, he claimed, he had been "betrayed" and placed in the "vile condition of an enemy in disguise within your posts."

The rider carrying André's papers to Washington returned, unable to deliver them because the commander in chief had taken the more northerly route back to the Hudson. Jameson added André's confession to the packet and sent it off again. This time he charged a captain to find Washington somewhere in the highlands.

The lieutenant bearing Lieutenant Colonel Jameson's two letters to Arnold was also on the road by that time, heading for the Robinson House. Apparently unaware of the nature of the material they carried, neither courier displayed any unusual sense of urgency. Losing much time waiting under cover for the rain to slacken, they found themselves still on the way when darkness fell. Each sought shelter and settled in for the night, intending to deliver their respective messages the next day.

After all day in the saddle, Washington himself made a last-minute decision to stop in Fishkill. He had unexpectedly met the French minister who wished to be briefed on the conference at Hartford. The Robinson House was only a few miles farther—he would ride there the next morning in time for breakfast.

MONDAY, SEPTEMBER 25, 1780

Up and on the road at dawn, as was his custom, General Washington rode south accompanied by Generals Knox and Lafayette and a number of aides. The rainy weather had blown by. The day was gorgeous, brightened by leaves turning to color. Spirits were correspondingly bright.

When the cantering group reached a trail leading up to the first of West Point's outlying forts on a hill east of the Hudson, the general suddenly wheeled onto it. He had made a brief visit to the fortress complex two months earlier, but he had not had the opportunity to inspect all of the works since he had lived there a year before. He planned to do that now and wanted to see this particular redoubt while he was so near it. A good-natured chorus of complaint arose from his aides. Mrs. Arnold was probably ready with breakfast. Why not eat first and then inspect?

"I know that all you young men are in love with Mrs. Arnold," he responded smilingly. If they were that eager, he said, they had his permission to ride on, but he intended to inspect this redoubt

and another on the way to the Arnolds' home. Chuckling, they all
followed him up the trail. Two officers, sent ahead to tell General
Arnold that Washington would be delayed, galloped south, happy
at their good fortune.

Arriving about nine o'clock, they found Benedict Arnold already at the breakfast table. Peggy was upstairs. Well, since General Washington would be delayed, would they care to join him?
Hungry from the brisk ride in the early morning air, they certainly
would.

As the three officers ate, the courier from Lieutenant Colonel
Jameson reined in and entered the house. Aides would normally
have screened messages arriving for Arnold, but fate had a hand
in events that morning. Because one of his aides was temporarily
away and the other was ill, Arnold beckoned the rider over and
took the two letters himself. Unhurriedly he opened them and
casually began to read. Messages from subordinate commanders
were routine.

However, the words leaping off these papers were anything but
routine. The general stiffened. Anderson captured . . . held at South
Salem . . . a pass signed by Arnold . . . documents concealed on
him . . . Washington notified.

Incredible! His entire scheme lay revealed! And Washington
himself would arrive any moment. As calmly as he could, the traitor left the table, pulled the messenger aside and told him to say
nothing to anyone about the capture of Mr. Anderson, ordered his
horse readied, and hastened upstairs to inform his wife. He had no
recourse other than to flee. Peggy would have to remain behind,
but she would be safe. Surely no one would suspect a young
woman and new mother of complicity in treason.

While the two were talking, an aide knocked on the door to
inform them that General Washington was nearing. Arnold bolted

downstairs, shouted over his shoulder that he was going across the river to West Point to prepare for Washington's visit, leaped on his horse, and raced down the steep trail to his barge. Head south, he ordered the surprised crew, and hurry!

Not long afterwards, General Washington dismounted at the Robinson House, finding some puzzled young officers and an unusual situation. Arnold was not there. He had rushed over to West Point just a short time before. Mrs. Arnold was in her room upstairs, indisposed. Breakfast was waiting, however, so he sat down to eat. With the meal over and still no word from Arnold, the commander in chief crossed the river to West Point expecting to find him there.

Instead, he stepped ashore to meet a very surprised Colonel John Lamb. That crusty colonel had not seen Arnold all day. Mystified, but not suspecting malfeasance, the commanding general toured the fortifications, sure that Arnold would soon show up with a good explanation for his strange behavior. For the next two hours he probed and questioned. He had anticipated finding problems, but nothing of the magnitude unfolding before him. West Point was far weaker than he would have imagined in his most pessimistic moments.

Dismayed and worried, bringing Colonel Lamb and the engineer along, he returned to the Robinson House for serious discussions with Arnold over the deteriorating status of the vital fortress. It was nearly two o'clock, and as yet there had been no sign of Arnold. Increasingly concerned over the continuing absence, Washington went to a room set aside for him and pulled off his coat and shirt to wash up. He could not fathom what could be keeping Arnold away.

The traitor, his dreams of retribution in ruins, had reached the *Vulture* shortly before noon, about the same time Washington was startling Colonel Lamb by landing unannounced at West Point. Climbing aboard the sloop to encounter a stunned Beverley Robinson, Arnold blurted out the staggering news. André was captured, Washington was at West Point, the plot had collapsed.

While Washington was inspecting the West Point defenses, Peggy Arnold had broken her silence, erupting in screeching hysterics. Wild screams from the top of the stairs jolted Richard Varick from his sickbed. Racing up the steps, he found Peggy running up and down a corridor, shrieking and pulling at her loose hair. She wore nothing except an unbuttoned gossamer gown floating behind her. Falling to her knees before the astounded aide, she pleaded with him to protect her from the men who wanted to kill her baby. With help from Major Franks and a doctor, Varick was able to put the ranting young woman back in bed and calm her somewhat. She was quiet by the time Washington returned from West Point.

As the perturbed commander in chief prepared to clean himself of the day's accumulated grime, the officer Jameson had dispatched more than a day earlier to find him arrived at the Robinson House. He handed his packet to Alexander Hamilton. The aide opened it—and immediately realized its awful significance. Arnold's strange disappearance now made sense.

Hamilton knocked urgently on Washington's door, entered, and spread the documents on a table. The general, clothed only in breeches and boots, scanned the papers. The terrible truth rolled over him. Benedict Arnold was a traitor! The erect Virginian sagged visibly under that blow, his torso slumping, consternation washing across his face. Arnold? It was utterly incomprehensible. Hamilton had never seen him so shaken by emotion. It took supreme willpower for the commander in chief of the Continental Army to pull himself together.

The traitor had in all likelihood made good his escape, but something may have delayed him. Washington ordered Hamilton and another officer to gallop to King's Ferry on the slim possibility that they could arrest the fugitive before he crossed into British control.

Dressing rapidly, the distraught general summoned Knox and Lafayette. There was no way of knowing how many others might have been involved in the conspiracy, so for the time being only close members of his personal party were to be trusted.

As the two men entered his room, Washington met them with a cry escaping from the depth of his wounded heart: "Arnold has betrayed us!"

CHAPTER TWENTY-ONE

"ERASE FROM THE REGISTER"

--◆-◆-◆--

A FTER KNOX AND LAFAYETTE SCANNED THE PAPERS REVEAL-ing Arnold's treachery, they sat down with Washington to plan a course of action. Questions abounded. What might enemy intentions be? Where were the patriots most vulnerable? How imminent was the threat of attack? Were others involved with Arnold?

The Americans knew that British ships were prepared to transport troops up the Hudson on short notice. But General Clinton had probably not yet learned of André's capture. Even if Arnold had made good his escape, it would be night before he reached New York City. So it seemed safe to assume that no major attack could be launched until, at the very soonest, early the next day, and likely later. Clinton's men would need to be readied, and weather would be a major factor to consider before attempting to sail up the river. Heavy skies were already showing signs of rain.

Washington decided not to spread the alarm until Hamilton returned with definite information regarding Arnold.

Meanwhile, the Robinson House and the near vicinity had to be sealed off. Washington's security detachment went on full alert, allowing no one in or out. Arnold's two aides were placed under house arrest, and soldiers were sent to seize Joshua Smith. Who among others could be trusted? John Lamb. After having spent much of the day with the blunt colonel, Washington sensed clearly that he had not been in on the plot. He sent him south to take command at King's Ferry, where he would give early warning of any enemy approach. Lieutenant Colonel Jameson was obviously loyal, for he had sent the incriminating documents to Washington in the first place. The commander in chief directed him to have André brought under heavy guard to the Robinson House. What about Arnold's wife?

Peggy, verging once again on hysteria, was demanding to see General Washington. Having known her since she was fourteen, he did not suspect her of treason. The Virginian went to her bedside.

Raving about those who would kill her baby, about hot irons pressed into heads, about Arnold being gone forever, she appeared not to recognize the general. Her flailing arms caused her flimsy gown again to fall away. Embarrassed, Washington turned and left. He had not suspected her before; now he was fully convinced of her absolute innocence. Her hysteria—or histrionics—had worked. Not a man present that day ever had the slightest doubt of Peggy Arnold's innocence. In fact, her complicity in the conspiracy remained a secret for nearly two centuries, surfacing only after researchers found undeniable evidence in musty British Headquarters papers.

Word soon arrived from Alexander Hamilton. Arnold had escaped to the *Vulture*. From that ship he had written a hasty letter to General Washington. After claiming implausibly to have switched sides out of "love for my country," he asked his former friend and mentor to protect Peggy. "She is as good, and as innocent, as an angel, and is incapable of doing wrong," he lied. Joshua Smith and the aides, Varick and Franks, were "totally ignorant of any transactions of mine that they had reason to believe were injurious to the public." Showing the parsimonious streak lurking just under the surface of his personality in recent years, Arnold raised the issue of his abandoned personal belongings. He wondered if Washington would see to it "that my clothes and baggage, which are of little consequence, may be sent to me" in the city. He would pay for any expense incurred, he assured the commander in chief. With lives and treason and war at stake, the traitor's mind dwelt on the mundane.

Washington worked late into the night issuing orders for the disposition of forces to defend the Hudson highlands. He would personally command at West Point and vicinity, while General Nathanael Greene would continue in charge of forces already shifting to concentrate nearer the Hudson highlands.

In a day or two it became evident that the British were not moving. Whatever Clinton's original plans might have been, the unexpected capture of André and the flight of Arnold had apparently caused him to reassess. Without the benefit of having a traitor on the inside, having lost the element of surprise, and with Americans standing ready, there would be no assault of the fortress complex. Rainstorms pelting the area gave further comfort to the defenders. On September 27, general orders in the main army proclaimed the day's parole to be "West Point." Countersigns were "Fortune" and

"Favors," while the watchword was "America." The saving of West Point seemed to give proof that fortune indeed favored America.

Despite the downpour, Peggy Arnold left that day. Major Franks, who had brought the young woman to join her husband only thirteen days earlier, had the duty of taking her back to her family in Philadelphia.

A day later, on September 28, Washington relinquished personal command in the highlands and returned to the headquarters of the Continental Army at Tappan, New Jersey. The threat Arnold's treason had posed to West Point had passed. Now it was a matter of dealing with the persons concerned.

Mrs. Arnold was gone, a pitied innocent in the minds of Americans. Varick and Franks, Arnold's abused aides, were also quickly cleared. Joshua Smith did have a trial. He was found not guilty of treason, merely of being extraordinarily naïve. Major John André had a hearing, but it was essentially a formality. He had been captured behind patriot lines, dressed in civilian clothing, and carrying documents of military intelligence. That was the classic description of a spy. Although he had the sympathy of his captors, who blamed Benedict Arnold for the English officer's predicament, he would hang.

Henry Clinton tried everything he could to save his adjutant general. But under the rules of war, Washington would not, could not, budge. He did hint that he would bend those rules by swapping André for Arnold, but that was the one thing Clinton could not do. On October 2, a day sad in both armies, André was publicly executed.

That left only Benedict Arnold. George Washington ached to get his hands on the traitor. Though Arnold was apparently out of reach in New York City, Washington authorized a complex scheme, involving a fake deserter, in order to capture him. Clinton inadvertently thwarted the attempt when he sent Arnold on a raiding expedition to Virginia. Washington never lost his burning desire to capture Arnold—a desire that would drive events the following year.

Although the immediate threat to West Point had been averted, Washington worried that news of Arnold's defection would accelerate the downward slide of America's determination to continue the long war. But, in fact, the betrayal had exactly the opposite impact on patriot morale—it gave new life to revolutionary zeal.

Emotions swept America in three distinct waves. First came surprise, disbelief, and shock. Then on the heels of astonishment came anger—bitter, biting anger. Sheer hate for the scoundrel who would have sold his countrymen and the cause for money. Arnold became almost at once a figure despised and reviled as none other has been in the entire history of the United States. Washington himself virtually seethed with hatred, so vile did he consider the treason. Loathing was universal. The Congress resolved "to erase from the register of the names of the officers of the army of the United States the name of Benedict Arnold." The main bastion at West Point, known as Fort Arnold ever since it was built, got a new name within days. The traitor was on his way to becoming a nonperson, a caricature whose name would become synonymous with the basest of disloyalty to country.

The third wave had more to do with the nation itself than directly with Arnold. Frightened by the brush with disaster, and seeing the saving hand of "Providence" in the favorable outcome, Americans experienced something akin to a religious revival. They tended to see a heavenly intervention on their behalf. It was nothing less than a "providential train of circumstances" that had blocked Arnold, Nathanael Greene told his soldiers, which "affords the most convincing proof that the liberties of America are the object of divine protection." The Congress announced a day of thanksgiving and prayer to mark the role of "Almighty God" in saving the nation "at the moment when treason was ripened for execution." Thomas Paine wrote in typically ringing words that the most important point in the affair was the "providence evident in the discovery" of Arnold before he could succeed. "I think the providential discovery of so deep and dangerous a plot," wrote an army doctor in his diary, ought to be widely and loudly proclaimed, for it is "a happy omen for America."

Washington himself summed up the soaring national emotion of thanksgiving: "In no instance since the commencement of the war," he solemnly proclaimed, "has the interposition of Providence appeared more conspicuous than in the rescue of the post and garrison of West Point from Arnold's villainous perfidy."

As the sequence of words in general orders for October 27 implied, there was widespread agreement that fortune favored America. A spirit reminiscent of that of 1776 walked the land again.

It is an irony among ironies that Benedict Arnold managed to do what no one else had. He revitalized the Revolution.

CHAPTER TWENTY-TWO

NEW LONDON
AND YORKTOWN

———◆•◆•◆———

WITHIN DAYS OF HIS DEFECTION, BENEDICT ARNOLD wore a new red coat. Sir Henry Clinton appointed him a brigadier general in the British army and authorized him to raise an armed force comprised of deserters and loyalists.

No one trusts—or for that matter, likes—a traitor. For propaganda purposes British headquarters trumpeted the fact of Arnold's defection, hoping by his example to precipitate a flood of desertions, but he was far from popular among his new compatriots. Beneath the surface of their formally polite, if aloof, reserve bubbled resentment that their one-time foe was now a general. To them, he was a double traitor who had rebelled against the mother country before turning on his fellow Americans. And it was widely believed that had it not been for Arnold's negligence, Major John André would not have swung as a spy.

The turncoat's early weeks in New York City were painfully deflating in other ways as well. General Clinton flatly refused to give him more money than the minimum he had promised if the attempt to seize West Point failed. Few Americans followed Arnold and joined the British; in fact, his treason seemed to be having the opposite effect. Across the United States the once respected hero became an overnight star of effigy burnings. Nor did those close to him escape scrutiny. Philadelphia authorities, led by the detested Joseph Reed (how that must have stung), seized his papers looking for evidence to expose his previous shady behavior. Finding a suspicious letter from André to Peggy, they banished her from the City of Brotherly Love, forcing her into exile with her husband in crowded New York City. All in all, it was hard for Arnold to find any fruits of his treason. He gained neither fortune nor prestige, and certainly not esteem.

Counting on battlefield exploits to restore his reputation, Arnold let Sir Henry know that he was ready to lead British units in combat. The question was, where?

French troops under Rochambeau held a strong position in Rhode Island. Washington's main army occupied forbidding defenses in and around the Hudson highlands. Nathanael Greene, sent to replace the disgraced Horatio Gates, opposed General Charles Cornwallis in the southern theater. That left the middle colonies unprotected and vulnerable. A campaign there would seriously hinder America's already sputtering ability to supply the Continental Army and could draw strength away from rebel forces in the south or north, or both. Sir Henry decided to send an expedition to invade Virginia. Brigadier General Benedict Arnold would command it.

Arnold sailed from New York on December 21, 1780, leading a mixed contingent of some 1,600 British, Hessian, and loyalist troops. He reached the James River in the new year and headed straight for Richmond, the capital and a major supply center. Governor Thomas Jefferson and Virginia's legislators scattered at the approach of their former countryman. By the end of the first week in 1781 the hard-riding marauder had burned the town's warehouse district and laid waste to several other smaller depots in the area. Largely unopposed, he then established a base at Portsmouth. From there he stood poised to ravage at will.

Despite serious problems in the main army—and they were many—George Washington's mind kept coming back to Benedict Arnold. He could not stand the thought of the infamous defector running roughshod through Virginia. Lives and homes of friends and family were at risk. Mount Vernon itself could be burned. The Virginian was furious.

But Washington also recognized the tantalizing prospect that Arnold's raiders, far from Clinton in New York, could be cut off and captured. If French warships could keep the British navy occupied, temporarily isolating Arnold's relatively small contingent, a fast-moving and competent ground force might overwhelm him. The miscreant could then be brought to justice. Washington wanted to try. He approached Rochambeau, who agreed to support continental troops with French naval and land forces.

By mid-February patriot leaders had selected more than a thousand men, many from the West Point garrison, who were robust, well trained, and well equipped. To command the expedition, Washington chose the Marquis de Lafayette. Should Arnold "fall into your hands," the Virginian coldly told Lafayette, you are to execute him "in the most summary way." The patriots hastened south overland, aiming for Annapolis, Maryland, where French transports were to pick them up to complete the movement by sea.

Washington rode to Newport to confer with Rochambeau, intending to do everything he could to eliminate any snags in the planning. "I set out this morning for Rhode Island where I hope to arrive before the fleet sails," he informed Lafayette on the first day of March 1781.

Once more, however, the Americans were let down by the French navy. After a brief naval clash with the British—which resulted in minor damage to the allied admiral's fleet but major damage to his confidence—the French ships meekly returned to Rhode Island. Lafayette was left on his own, halfway to the objective.

Disappointed but grimly determined, Washington directed him to continue by land. He was to operate against Arnold with the forces he had until the commander in chief could send more. No matter what, Arnold was not to be left unopposed.

Following the withdrawal of the French fleet, General Clinton sent Major General William Phillips and some two thousand men to Virginia to reinforce Arnold. Phillips, as the senior officer, assumed overall command. In one of the war's many coincidences, Phillips had faced Arnold in the battles of Saratoga back in 1777. Now he found himself fighting alongside his former opponent.

The British, with an even greater military superiority thanks to Phillips's reinforcements, continued their ruinous attacks through April. With Phillips directing operations and Arnold leading raiding columns, the invaders ranged Virginia at will.

Then, on April 30, the redcoats were surprised to find continental units facing them. Lafayette had arrived.

General Phillips prudently withdrew to a base on the James River to assess the new situation. There, early in May, he learned that General Charles Cornwallis was marching north from the Carolinas to join him in Virginia. That would change the balance of power again.

General Cornwallis arrived on May 20 and pushed north to trap Lafayette, allegedly boasting, "The boy cannot escape me." But Lafayette eluded Cornwallis, slipping safely north of Fredericksburg by early June. Without the services of Phillips (who had died of fever) or Arnold (who had returned to New York), Cornwallis stopped his pursuit and turned his attention to launching destructive sweeps across the state.

At that point, Anthony Wayne and a strong body of soldiers joined Lafayette, giving the Americans sufficient strength to discourage freewheeling raids. Cornwallis moved slowly back south and east, with Lafayette cautiously following.

By July the English commander was thoroughly frustrated by the slippery patriot forces and by General Clinton's orders that he occupy a base on the coast. By late August most British elements in Virginia were ensconced behind earthworks thrown up around the small port town of Yorktown.

Washington had not captured Benedict Arnold, but the forces he had sent south helped precipitate the decisive battle of the Revolutionary War.

Momentum shifted in May 1781. While Anthony Wayne was marching to reinforce Lafayette in Virginia, news arrived that more ground troops were on the way from France and a powerful French fleet under the respected Admiral de Grasse might sail north from the West Indies to participate in an attack. Late that month Washington and Rochambeau met at Wethersfield, Connecticut, near Hartford, to plan the coming campaign. Washington had struggled for years to orchestrate "one great vigorous effort" against a British stronghold, and that opportunity appeared to be finally materializing.

Their planning had to be flexible—so much depended on the French navy. American and French land forces would link up on the Hudson River above New York City, where they would pose a threat to that city and could act in any direction according to developments at sea. Even the very objective of their campaign could not be selected until questions regarding the fleet's destination could be answered. New York? Somewhere in the south? Elsewhere?

By July the two armies had united and were posturing as if to attack Clinton's northernmost outposts on Manhattan Island. But however much he may have burned to recapture the city he had lost five long years before, Washington could take no decisive steps until first hearing from de Grasse. Without a navy nothing would work.

Then, in mid-August, came thrilling news: the admiral was sailing for the Chesapeake with a mighty fleet and about three thousand soldiers. He would be there early in September and remain until mid-October. On that same day arrived word that Cornwallis was digging in at Yorktown. Here was the long-awaited chance to strike a telling blow, and a place and timetable for doing it.

That was all the information Washington and Rochambeau needed. They would fall on Cornwallis, who might be trapped with perhaps as much as a fourth of all of Great Britain's forces in America. To have a chance of working the plan would have to achieve surprise, and that would require speed. Within mere days the two generals had their combined armies in motion for a rendezvous with de Grasse in Virginia.

In as superb an operational maneuver as was seen in the war—or in any war, for that matter—allied forces feinted at New York City to hold Clinton in place, and then raced more than four hundred miles south to surprise and surround their prey at Yorktown. Moving not only men but enormous quantities of supplies and equipment, both over land and on water, needing food and forage all the way, Washington was attempting a feat to tax the most professional of armies.

Meanwhile, the French navy made up for nearly four years of ineptitude by outsailing and outfighting the British fleet and joining Washington and Rochambeau in besieging Yorktown.

The "great vigorous effort" bagged Cornwallis. On October 19 he formally surrendered his entire army. Although two more years were to pass before final terms for a peace treaty could be worked out, the war was essentially over. America had won its independence.

———•—•———

Benedict Arnold had one last bloody scene to play. After returning to New York City, he had watched Washington and Rochambeau threaten Manhattan Island. Like his British colleagues, he was surprised when the combined force suddenly disappeared.

A worried Sir Henry Clinton quickly ordered a diversionary attack into New England, hoping to draw units away from Washington's forces heading south. He selected New London, Connecticut, as the objective. That town had long been high on his list of potential targets. It was Connecticut's leading wartime seaport, it was a haven for privateers, it held large stores of valuable rebel supplies, and it was close to New York. Moreover, the area was well known to one of Clinton's generals. Benedict Arnold had been born and raised in Norwich, a few miles up the Thames River from New London. He got the mission.

Arnold began landing troops on both banks of the Thames on the morning of September 6. New London stood basically defenseless on the west side of the river while a single bastion, Fort Griswold, guarded the east side. Arnold personally led the attack against the port town, where shipping jammed wharves and stacks of supplies filled warehouses. Soon New London was ablaze, buildings and ships alike going up in flame. Across the river, militiamen manning Fort Griswold refused to surrender without a fight, obliging the raiders to take the fortification by storm. As enemy soldiers breached the ramparts, patriots laid down their arms—or tried to. Infuriated attackers, their blood up and angered by the casualties they had sustained in the assault, began to massacre the garrison, not stopping until some eighty defenders had been slain in cold blood. Arnold quickly withdrew, sailing back to New York.

The burning of New London and the gruesome atrocity at Fort Griswold deepened the already visceral hatred Americans felt for Benedict Arnold. The raid itself had absolutely no impact on General Washington's march to Yorktown.

That was the last time Arnold ever commanded troops in battle.

CHAPTER TWENTY-THREE

LEGACY

⫘⬥⫘

O NE CAN SUM UP THE LEGACIES OF THE TWO MEN IN A
simple truth: George Washington became the father of
his country while Benedict Arnold became a man without a country.

Washington lived for nearly two more decades after the treason;
Arnold outlived him by only eighteen months. In those years
George Washington rose to new heights of renown while Benedict
Arnold dwelt in the depths of infamy.

So soaring was Washington's fame that historians still struggle to
portray him as really human, a man with strengths and weaknesses, not some sort of super being placed on earth for the specific purpose of creating the United States of America.

Arnold, on the other hand, was almost at once removed from
the register of American heroes. His villainy erased his heroic
deeds. Historians struggle with him, too, trying to reconcile his

intrepid leadership in the first three years of the Revolutionary War with his later treachery.

It may well be that the complete story of those two patriots will linger always just beyond the reach of even the best of analysts to explain. It is relatively easy, however, to relate what each did in the years after they became enemies.

Following the triumph at Yorktown, General Washington held the army—and the country—together until a favorable peace treaty could be forged. He then resigned his commission and returned to Mount Vernon. When the new nation began to come unglued under the inoperable Articles of Confederation, he chaired the convention that wrote our Constitution, and played a key role in its ratification. As America's first president—the only popularly elected ruler in the entire world at that time—he established the policies and precedents that assured the enduring nature of the infant republic. After eight years in office (1789–1797) he once again turned his back on power and retired to Mount Vernon, where he died in 1799. He was indeed, in the immortal words of "Light-Horse Harry" Lee, first in war, first in peace, and first in the hearts of his countrymen.

Three months after his futile raid on New London, General Arnold left for England, never to return to the country of his birth. Initially he was well received. The king and his ministers conferred with him on American affairs, and lifetime pensions were granted to him and his family. But the novelty surrounding the celebrated turncoat soon wore off, and he found himself more or less isolated in a land where he was neither fully trusted nor liked.

Denied a command in the army, he turned back to commerce, going in 1785 to New Brunswick in Canada and starting again as a merchant-shipper. That did not work out advantageously. For one thing, the many loyalists who had settled there were unable to for-

get that his long-ago heroics as a patriot warrior had been so instrumental in their ouster from the United States. Barred on pain of
death from entering the United States, and recognizing that he
would never be accepted in Canada, he returned to England in
1791. But even there his past was not forgotten, leading him to fight
yet another duel to stifle slights leveled against him. Then began a
decade of decline in which nothing seemed to work out for him.
During the war with France he tried his hand at outfitting privateers, with scant success. In that venture as in most during those
years, he lost more than he gained.

Constant setbacks wore him down. He died in June 1801, a
beaten man looking back on a largely wasted life. Peggy told her
firstborn son (the infant she had clasped so dramatically to her
breast at the Robinson House back in 1780) that Benedict's
"numerous vexations and mortifications...had broken his spirits
and destroyed his nerves." He left his family a stack of debts—and
a name reviled in history.

One author labeled George Washington "a Man of Monuments." From Mount Rushmore to the majestic obelisk in our
nation's capital, he is honored by so many markers that no actual
count of them exists. And monuments are the least of it. The face
on the dollar bill, paintings and prints without number, buildings
where he slept, books too numerous for any one person to read,
places and people named for him—the list of tributes to George
Washington is endless.

The opposite is true of Benedict Arnold. His name is on a
memorial stone (of Vermont granite, by the way) in the small
church of St. Mary's Battersea in London, but his bones lie mixed
there with others in a common grave. A stream near his marching
route to Quebec is called Arnold River—but it runs only on the
Canadian side of the border. At the spot where he was wounded

as he broke the British line during the Second Battle of Saratoga stands a memorial of sorts: a disembodied leg, clad in a military boot. That strange edifice recognizes his extraordinary deeds in the battle and the crippling wound he sustained, but he is neither represented nor even named. For sure, the register has been virtually erased.

Nowhere is the difference in the legacies of the two men more starkly portrayed than at the very vortex of the treason itself.

Go to West Point. Right at the center of that fabled ground, overlooking the cadet parade field, stands a larger-than-life statue of General Washington. Mounted on a mighty stallion, erect, outstretched arm pointing bravely to the future, the most heroic figure of any honored there, he dominates the scene as completely as he dominated events in his own lifetime.

Now walk from there along (what else?) Washington Road to the cemetery, where the earliest graves are of Revolutionary War soldiers. Enter the old chapel and look at the wall to your right. There, high and in a row from front to back, hang plaques commemorating generals of the Revolutionary War. Striking in their simplicity, each contains only four entries: a rank, a name, a date of birth, and a date of death. Except for the final one, almost lost to view up by the choir loft. It shows only a rank—major general—and a date of birth. The message is inescapable: non-persons have no name and traitors never die, they simply cease to exist.

The Arnold family plot in Norwich's Colonial Cemetery contains the graves of Benedict's parents and four of his siblings who died in childhood. Two headstones are missing, however, that of his father (Benedict IV) and of his older brother (the first Benedict V). Apparently, some townsmen took literally the injunction to remove Benedict Arnold's name wherever it might appear.

George Washington fathered no children. But his name lived on, carried proudly by American boys generation after generation. Benedict Arnold sired nine offspring. His eldest son, Benedict VI, died in battle fighting for Great Britain against French forces in 1795, the last in a line of Arnolds of that name. There would be no more. For, by his treachery, Benedict Arnold had turned an esteemed name into an evil epithet.

CHAPTER TWENTY-FOUR

CHARACTER

———◆◦◆◦◆———

IN 1802, NOT LONG AFTER THE DEATHS OF GEORGE WASHINGTON and Benedict Arnold, President Thomas Jefferson signed into law the act founding the United States Military Academy. The school was to be located at West Point, on the very ground so central to Arnold's treason. Its purpose—at the time and over the centuries since—was to provide the young republic with military officers who would be leaders of character. That phrase is irreducible, the three words comprising one indivisible concept. Not simply leaders was West Point to produce, but leaders of character.

Establishing at that place an institution having such a purpose is the final irony in the story of Washington and Arnold.

The tale of the two patriots, who left such diametrically opposite legacies despite life trajectories that were at one time so parallel, is only partly told by addressing *what* happened. To be complete it must also address the *why*. Why did one man stay on the road to historical immortality while the other plunged over the cliff of infamy?

The easy answer is to say that one had strength of character while the other did not. But what exactly does that mean? What is character? And how did it shape so extraordinary an outcome?

Character is a deceptively simple word with meanings ranging from the objective ("the aggregate of features and traits that form an apparent individual nature of some person or thing") to the descriptive ("qualities of honesty, courage, or the like") to the subjective ("moral or ethical quality; good repute; integrity"). Not surprisingly, therefore, the word is often paired with a modifier: sterling character; bad character; strong character; weak character; fine character; and so on. It is in fact a chameleon word.

Philosophers have wrestled through the ages with the concept of character. The ancient Greeks reduced it to the sum of four virtues. *Fortitude*: strength of mind along with the physical and moral courage to persevere in the face of adversity. *Temperance*: self-discipline to control passions and appetites. *Prudence*: practical wisdom and the ability to make the right choice in specific situations. *Justice*: fairness, honesty, lawfulness, keeping promises. A person of good character, the ancients thought, kept those four virtues in balance.

The advance of thousands of years has not appreciably improved that formulation. A group of modern educators and philosophers, meeting in 1992 in Aspen, Colorado, listed what they concluded were the core elements of character: trustworthiness, respect, responsibility, caring, fairness, and citizenship. Those six elements embrace two of the Greeks' virtues, temperance and justice, but seem to relegate to lesser status such traits as moral courage and practical wisdom.

A Civil War hero, Major General Joshua Chamberlain, gave a warrior's version of what the word means, telling a gathering of Union veterans that character plays a paramount role in battle: "I do not mean bravery. Many a man has that. What I mean by character is a firm and seasoned substance of the soul. I mean such qualities as intelligence, thoughtfulness, conscientiousness, right-mindedness, patience, fortitude, long-suffering and unconquerable resolve."

"A firm and seasoned substance of the soul." Maybe there is no better way of saying it.

If it is so vague a concept, why is it so important, particularly for military leaders? Numerous individuals have made an effort in the last couple of centuries to answer that very question. Napoleon thought that for generals, the base (character) must equal the height (intelligence). Clausewitz believed that senior wartime leaders must have great strength of character. Joshua Chamberlain held that in battle it is character that tells. General Matthew Ridgway said that character is the bedrock on which the whole edifice of leadership rests. According to Ronald Reagan, character takes command in moments of crucial choices.

Perhaps, therefore, most of us can agree that character is an essential element in the makeup of military leaders. If so, can we define leaders of character? Here, for our purposes, is a distilled definition: leaders of character know the difference between right and wrong and have the courage to act accordingly; that is, they have the moral fiber to take the harder right instead of the easier wrong.

What, then, can be said about the character of George Washington on the one hand, and of Benedict Arnold on the other?

Washington is the easier of the two to deal with, if for no other reason than that so many individuals during his life and ever since have explored virtually every facet of his personality.

Richard Brookhiser, a modern historian with deep insights into Washington's character, described one of his guiding qualities as "an absolute unwillingness to be led astray by personal gain or ideological distractions." Moreover, "Morals integrated him and held his being together, even as they connected with his fellow Americans." Brookhiser was especially impressed with the general's civility. That a man possessed of so volcanic a temper kept it mostly under control through a long and bruising public existence is indeed exceptional. Despite much provocation, George Washington never offered or fought a duel.

David Abshire, former president of the Center for the Study of the Presidency, said that Washington "was defined by maturity and a capacity for growth." He added, "For George Washington, who he was, and what he did were the same ... the heart of Washington's leadership was pure character." No one has ever described the commander in chief's essence more succinctly.

Don Higginbotham, a noted historian of the Revolutionary War, spoke admiringly of Washington's personal equilibrium in the unforgiving spotlight of fame. "Lionized by men of affairs, sought out by visiting dignitaries, all but deified by hosts of his countrymen, he kept his prewar values and priorities in place, something no narcissist could do."

Thomas Jefferson, who disagreed with Washington on many issues and was not above peevishly disparaging him, nevertheless recognized the centrality of his character in the creation of the new country. After Washington had by sheer force of will extinguished a nascent revolt by army officers near the war's end, Jefferson generously and accurately gave full credit for preventing the subversion of the Revolution to "the moderation and virtue" of a single man, that is, to the character of George Washington.

In light of nearly universal expressions such as those above, one might argue that Washington's life itself could serve as an exemplar for strength of character.

Arnold presents a very different case. His villainy colored everything he did before or afterward. It also limited the number of historians eager to learn more about him, leaving much of his life and personality still open to analysis and appraisal. It seems impossible to integrate the images of Arnold the patriot and Arnold the traitor. The man remains no less an enigma in the twenty-first century than he was in his own lifetime.

How, therefore, can one examine his character? Recognizing limitations inherent in the approach, we are obliged simply to look at the facts available and attempt to integrate them into a mosaic. For a workable framework, the one handed down by those early Greek philosophers will do just fine. Let us see how Benedict Arnold stacks up in each of their four virtues, as well as in overall balance.

Fortitude: strength of mind along with the physical and moral courage to persevere in the face of adversity. Strength of mind he definitely possessed. No one has ever doubted Arnold's intellect. He also had exceptional physical courage, displayed repeatedly in the crucible of mortal combat. Moral courage is less demonstrable and not without question, but in the sense that he never backed down from what he saw as positions of principle he can be accorded this trait.

Temperance: self-discipline to control passions and appetites. Here he fails miserably to measure up. Throughout his life his passions all too often overwhelmed him, and in the end his appetites consumed him.

Prudence: practical wisdom and the ability to make the right choice in specific situations. In this area the record is mixed. In business and war Arnold excelled as few men ever have. In politics and human relationships he fell flat, being neither wise nor of good judgment.

Justice: fairness, honesty, lawfulness, keeping promises. In these traits Benedict Arnold was an abject failure. His record itself damns him beyond redemption.

Thus, by the scale of those four virtues, Arnold's character score is one positive, one mixed, two negative. No balance exists among them.

What of the distilled definition of leader of character cited earlier: to know the difference between right and wrong and to have the courage to act accordingly? In a purely legal sense, of course, Arnold knew the difference between right and wrong. But, in a personal sense, that knowledge bordered on irrelevance. The historical record is replete with evidence to indict him as a thoroughgoing narcissist, ego-centered in the extreme. "Right" was whatever seemed good for him; "wrong" was whatever seemed bad for him.

When right for him happened to correspond with what was right for causes outside of self, he was a hero. When right for him conflicted with other causes, however, his narcissism led him into dissension—and eventually to dishonorable behavior. Although Arnold dwelt much on "honor," and struck back ferociously when his was threatened, he had a warped sense of what the word meant. As shown by his own words and actions, in his mind honor was more akin to reputation than it was to noble traits such as integrity. Duels fought to preserve his honor were really fought to protect his reputation.

Benedict Arnold did not possess Joshua Chamberlain's firm and seasoned substance of soul. Indeed, it is quite clear that America's Hannibal suffered from a near-absence of character as envisioned by Chamberlain. Instead of substance, Arnold had an emptiness at the center.

Perhaps the last word on the matter may have been stated by Len Marella in a book on ethical leadership. To paraphrase the author:

> Your thoughts become your words.
> Your words become your actions.
> Your actions become your habits.
> Your habits become your character.
> Your character becomes your destiny.

The lives of George Washington and Benedict Arnold bear profound witness to the proposition that character is destiny.

Suggested
Readings

U SING TWO REVOLUTIONARY WAR GENERALS AS CENTRAL characters, this book follows the trajectories of their lives and careers, at first so parallel and then diverging dramatically. Here are some thoughts to help guide the reader wanting to dig more deeply into the personality of either man or to explore more comprehensively the war in which they fought.

George Washington

Two problems are encountered immediately in trying to compile any list of works on Washington. First, there are simply more in print than any one person can grapple with short of a lifetime of study. Second, historians have been frustrated more often than not in their struggle to discover and depict the colossus who was the father of our country. Fortunately, several modern scholars have made major advances in moving the marker closer to the ultimate attainment of that daunting goal. Perhaps the best place to begin is with James Thomas Flexner's four volume biography, *George Washington* (Boston, 1965–1972). Then, for a short but insightful study of Washington the person, see Richard Brookhiser, *Founding Father* (New York, 1996). Joseph Ellis adds more dimension to the great man's elusive personality in *His Excellency* (New York, 2004). The most recent of such volumes is one that may well be destined to become a classic—Peter R. Henriques, *Realistic Visionary* (University of Virginia, 2006). Finally, for a concise portrayal of Washington as a soldier, one that can be read in a single long airplane flight, check Dave Palmer, *First in War* (Mount Vernon, 2000).

BENEDICT ARNOLD

The situation is reversed in the case of Arnold. The man whose very name became a synonym for treason has not attracted a host of historians eager to devote the time and effort to portray him. That has been changing in recent years, with a spate of books and even a number of television documentaries attempting to explore and expose the contradictions in his character. The first solid study was Willard M. Wallace, *Traitorous Hero* (New York, 1954). Willard Sterne Randall, *Benedict Arnold, Patriot and Traitor* (New York, 1990), is a comprehensive tome, but is less than rigorous with facts. A volume attempting to psychoanalyze Arnold, ending up being both intriguing and disappointing, is Clare Brandt, *The Man in the Mirror* (New York, 1994). Far and away the best book on Arnold's life up to and through the treason is James Kirby Martin, *Benedict Arnold: Revolutionary Hero* (New York, 1997).

The American Revolutionary War

There seems never to have been a shortage of good accounts of the War of Independence, and an increased flow has added to that number ever since the celebration of the bicentennial in the mid-1970s. Any list, therefore, is at best an arbitrary starting point for further study. For an overall strategic framework to the war, see Dave Palmer, *The Way of the Fox* (Connecticut, 1975). David McCullough, *1776* (New York, 2005) is an acclaimed recent book focusing on a single period of the war, while Stephen R. Taaffe, *The Philadelphia Campaign, 1777–1778* (University of Kansas, 2003) is an example of one focusing on a single campaign. To begin a deeper investigation into the essence of the war, read Don Higginbotham, *The War of American Independence* (New York, 1971).

Leaders of Character

While this topic is the subject of an entirely different field of study, it should not be left dangling. For, at its very core, *George Washington and Benedict Arnold: A Tale of Two Patriots* is about the importance of principled leadership–leaders of character. A good place to start before branching out is Len Marrella, *In Search of Ethics* (DC Press, 2001).

MAPS

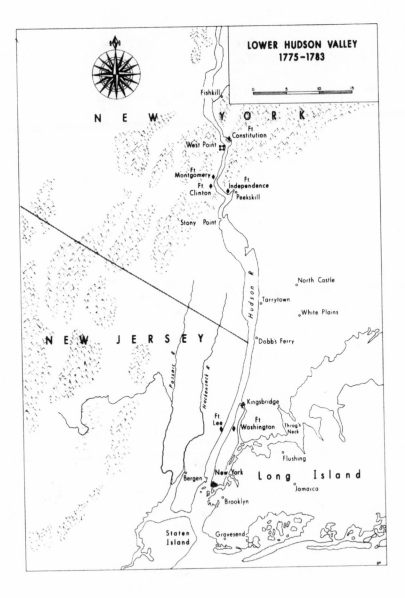

LOWER HUDSON VALLEY
1775-1783

Fishkill

N E W   Y O R K

Ft.
Constitution

West Point

Ft.
Montgomery
Ft.   Ft.
Clinton   Independence
Peekskill

Stony Point

Hudson R.

North Castle

Tarrytown
White Plains

N E W   J E R S E Y

Dobb's Ferry

Kingsbridge

Ft.
Lee   Ft.
Washington   Throg's
Neck

Flushing

Bergen   New York   Long   Island

Brooklyn   Jamaica

Staten
Island   Gravesend

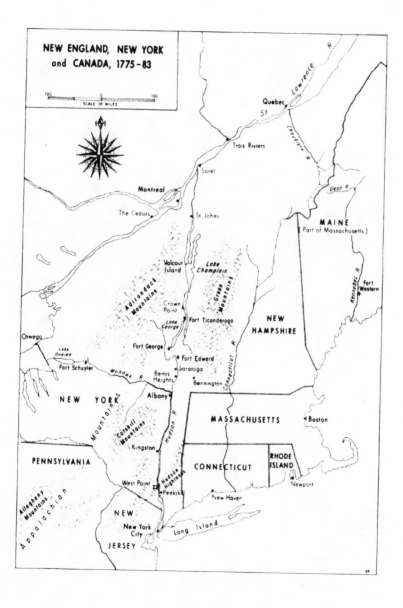

NEW ENGLAND, NEW YORK
and CANADA, 1775-83

SCALE OF MILES

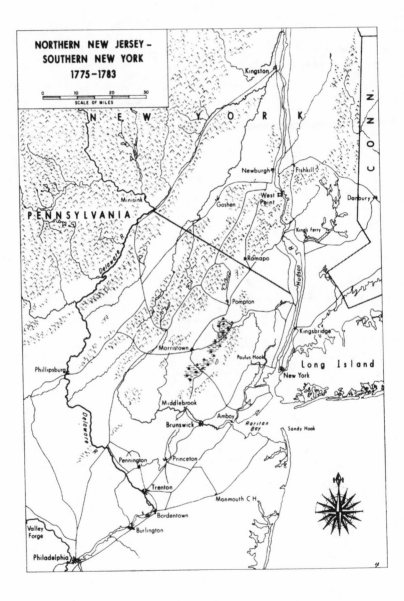

NORTHERN NEW JERSEY -
SOUTHERN NEW YORK
1775-1783

0   10   20   30
SCALE OF MILES

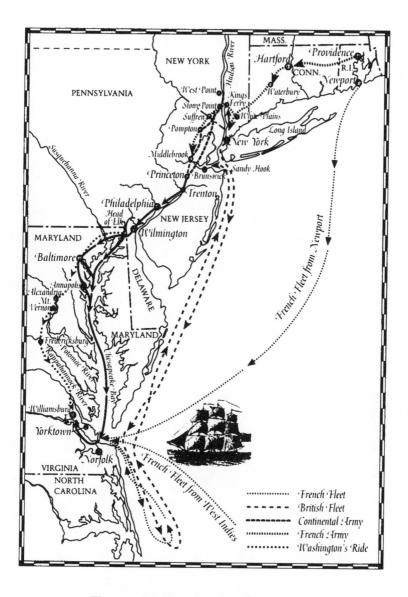

The central theater of combat, showing the
maneuvers of the Yorktown Campaign.

LIST OF
ILLUSTRATIONS

FRONTISPIECE

George Washington (1732–1799)
Courtesy of Mount Vernon Ladies' Association
Oil on canvas by Rembrandt Peale (1778–1860), American,
ca. 1855–1860. Bequest of Luisita L. Cofer, 1956, H-2062.
Photographed by Ed Owen, 1997.

Benedict Arnold
Courtesy of Bill Stanley, president of the Norwich Historical
Society.
Previously unpublished portrait of Benedict Arnold, in oil by
Doug Henry.

PHOTOGRAPH SELECTION

George Washington, the soldier.
Courtesy of Mount Vernon Ladies' Association
George Washington after the Battle of Princeton, oil on canvas by
Charles Willson Peale (1741–1827), American, 1780. Bequest of
Jane J. Boudinot, 1925, H-17. Photographed by Ed Owen, 1997.

**George Washington taking command of the
Continental Army.**
The Granger Collection.

The father of his country.
Courtesy of Mount Vernon Ladies' Association
Portrait of George Washington (1732–1799), oil on canvas by
Charles Willson Peale (1741–1827), American, ca. 1795. Gift of
Mrs. Wallace H. Cole and Mrs. John C. Jansing, 1995, M-3761.
Photographed by Harry Connolly, 1995.

An epic moment.
Courtesy of Mount Vernon Ladies' Association
George Washington Crossing the Delaware [December 15, 1776].
Engraving by Paul Girardet (1821–1893), 1853 after painting by
Emmanuel Gottlieb Leutze (1816–1868). Published by Goupil &
Co., New York. Gift of Mr. and Mrs. Robert B. Gibby, The
Willard-Budd Collection. RP-444, WB-26A1. Photographed by
Ed Owen, 1998.

The house that became his monument, Mount Vernon.
Courtesy of Mount Vernon Ladies' Association
East View of Mt. Vernon Mansion, lithograph published by

N. S. Bennett, 1859. Alexander Robertson, [Jacob or Henry] Seibert, James A. Shearman, engravers. Photographed by Paul Kennedy, 1987.

General of the Continental Army.
Courtesy of Mount Vernon Ladies' Association
Equestrian Portrait of George Washington, oil on canvas attributed to Rembrandt Peale (1778–1860), American, ca. 1830. Gift of Sarah Potter Tatham in memory of her husband, Edwin Tatham, 1934, H-54. Photographed by Hal A. Conroy, 1991.

Plotters: Horatio Gates and John Adams.
Courtesy of Mount Vernon Ladies' Association
Gates etching by H. B. Hall, 1872 after painting by Gilbert Stuart (1755–1828), American, 1793–94.
Adams etching by unknown artist, no date. Gift of Paul A. Halvorsen, 1997.

Alexander Hamilton as statesman and soldier.
Left photo: Courtesy of Mount Vernon Ladies' Association
Etching by unknown artist, no date. Collection of the Mount Vernon Ladies' Association.
Right photo: The Granger Collection.

Benedict Arnold's official appointment as Major General of the Continental Army.
Courtesy of Mount Vernon Ladies' Association
Commission of Benedict Arnold to Major General by John Hancock, President of the Continental Congress, May 2, 1777. Purchased with funds donated by the Honorable and Mrs. Togo D. West, Jr. RM-1035, MS-5670.

Conspirators: Arnold tells Major John André to conceal the plans of West Point in his boot at their meeting on September 21, 1780.
The Granger Collection.

Previously unpublished portrait of Benedict Arnold, in oil by Doug Henry.
Courtesy of Bill Stanley, president of the Norwich Historical Society.

ACKNOWLEDGMENTS

A WRITER OF HISTORY IS ALWAYS INDEBTED TO THE LEGIONS of scholars whose work over the decades has provided the essential resources undergirding his or her work. Editors who published original material, archivists who compiled document collections, professors who maintained interest across the generations, researchers who retrieved priceless items from the mists of time, authors who wrought meaning from incomplete evidence, historians who kept the human stories alive, and on and on. This book reflects the fruits of their labor and owes more to them than to my small role in distilling the narrative from their contributions. I am indeed in their debt.

A host of individuals helped directly over the years, many by extending encouragement, others by sharing information, some by reading parts of the manuscript and commenting. I dare not try to name all of them here, but a few must be mentioned for the very reach of their generosity. Bill Stanley, longtime leader in the city of Norwich, Connecticut, was a veritable treasure trove of information about Benedict Arnold, especially of his youth in Norwich. Bill's tireless efforts to balance the historical record regarding Arnold and his constant eagerness to assist historians of all stripes surely mark him with angel dust. Arthur Lefkowitz, whose inimitable caliber of research make him a one-of-a-kind resource, is the preeminent expert on Arnold's exploits in the autumn of 1775, and he is blessed with a keen editor's eye. Eric Schnitzer, park ranger and historian at Saratoga National Historical Park, is simply *the* person to consult on details of the fighting in that region, and he made time in his packed schedule to provide invaluable insights. Alan Dietz, a dedicated researcher at the Schuyler Mansion in Albany, New York, was unflagging in helping me chase down obscure facts to fill in the historical record. The late Edward Krasnoborski, whose work for many decades as a cartographer in the History Department at West Point left a legacy of excellence, lent his talent to the drafting of the maps. To those five I could never express my appreciation too fully.

Much credit goes to James Rees and his outstanding staff at Mount Vernon. Besides cheerleading the effort from the outset, they helped refine the manuscript, handled the plan for illustrations, and were instrumental players in the publication process itself.

Finally, I have nothing but unstinting praise for the superb staff at Regnery Publishing—Marjory Ross, Harry Crocker, and their entire crew were a "dream team" that was a genuine pleasure to work with. Special kudos to Kate Morse, Amanda Larsen, and Paula Decker for their patience with me. I am grateful to have benefited so very much from their professionalism, and this book is a better one for their contributions.

INDEX